THE GREAT PARTITION

THE GREAT PARTITION

The Making of India and Pakistan

YASMIN KHAN

YALE UNIVERSITY PRESS
NEW HAVEN AND LONDON

For information about this and other Yale University Press publications, please contact:
U.S. Office: sales.press@yale.edu   yalebooks.com
Europe Office: sales@yaleup.co.uk www.yaleup.co.uk

Set in Minion by J&L Composition, Filey, North Yorkshire
Printed in the United Kingdom by St Edmundsbury Press, Bury St. Edmunds, Suffolk

Library of Congress Cataloging-in-Publication Data

Khan, Yasmin, 1977–
   The great Partition: the making of India and Pakistan/Yasmin Khan.
     p. cm.
   Includes bibliographical references and index.
   ISBN 978–0–300–12078–3 (alk. paper)
   1. India—History—Partition, 1947. 2. Nationalism—India—History.
   3. Nationalism—Pakistan—History. I. Title.
     DS480.842.K49 2007
     954.04'2—dc22

                                                                    2007006713

A catalogue record for this book is available from the British Library.

10 9 8 7 6 5 4 3 2 1

For Javed Khan, in memory

Contents

Illustrations

1. Communist delegates marching during the Punjab Provincial Delegates Conference, 1945 © Sunil Janah, 1945, 2007. From the web archive at members.aol.com/sjanah (email: sjanah@aol.com).
2. Royal Indian Navy mutineers, Bombay, 1946 © Nehru Memorial Museum and Library.
3. Muslim League leader Mohammed Ali Jinnah holding a press conference, Bombay, January 1946. Photograph by Margaret Bourke-White © Time & Life Pictures/Getty Images.
4. People in Bombay lining up to vote in the general elections, 1946 © Sunil Janah, 1946, 2007 (sjanah@aol.com, members.aol.com/sjanah).
5. A co-educational zoology class at Aligarh Muslim University, May 1946. Photograph by Margaret Bourke-White © Time & Life Pictures/Getty Images.
6. Lord Pethick-Lawrence, member of the British Cabinet Mission delegation, looking over papers, 1946 © NMML.
7. A peace procession after the riots in Calcutta, 1946 © Sunil Janah, 1946, 2007 (sjanah@aol.com, members.aol.com/sjanah).
8. Villagers in boats fleeing under cover of darkness from their burning villages during riots in Noakhali, an eastern district of undivided Bengal, 1946–7 © Sunil Janah, 1947, 2007 (sjanah@aol.com, members. aol.com/sjanah).
9. Crowds look on during Gandhi's visit to encourage Hindu–Muslim unity in Noakhali © NMML.
10. Muslims and Hindus attempt to promote peace by jointly flying the flags of the Muslim League and the Indian National Congress, Calcutta, 1946 © Sunil Janah, 1946, 2007 (sjanah@aol.com, members.aol.com/ sjanah).

Maps

Acknowledgements

I was born in London two generations after the events described in this book. Nonetheless people sometimes ask about my own 'Partition story'. Both my grandfathers were bit-players in the story of Partition as it unfolded in the subcontinent and both had their own lives profoundly shaped by the ending of the British empire. One was stationed as a British officer in an Indian Army tank regiment. He stayed in the subcontinent during the postcolonial transition and saw at first hand, from a base in Punjab, the creation of the two new states of India and Pakistan. At the same time, not far away, my other grandfather who was born in North India was supporting the Muslim League. He campaigned as a candidate in the 1946 provincial elections and moved part of his family to Pakistan after the new state was created.

Neither of them, I suspect, would have agreed very much, if at all, with my interpretation of events here. Their walk-on parts in the Partition story, though, and the stories that grew up around them, encouraged my interest in history, and provoked my curiosity about the origins of modern India and Pakistan – two states which are supposedly so different and yet have such recently intertwined roots. I am very grateful to friends and family in India, Pakistan and Britain who lived through the Partition of 1947 and who shared their thoughts with me. The subtext to this book is a will for peaceful rapprochement in South Asia and I very much hope it will be read in this light.

My debts have been building up for many years now. I was fortunate to start studying history under the careful eye of Lawrence Goldman at St Peter's College, Oxford. Judith Brown and Ian Talbot both guided this work through earlier incarnations and have been consistently generous since. At my way stations over the past decade – Oxford University, the University of Edinburgh and Royal Holloway, University of London – my thanks to: Sarah Ansari,

Henry Mayr-Harting, Henrietta Leyser, Peter Carey, Roger and Patricia Jeffery, Anna-Maria Misra, Francis Robinson, Crispin Bates, Imre Bangha, David Washbrook and John Darwin. Alpa Shah is both friend and honest critic and helped improve the manuscript. Markus Daechsel, likewise, and his own book has left an imprint on my thinking about 1947. Heather McCallum at Yale has been a source of encouragement and constructive ideas and my thanks to Yale for the care with which the book has been produced.

The National History Center seminar on the subject of decolonisation held in Washington DC in the summer of 2006 enabled me to see things from new angles; I am grateful to Wm Roger Louis, Pillarisetti Sudhir and the other conveners and participants. Colleagues in the politics department at Royal Holloway have been entirely supportive. Lance Brennan and Professor Anthony Epstein both generously shared previously unpublished documents and Sunil Janah's photographs add much to the text. Benjamin Zachariah, Shabnum Tejani, Andrew Whitehead, William Gould and Kaushik Bhaumik provided comments and discussion at critical moments. My research would not have been possible without the support of the Arts and Humanities Research Council and the British Academy which have sustained me throughout my graduate years and beyond. Countless expert librarians and archivists made research a more pleasurable experience; particular thanks to Teen Murti Bhavan, Delhi, and the Indian Institute, Oxford.

For hospitality and companionship in Karachi, Lahore, Delhi, Lucknow, Oxford, Edinburgh and London, my thanks to: Jan-Peter Hartung, the Wright family, Ram Advani, Dr and Begum Siddiqui, Umbreen Daechsel, Seema Ansari and family, Pippa Virdee, Alexander Morrison, Timothy Phillips, Anthony Bale, Orlanda Ruthven, Rebecca Loncraine, Saleema Waraich, Swati Roy, Naomi Foxwood, Blanche Rugginz, Amy Longrigg, Henry Longbottom, and Melody and Nat Hansen. Most important of all, my mother, Finola Khan, and brother, Jamie Khan. And, at last, I can finally record my gratitude to Ben Wright – for everything else.

Although I have tried to acknowledge sources faithfully, every chapter bears the hallmark of a broader debate among numerous researchers and academics. This may be a starting point for further reading about 1947: suggestions for this are provided in the bibliography, particularly on the experience of Partition in Bengal which deserves a volume of its own. Errors of fact and omission are, needless to say, my own.

Abbreviations

AICC — All India Congress Committee
AIHM — All India Hindu Mahasabha
CPI — Communist Party of India
CWMG — *The Collected Works of Mahatma Gandhi* (New Delhi: Publications Division, Ministry of Information and Broadcasting, Government of India, 1958–)
FNR — Fortnightly Reports
ICS — Indian Civil Service
INA — Indian National Army
IOR — India Office Records
JP — *Quaid-i-Azam Mohammad Ali Jinnah Papers*, ed. Z.H. Zaidi (Islamabad: National Archives of Pakistan, 1993–)
NAI — National Archives of India, New Delhi
NMML — Nehru Memorial Museum and Library, New Delhi
NWFP — North West Frontier Province
R&R — Relief and Rehabilitation
RSS — Rashtriya Swayam Sevak Sangh
SPC — *Sardar Patel's Correspondence, 1945–50*, ed. D. Das (Ahmedabad: Navajivan, 1971)
SWGBP — *Selected Works of Govind Ballabh Pant*, ed. B.R. Nanda (New Delhi and Oxford: Oxford University Press, 1993–)
SWJN — *Selected works of Jawaharlal Nehru*, ed. S. Gopal, series 1 (New Delhi: Orient Longman, 1972–1982), series 2 (New Delhi: Jawaharlal Nehru Memorial Fund; distributed by Oxford University Press, 1984–)

TOP	*Constitutional Relations between Britain and India. The Transfer of Power, 1942–7* ed. Nicholas Mansergh and E.W.R. Lumby (London: H.M. Stationery Office, 1970–83)
UP	United Provinces. The state was renamed Uttar Pradesh (literally 'Northern Province') in 1950
UPSA	Uttar Pradesh State Archives, Lucknow
USSA	United States State Department Archives, Washington DC

Glossary

ahimsa	non-violence; policy of non-violence used by Gandhi
akhara	gymnasium; club
anna	small unit of Indian money
azadi	freedom
Bakr-Id	Muslim festival during which animals are sacrificed
bania	shopkeeper; grocer
bhadralok	Indian elite, especially in Bengal
bustees, bastis	shanty towns
charpoi	bed or seat made from wood and rope
crore	ten million
dalit	literally, oppressed; untouchable, outcaste
fatwa	notification of a decision of Muslim law; decree; verdict
ghat	river bank; cremation site
goonda	criminal, thug
harijan	literally, children of God; untouchable, outcaste
hartal	strike or protest, specifically, shutting the shops in a market
Holi	Hindu spring festival during which coloured water or coloured powder is splashed on friends, family or passers-by
Jai Hind	Victory to India
jatha	organised group, gang or band
kafan	funeral shroud
kafila	caravan or foot column
Kalma	Islamic recitation
khadi	homespun cloth
kisan	cultivator, farmer

lakh	one hundred thousand
lathi	a staff or club
maulana	title of respect for a Muslim learned man
maulvi	a man learned in Muslim law; a teacher, especially of Arabic or Persian
mela	fair or festival
mohalla	quarter of a town; ward
Muhajir	term used to describe a Partition migrant from North India to Pakistan; literally, the companions of the Prophet Muhammad who fled from Mecca to Medina
Pakistan Zindabad	Long Live Pakistan
panchayats	village councils
pir	descendant and trustee of Sufi shrine
qasbah	town
raj	literally, rule; Raj is also used to describe the British empire in India
sabha	organisation
sadhu	Hindu holy man, an ascetic
satyagraha	literally, truth-force; Gandhian philosophy and practice of non-violent resistance
shariat	law of Islam
swadeshi	self-sufficiency; anti-colonial movement
swaraj	sovereignty, self-rule
zamindar; zamindari	landholder; system of landholding in India

Timeline of Major Events, 1945–1950

1945

7 May	End of the Second World War in Europe
14–15 June	Congress Working Committee released from jail
5 July	General Election held in Britain
25 June–14 July	First Simla conference fails to form an executive assembly
26 July	Labour landslide victory in British elections
21 August	Viceroy Wavell announces Indian elections to be held in the winter
5 November	Indian National Army trials start
Mid-December	Polling for the Central and Legislative Assembly elections begins
Late December	Results of elections to Central Legislative Assembly announced

1946

11 January	Muslim League celebrate 'Victory Day'
18–23 February	Royal Indian Navy mutiny
19 February	Secretary of State for India announces Cabinet Mission will visit India
22 February	Communist Party of India calls for a general strike
25 March	Cabinet Mission arrives in New Delhi
28 March	Governors report results of the provincial elections
April	Formation of provincial ministries
3–17 April	Meetings between Indian leaders and the Cabinet Mission

7–9 April	Meeting of League legislators in New Delhi
5–12 May	Cabinet Mission convenes unsuccessful tripartite meeting in Simla
16 May	Cabinet Mission puts forward its own federal solution in a statement; broadcast on radio to Indian people
26 June	Negotiations over an interim government fail
29 June	Cabinet Mission leaves India
8 August	Viceroy invites Congress to proceed in an interim government without the League's participation
16–18 August	The League's 'Direct Action Day' ends in violence in Calcutta
24 August	Viceroy broadcasts on the radio regarding formation of an interim government
2 September	Interim government takes office without the League's membership; members are sworn into office
Early September	Ahmedabad, Allahabad, Bombay: violent clashes
Mid-October	Massacres in Noakhali and East Bengal
26 October	League members join the interim government
October–November	Massacres in Bihar
6 November–2 March	Gandhi remains in Noakhali
Early November	Garhmukhteshwar killing in United Provinces
9 December	Constituent Assembly formed without League members, adjourned until 20 January

1947

24 January	Muslim League starts agitation for 'civil liberties' in Punjab
20 February	Attlee's statement that the British intend to grant independence not later than June 1948
2 March	Resignation of the Unionist Coalition Prime Minister, Khizr Tiwana, in Punjab
March	Widespread destruction in Lahore and Amritsar Gandhi goes to Bihar
15 April	Joint appeal for peace made by Gandhi and Jinnah
May	Mass violence in Lahore
End May	Widespread fighting and destruction of villages in Gurgaon

3 June	The plan to partition the subcontinent is agreed and made public
20 June	Bengal and Punjab Legislative Assemblies vote on partitioning the two provinces
June	Violence in Lahore, Amritsar and Punjabi villages
1 July	Partition Council formed (takes over from a special committee of the Cabinet)
1–10 July	Serious rioting in Lahore and Calcutta
8 July	Radcliffe arrives in India
16–24 July	Bengal Boundary Commission holds public sittings in Bengal
20–30 July	Punjab Boundary Commission holds public sittings in Lahore
28 July	Indian Constituent Assembly sub-committee votes against separate electorates for Muslims in India
14 August	Independence Day in Pakistan
15 August	Independence Day in India
17 August	New ferocity in Punjab
	First British troops sail from Bombay
	Boundary Commission Award is announced
18 August	Prime ministers Nehru and Liaquat Ali Khan issue a joint statement from Amritsar after visiting affected areas
28 August	Nehru announces the Indian government will have to rethink policy regarding transfer of populations
31 August	Punjab Boundary Force dissolved; replaced by two military evacuation operations
	United Council for Relief and Welfare formed under the co-ordination of Lady Mountbatten
2 September	Jinnah appeals for help for Pakistani refugees
3 September	Joint dominion conference held in Lahore
7 September	K.C. Neogy appointed first Indian Minister for Relief and Rehabilitation of Refugees; Emergency Cabinet Committee established in India
19 September	Iftikhar-ud-din sworn in as West Punjab Refugees Minister
21 September	Joint statement of Nehru–Liaquat Ali from New Delhi

21 November	Numbers of evacuations in Punjab exceed eight million people
6 December	Inter-dominion Conference, Lahore: operation to recover and restore abducted women agreed
December	A.K. Azad recommends Indian Muslims join the Congress at a convention in Delhi
14–15 December	All-India Muslim League Council meeting, Karachi. The League splits into two branches: the Pakistan Muslim League and the Indian Union Muslim League

1948

12 January	Atrocity against trainload of refugees at Gujrat, Pakistan
30 January	Assassination of Mahatma Gandhi
	Ban on the RSS and Muslim National Guard in India
14 February	Two weeks of mourning in India end; Gandhi's ashes immersed at Allahabad
28 February	Last British troops in India depart
March	Refugee–local conflicts in Godhra, Gujarat
	Inter-dominion arbitral tribunal meets
Early July	Hindu–Muslim riots in Bombay
July	Over 15,000 abducted women recovered by both governments since December 1947
	Permit system introduced in West Pakistan
12 September	Jinnah dies
Mid-September	'Police Action' in Hyderabad and accession of the Nizam to India
30 September	Indian banknotes no longer legal tender in Pakistan
November	RSS initiates civil disobedience against the ban on the organisation
11 November	Inter-dominion agreement sets out terms for recovery of abducted women
15 December	Godse and Narain Apte hanged for Gandhi's murder
21–23 December	Idols found installed in the temple at Ayodhya, Uttar Pradesh.
December	RSS begin a campaign against Golwalkar's detention

1949

1 January	United Nations-sponsored ceasefire announced in Kashmir
19 February	Tara Singh jailed for leading agitation for a Sikh homeland
12 March	Objectives Resolution adopted by Pakistani Constituent Assembly
May	Indian Constituent Assembly votes against reserved seats for religious minorities
29–30 July	All-India Refugee Conference, New Delhi
12 July	Ban on RSS lifted in India
19 December	Abducted Persons (Recovery and Restoration) Bill passed in India

1950

26 January	Inauguration of the Republic of India
January–March	Attacks on non-Muslims in East Bengal, especially in Khulna, Chittagong, Barishal and Sylhet
Early March	Attacks on Muslims in west Uttar Pradesh
8 April	Nehru and Liaquat Ali sign pact on protection of minorities in New Delhi, followed by further talks in Karachi
19 April	Nehru accepts resignation of K.C. Neogy and S.P. Mukherjee owing to disagreements over Pakistan
28 June	Agreement signed on settlement of moveable assets lost during Partition
30 July	All-India Refugee Conference, Delhi
15 December	Death of Vallabhbhai Patel, Indian Deputy Prime Minister

1   India before Partition

KASHMIR

·—·—· International boundary
············· State boundary
- - - - Ceasefire line
·—··—··— International boundary
between India and Pakistan

AFGHANISTAN
Peshawar

Lahore

TIBET

WEST
PAKISTAN

Delhi
Aligarh
NEPAL
BHUTAN

IRAN
Lucknow

Karachi

Arabian Sea

Ahmedabad
Calcutta Dacca

INDIA
EAST
PAKISTAN
(Bangladesh
from 1971)

BURMA

Bombay

Hyderabad
Bay of Bengal

Indian Ocean

Madras

Indian Ocean

600 miles

600 km

CEYLON

2   India and Pakistan after Partition

3 The Radcliffe Line in Punjab

Map Legend

- - - - - - District boundary
— — — — Radcliffe Line
—··—··— Boundary of undivided Bengal including princely states

50 miles

100 km

NEPAL

BHUTAN

DARJEELING

JALPAIGURI

COOCH BEHAR

ASSAM

RANGPUR

MEGHALAYA

DINAJPUR

MALDA

BOGRA

Sylhet

MYMENSINGH

RAJSHAHI

MURSHIDABAD

PABNA

• **Dacca**

DACCA

TRIPURA STATE

BIRBHUM

NADIA

EAST PAKISTAN

TIPPERA

BURDWAN

JESSORE

FARIDPUR

WEST BENGAL

BANKURA

NOAKHALI

HOOGHLY

HOWRAH

• **Calcutta**

KHULNA

BAKARGANJ

CHITTAGONG

MIDNAPORE

CALCUTTA

Chittagong •

CHITTAGONG HILL TRACTS

BIHAR and ORISSA

Bay of Bengal

4   The Radcliffe Line in Bengal

Introduction: The Plan

South Asians learned that the British Indian empire would be partitioned on 3 June 1947. They heard about it on the radio, from relations and friends, by reading newspapers and, later, through government pamphlets. Among a population of almost four hundred million, where the vast majority lived in the countryside, ploughing the land as landless peasants or sharecroppers, it is hardly surprising that many thousands, perhaps hundreds of thousands, did not hear the news for many weeks afterwards. For some, the butchery and forced relocation of the summer months of 1947 may have been the first that they knew about the creation of the two new states rising from the fragmentary and terminally weakened British empire in India.

People who owned or could gather around wireless sets in family homes or in shops, marketplaces and government offices, heard the voices of four men carrying across the airwaves from the broadcasting station of All India Radio in the imperial capital, New Delhi, at 7 p.m. Indian Standard Time on the evening of 3 June. They were informed of the plan to divide up the empire into two new nation states – India and Pakistan. A live link-up from Westminster, where Prime Minister Attlee was making the announcement to the assembled benches of the House of Commons, was relayed via Delhi across the Indian empire's 1.8 million square miles, twenty times the size of Britain itself. In cities from Quetta to Madras, Calcutta to Bombay, these voices carried out along the streets, 'By the evening of June 2, 1947, the atmosphere in Karachi was one of suppressed excitement over the new plan for India and the Viceroy's coming broadcast,' observed an American vice-consul stationed in the port city. 'Thousands of persons from all classes of society had assembled in the streets and public parks to hear the broadcast, while radio shops and stores put on loud-speakers to give passers-by an opportunity to hear the announcement.'[1] In Bombay, the writer and producer Khwaja Ahmad

Abbas was at a colleague's house discussing a new film project at the time. 'Literally millions all over the yet-united India sat glued to their own or their neighbours' radio sets, for the fate of India was to be decided that day,' he later remembered. 'From Peshawar to Travancore, from Karachi to Shillong, India became an enormous collective ear, waiting for the broadcasts breathlessly, helplessly and hopelessly.'[2] Far away from Bombay, in the Himalayan foothills of Assam, where flooding and postal delays had cut off communications with the rest of India, the Governor invited local politicians to his house to hear the live announcement.[3] In Delhi, as the Viceroy and the Indian politicians approached the All India Radio studio in their cars, 'officials were leaning out of all the windows and cramming the balconies'.[4]

In the tense studio in Delhi four statesmen spoke one after the other; first, the British Viceroy, Mountbatten, then the Congress Party leader and future Prime Minister of India, Jawaharlal Nehru, followed by Jinnah, the Muslim League leader and Governor-General of Pakistan in waiting and, finally, Baldev Singh, representative of the Sikhs.

It was a burning hot summer's evening. Rumours had been flying in all directions that an announcement was imminent. Journalists had been well primed and copies of the pre-prepared scripts that the leaders would read from had been circulated in advance to give the press a head start in preparing the special editions that would be rushed to print as soon as the broadcast had finished. After almost two centuries of imperial rule in India, the collapse of the Raj and its recreation in the shape of two nation states was being declared. Independence and Partition were mutually entwined.

The speeches themselves, though, were oddly flat. Even Mountbatten who prided himself on his persuasive rhetoric gave a muted and hesitant performance. Furthermore, the British announcements were masterpieces of obfuscation. It was stated that power would be handed to the Indian people before June 1948. In fact, within days, the real date would be proclaimed: 15 August 1947, ten months earlier than anticipated. The plan paved the way for the partitioning of the highly contested provinces of Punjab and Bengal between the Congress and the Muslim League, and Indian representatives of the legislative assemblies in these two provinces, in the words of the British Prime Minister, 'will be empowered to vote whether or not the Province should be partitioned'. If Partition was decided upon, in Attlee's oblique words, 'arrangements will be made accordingly'.[5] This meant, for those who could read between the lines, that the campaign for a Muslim South Asian state, Pakistan, had succeeded. These provincial fragments would be made into a separate sovereign state and hived off from the remaining parts of British India, which would become independent India. Yet, in these momentous and long-awaited announcements, neither Mountbatten nor Attlee mentioned the word 'Pakistan' once. The Viceroy went further and couched the whole proposal as a theoretical question, dependent on 'Whichever way the decision of the Indian people may go'. This was diplomatic frippery. The votes in the assemblies were a foregone conclusion and the plan itself had been painfully hammered out in months of intense debate between Indian leaders. It was self-evident to everyone who had lived through the tumultuous months that preceded this announcement, who had witnessed rioting and murders that stretched across North India from Bengal and Bihar to Bombay, and had followed the near-misses of alternative peace proposals and the collapse of the Cabinet Mission talks in 1946 that almost resulted in a federal India, that these statements meant one thing: Pakistan was going to be created, no matter what else happened.[6]

What did the creation of Pakistan mean? Nehru did not mention the P word either, only once allowing that the plan laid down 'a procedure for self-determination in certain areas of India'. Although he encouraged his listeners to accept the plan that was being presented, it was 'with no joy in his heart' and although he was clearly talking of a major change in the territorial map of the subcontinent, he told his listeners, confusingly, that 'The India of geography, of history and traditions, the India of our minds and hearts cannot change.'[7] Nor were there any maps to help even the most well-informed English-speaking listener understand what was happening. It was left to the newspapers to publish their own creative interpretations of exactly where a new borderline, snaking through Bengal in the east and Punjab in the west, might fall once the country was divided. The real line would not be presented to the public until two days after the new states had come into existence, on 17 August, and would be hurriedly marked on maps using censuses of 'minority' and 'majority' populations. The border would be devised from a distance; the land, villages and communities to be divided were not visited or inspected by the imperial map-maker, the British judge, Cyril Radcliffe, who arrived in India on 8 July to carry out the task and stayed in the country only six weeks.

It was only Mohammed Ali Jinnah, the Muslim League leader, dressed in a white linen jacket and tie, who talked of Pakistan. Jinnah claimed to be the leader of almost one hundred million South Asian Muslims who lived primarily in the north-eastern and north-western corners of British India but were also threaded in their millions throughout the subcontinent's population in towns, villages and princely states. However, he showed little sign of triumphalism. Jinnah had initially been reluctant to talk at all and then hedged his speech with qualifications and sub-clauses: 'It is clear that the plan does not meet in some important respects our point of view; and we can not say or feel that we are satisfied or that we agree with some of the matters dealt with by the plan,' he announced. It would be up to the Muslim League to decide whether they should accept the partition plan as 'a compromise or as a settlement'. Rarely has the birth of a new country been welcomed with so many qualifications by its foremost champion. Clearly something strange and unprecedented was taking place.[8]

Over the next few days, in press conferences and speeches, the outlines of the sketchy Partition plan would be fleshed out and greeted with a mixture of joy, horror, bewilderment and fury. It is little wonder that the reactions to the 3 June plan were confused, contradictory and violent. The plan – for all its superficial complexity and fine detail – was wafer thin and left numerous critical aspects unexamined and unclear. Where was India and where was Pakistan? Who was now an Indian or a Pakistani? Was citizenship under-pinned by a shared religious faith, or was it a universal right, guaranteed by a state that promised equality and freedom to all? Were people expected to move into the state where their co-religionists resided in a majority? The tragedy of Partition was that by the time people started to ask and try answering these questions, unimaginable violence had escalated to the point of ethnic cleansing.

All in all, it was probably very difficult indeed in 1946 – without the aid of fortune-telling powers – to imagine what a free South Asia was going to look like. It was evident that two *parties*, the Congress and the League, would be at the forefront of leading and designing the new state, or states, and that the most prominent leaders – Nehru, Jinnah and Gandhi – would be central to carving out the future political orientation of the countries. Questions about economic and social policy, national borders, political sovereignty and consti-tutional rights, however, had barely been addressed or were highly contested. And yet by 1950 two nation *states* stood alongside each other in South Asia, with membership of the United Nations, full sovereignty and complete political independence.

This book is about these months of transition and how, at the end of the British empire, two states emerged from the South Asian landmass, unfortu-nately with deep-rooted and lasting antipathy towards each other. It aims to dig beneath the often hostile and justificatory rhetoric about Partition, as well as imperial stories of a smooth and seamless 'transfer of power', to show just how disorderly the whole process was and how it threatened the very existence of the two new states. It also underscores how uncertain and ambiguous the meanings of Partition and Pakistan were to people living through these events.

The brilliant success of the Congress and the League in writing post-dated histories and retrospectively ascribing meaning to the support that they gained at the time has obscured the ways in which notions such as *swaraj* (literally meaning self-rule, and invoked by Gandhi to convey freedom from imperialism) and 'Pakistan' were understood by people in 1947. There were various vocabularies of freedom in circulation in the late 1940s. The story of the 'transfer of power' used by both the outgoing imperialists and the incoming nationalist powers has been so effective, well disseminated and uncompromising that it has obscured the meanings of freedom at the time. Partition for many South Asians was far more complicated and was the beginning of a process of their construction as new national citizens, rather than simply the end point of nationalist struggles. The words 'Pakistan', '*swaraj*' and 'Partition' have acquired concrete meanings in the intervening sixty years. In contrast, 'freedom' was not clearly defined in 1947. This was a time before these histories and national images had become standard.[9] It will become apparent that the meanings ascribed to these words in 1947 were regularly at odds with the ways that we understand them now so that nobody – from Mountbatten to the most humble farmhand – foresaw their true meaning or what the future would deliver. The plan to partition the Punjab and Bengal – which in the event delivered one of the worst human calamities of the twentieth century – was heralded by a leading newspaper's special correspondent with great enthusiasm as a day which would be 'remembered in India's history as the day when her leaders voluntarily agreed to divide the country and avoid bloodshed'.[10]

Both the Indian and Pakistani states have proved extremely adept at papering over these differences and muffling the multiple voices that made up the 'nationalist' groundswell in the late 1940s. The apparent support for the League and the Congress as displayed in rallies and general elections in 1946 was enough sanction, and sufficient proof, that the modern nation states of India and Pakistan had been envisaged collectively and that their citizens had willed them into existence. A history-writing project was commenced immediately after Independence in both states, which slotted these nationalist upsurges into a straightforward teleology that can still be viewed in the black and white photographic exhibitions in the national museums of South Asian cities or in schoolchildren's history textbooks. In short, both states have been good at promoting themselves. The growth of the nationalist parties blends seamlessly into the successful foundation of new countries. Nehru had this in mind even before India had achieved freedom, suggesting exactly a year before Independence that 'we might hold an all India exhibition of the Congress struggle of 1920–1946'. Meanwhile, the first Prime Minister of Pakistan, Liaquat Ali Khan, was considering the displays in a new national museum days before Pakistan even came into existence.[11] All the states involved, including Britain, have projected back on to events their own nationalistic, and indeed skewed, readings of why and how the subcontinent was partitioned.

Even by the standards of the violent twentieth century, the Partition of India is remembered for its carnage, both for its scale – which may have involved the deaths of half a million to one million men, women and children – and for its seemingly indiscriminate callousness.[12] Individual killings, especially in the most ferociously contested province of Punjab, were frequently accompanied by disfiguration, dismemberment and the rape of women from one community by men from another. Muslims, Sikhs and Hindus suffered equally as victims and can equally be blamed for carrying out the murders and assaults. The killings bridged the barbaric and the calculatedly modern, they were both haphazard and chillingly specific. A whole village might be hacked to death with blunt farm instruments, or imprisoned in a barn and burned alive, or shot against walls by impromptu firing squads using machine-guns. Children, the elderly and the sick were not spared, and ritual humiliation and conversions from one faith to another occurred, alongside systematic looting and robbery clearly carried out with the intention of ruining lives. It seems that the aim was not only to kill, but to break people. A scorched earth policy in Punjab, which would today be labelled ethnic cleansing, was both the cause and the result of driving people from the land. Militias, armed gangs and members of defence organisations went on the rampage. All this both preceded and accompanied the migration of some twelve million people between the two new nation states of India and Pakistan.

The generality of these stories does little justice to the horror of individual tales, which are difficult even for the most hardened and dispassionate reader to digest. Small details give only a glimpse of a deeper tragedy, expressed in the cries of an unknown refugee who, when meeting Nehru as he toured the refugee camps, slapped him on the face, crying, 'Give my mother back to me! Bring my sisters to me!' or in the grief of an unnamed villager 'whose family had been wiped out', who on meeting Jinnah as he toured the Pakistani camps in 1947, 'sobbed uncontrollably'.[13]

In New Delhi, politicians and officials created reams of memos and press releases, and held heated debates as they thrashed out the formation of

Pakistan and India. This means very little, though, without reference to the millions of people whose lives were being shaped. The histories of Partition have had a tendency to segregate two sub-genres artificially: the histories of Partition victims, or survivors, and their epic journeys across the ruptured Punjab, and the histories of bureaucratic and political intrigue acted out in the marble-floored rooms of Lutyens's New Delhi. This human story is a very political one, though. After all, what is the history of Pakistan and India without reference to Pakistanis and Indians? Ordinary Indians suffered and were affected but also shaped the outcomes of 1947. Any suggestion that the political games in New Delhi were unrelated to the violence that occurred during Partition should be dispensed with by Mountbatten's revealing admission of almost breathtaking callousness when he admitted, on hearing that over sixty villages had been wiped out in Gurgaon, in Delhi's hinterland, 'I could not help feeling that this renewed outbreak of violence, on the eve of the meeting with the leaders, might influence them to accept the plan which was about to be laid before them.'[14] The Partition plan itself was brought about through acts of violence. Partition's elitist politics and everyday experiences are not as separate as they may seem at first glance because mass demonstrations, street fighting and the circulation of rumours all overlapped with the political decision-making process.

I would argue for a more all-encompassing, and expansive assessment of Partition. It swept up people in very large territorial tracts of the subcontinent. Punjab, in the north-west of undivided India, has rightly been the focus of much recent writing about Partition, as this was the province most brutally sliced into two parts in 1947, and was the bloody battlefield of Partition where by far the greatest number of massacres of Hindus, Sikhs and Muslims occurred. Judging the limits of Partition and its social, economic and political penetration of South Asia is hardly a precise science, and although I have attempted to give specific locations and examples of Partition 'beyond Punjab', and to draw attention to regional variations, there are inevitably times when this slides into generalisations. Yet to fail to do so, it seemed to me, would run counter to findings that paint Partition as a pan-continental event. Partition went far beyond the pinpointed zones of Punjab and Bengal and caught up people in hundreds or thousands of towns and villages in numerous ways.

Beyond Punjab and Bengal, rioters wreaked havoc in many cities. Cities that declared riot zones at different times between 1946 and 1950 included Delhi, Bombay, Karachi and Quetta; in the province of Uttar Pradesh, the towns of Varanasi, Shahjahanpur, Pilibhit, Moradabad, Meerut, Kanpur, Lucknow,

Bareilly, Garhmukhteshwar, Allahabad, and Aligarh among others; the hill stations of Simla and Dehra Dun; in the province of Gujarat, Ahmedabad, Godhra and Vadodara; and Ajmer and Udaipur in Rajasthan. Stretching into central and western India, Amraoti, Sangamner, Saugor, Nagpur, Lashkar and Gwalior were afflicted, and Chapra, Jamalpur and Jamshedpur in Bihar. A few outbreaks of Partition violence even occurred in the south, which in general stayed remarkably untouched by the conflict unfolding in the north, in riots in Secunderabad, in present-day Andhra Pradesh in 1947 and 1949.[15] Princely ruled territories, especially Kashmir and Hyderabad, were involved as well as the directly controlled British locales. This was nothing short of a continental disaster.

There are no doubt cities which have been, for specific if contested reasons, particularly riot-prone in South Asia's past, while others have remained especially peaceful. Each riot had its own causes and could be written about individually. There were also powerful countervailing forces against violence, not least the well-honed provincial identities and regional patriotism marking out some areas and the work of peace groups, Gandhians and activists, especially on the Left. Nevertheless, riots, beyond the limits of Punjab and Bengal, added immeasurably to the social dislocation of Partition and generated their own economic crises, wrenching refugee upheavals and visible destruction. Add to this the random stabbing attacks that started to become a feature of life in other towns of North India and the anxiety of people with relatives living in the war-torn Punjab, or with children studying at faraway educational institutions or who suffered from dishonoured business contracts, who worried about the fear of violence, even when this did not materialise, and the number of people touched by Partition in one way or another starts to swell.

The South Asian middle class became particularly implicated in, and affected by, Partition's violent repercussions. Urban wage-earners, bureaucrats, clerks and peons in government service, teachers, landlords, traders and stallholders, and petty manufacturers are the subject of many of the stories presented here. This is partly because the evidence about them is more immediately accessible in archival and newspaper sources than is that of the rural peasantry, but mostly because it was these groups that provided the manpower behind many Congress and League campaigns. The middle class spread the nationalist ideals and became closely interconnected with 'nation-building' in the post-Independence era, through work in government institutions, the media and business.

The refugee crisis had a shocking visibility in places far away from the Bengali and Punjabi focal points as refugees drained away from Punjab and made their homes in the further corners of the subcontinent, whether by their own initiative or through the forced dispersal of government relocation projects. Most conspicuously in New Delhi, where large numbers of journalists and civil servants were on hand to record the devastating scenes for future historians, but also in many other provinces; there were more than 160 government-operated refugee camps in independent India with three in Madras, 32 in Bombay presidency and 85 in East Punjab. Refugees resettled as far north as Peshawar and as far south as Madras, and some Bengali refugees were rehoused in the Andaman and Nicobar archipelago in the Indian Ocean. Press coverage, propaganda (well circulated either by political partisans or by the state itself) and the radio spread news of the crisis. Stories of Partition evoked feelings of fear, sympathy and horror long distances away. This was the full force of Partition.

During Partition and its aftermath, an empire came to an end and two new nation states were forged from its debris. This 'operation', which is often described using the metaphors of surgery, was far from clinical. Partition played a central role in the making of new Indian and Pakistani national identities and the apparently irreconcilable differences which continue to exist today. We could even go as far as saying that Indian and Pakistani ideas of nationhood were carved out diametrically, in definition against each other, at this time. Partition, then, is more than the sum of its considerable parts – the hundreds of thousands of dead, the twelve million displaced. It signifies the division of territory, independence and the birth of new states, alongside distressing personal memories, and potent collective imaginings of the 'other'. Partition itself has become a loaded word, with multiple meanings in both English and the vernaculars, and triggers complex feelings with deep psychological significance.[16]

The history of Partition is very much a work in progress, with major oral history projects still under way and new archival sources still to be unearthed, and there have been seismic reappraisals of Partition in the past decade. Many writers in recent years have been rather allergic to national histories, preferring to deal with provincial, local or regional arenas, sensitive to the risk of oversimplification and the constraints imposed by attempting national narratives. The continental dimensions and domestic variations in South Asia, of language, caste and religion, and the local peculiarities and sensibilities of these communities, are legendary. Often what might be a critically important regional event in one place bears little relevance to the wider nation. Instead, the trajectory has been towards micro-histories, inflected by anthropology, sociology and theory, which rightly resurrect the ordinary, everyday Indian in the picture and restore him or her to the past. Urvashi Butalia, the foremost chronicler of Partition voices, expressed her distaste with the clinical neutrality which characterised some of the earlier works about 1947 and her deep suspicion of histories 'that seem to write themselves'.[17] She is right: Partition stories are personal, intensely subjective, constructed through memory, gender and ideas of self, and span the subcontinent.

This book engages with the idea of two nations, however, as it seems difficult to overlook the fact that two antithetical states emerged in 1947. For all their domestic heterogeneity and irrespective of widespread and popular demands for peace, the reality is that these states have repeatedly fought wars against each other, restricted trade and interaction between their citizens, spent vast amounts on arms, developed nuclear weaponry and are suspended in ideological conflict. The gross tragedy for ordinary people which Partition involved – the migration of huge numbers to unknown places, the violence which deliberately targeted refugees and minorities, and the particular terrors for women – sit alongside the immense problems families faced in reconstructing their lives anew. These histories are intrinsically important but also part of this broader story of national reconstruction and international rivalry.

Individuals were caught between the pull of two opposing nationalisms and had their citizenship settled and fixed as Indian or Pakistani. The Indian and Pakistani governments had to undertake the complex governmental business of teasing out two new states, with full administrative and military apparatus. All this took place just at the time when social uncertainty, the loss of trained manpower and the lack of resources were testing their administrative abilities to the utmost. India and Pakistan were built on messy and turbulent foundations. Partition set in motion a train of events unforeseen by every single person who had advocated and argued for the division. Above all, this book revisits how and why this happened; how the British empire disintegrated in South Asia, and how two new nations materialised. The grave implications of this stretch into the present day for these two vitally important, and now distinctive, countries.

1

In the Shadow of War

The eccentric and itinerant retired Indian civil servant Malcolm Darling toured North India on horseback at the end of 1946 to ascertain 'what the peasant was thinking' and 'how his way of life had been affected by the war'. It was clear that the end of the British empire in India was imminent and Darling was fully conscious of the momentous days that he was witnessing. The Second World War was over and change was afoot. Darling desired to know what Independence would mean for ordinary Indians living in villages and small towns on the Punjabi and North Indian plains. He could, of course, have chosen to travel by motor car, but Darling intended to chronicle the end of the empire as an equestrian, self-consciously styling himself as the direct heir to Arthur Young who had ridden across France in the eighteenth century. By doing so, Darling suggested that the end of the British Raj in India was a historical moment directly comparable with the French Revolution. He was interested in observing a panoply of concerns, including improvements in living standards, the status of women and the uptake of novel farming techniques, but one of the questions which preoccupied him – and which he asked repeatedly of the hundreds of villagers, soldiers and administrators who provided hospitality, hot tea and chit-chat along the way – was what people wanted from Independence; what their dreams of a life free from imperial rule looked like.

Darling met hundreds of villagers on his ride and they all answered his questions about *azadi*, or freedom, differently: among a group of Punjabi Muslims, he noted, 'The village headmen riding with me were all supporters of the League. "What is its object?" I asked them. "*Sanun kuchh patta nahin –* we have no idea," said one of them and another added: "It is an affair of the Muslims".' A third was more explicit and said: 'If there were no League, the Hindus would get the government and take away our land.' In another village named Balkassar, he met prosperous members of the Khatri Sikh community who told him, 'Sikh and Muslim . . . had lived together in harmony, but now, with the cry for Pakistan, each eyes the other critically and keeps apart.' 'But surely you want *azadi*?' Darling asked. '*Azadi*', said one of the younger men 'is *bebadi* – destruction, and Pakistan is *kabaristan* – a graveyard.' In another village, Miani Gondal in Punjab, he asked the difference between the Congress and the League. Someone piped up saying, 'we don't bother about that' and another attempted to explain the meaning of Pakistan. 'Our area', he said, 'must be separate, and the Hindu area must be separate.' When he asked a group of Sikhs on the other side of the Chenab River in a central Punjabi village in the district of Lyallpur, 'What would they do with freedom?' he recorded, 'When the word *azadi* – freedom – was mentioned there was no dissentient voice. All wanted it and when I asked what they would do with it when they got it, a Sikh replied, "Now we are slaves. When we are free we shall serve ourselves and do as we like. Then we shall gladly pay more taxes." Another colonist, one of the more educated present wearing a fine black achkan [long coat] said that when they were free they would have prosperity.' Darling could not help but conclude that *azadi* is 'the word which comes up sooner or later at every meeting'.[1]

Darling's account must be handled with suspicion because he was, for all his liberal compassion and interest in Indians, ambivalent about the end of the Raj. His stories play down the great strength of nationalist feeling in India at the time and can be read as justification for the prolongation of empire. There was absolutely no shortage of well-educated, articulate and fiercely political Indians alive at the end of the war, determined to start shaping the fate of their own state. The central question though was a valid one. What did ordinary Indians expect from Independence and what were the hopes and dreams at the end of the Second World War as people felt themselves to be on the brink of a revolution? Above all, Darling was right about one thing. 'What a hash politics threaten to make of this tract, where Hindu, Muslim and Sikh are as mixed up as the ingredients of a well-made pilau', he predicted as he rode across the fertile Punjabi plains that winter.[2] Within a year this region would be divided in half and many of the people he met along the way in these 'mixed-up' populations would have been wrenched out of their homes, made destitute or murdered.

The land which Darling rode through was much changed from the pre-war years. At the end of the war India was either an exciting and exhilarating or a dangerous place, depending on your particular circumstances and viewpoint. The divisive question about how best to settle the representation of Hindus,

Sikhs and Muslims in a future Indian state was only one of numerous problems facing the British government as it tried to resume service after the summer of 1945, and it was by no means certain that it would become the most critical. The demands and compromises made during the war had badly cracked the foundational scaffolding of the Raj. This structure, which was so good at giving the illusion of permanence and durability, was actually built on specific sets of relationships between British administrators and an unlikely coalition of Indian princely rulers, self-promoting landed oligarchs, hand-picked civil servants, locally hired policemen and soldiers. By the end of the Second World War, a thread had loosened in the political fabric of the state. An unparalleled naval mutiny shook the authority of the Raj to its foundations and strikes, student activism and peasant revolt reverberated throughout the country, while an ill-advised attempt to prosecute members of the rebellious Indian National Army became a national *cause célèbre*. Above all, this was a time of transition, and India, and its old colonial system of governance, was irreversibly altered by the tremendous economic, social and psychological consequences of war.

Just as it had in Britain, the war effort strained, and ultimately reconfigured, the very nature of the political economy of the state and the partition that followed is difficult to comprehend in isolation from this upheaval. Daily terror and dread of an impending attack by the Axis powers had suffused life during the war years for many, especially once Singapore toppled to the Japanese in 1942. Even though such an attack failed to materialise on Indian soil, apart from the oft-forgotten Japanese bombing of Bengal, fear of imminent invasion had been inculcated quite deliberately by government propaganda. In North India blackouts and bomb shelters were not unusual in the homes of the wealthy, and fearfulness and rumour had become a feature of public life well before Partition appeared on the political horizon, as is attested by the withdrawal of bank savings and their conversion into cash and jewellery in Punjab.[3] At the war's cessation, thousands of troops, fired up by exposure to new political ideas and expecting some recompense for the rigours of military service, returned to their villages. Troops housed in one camp twenty miles from Delhi, 'had become accustomed to a new standard of living in Germany . . . some had the conviction that they were coming to a free India' and others wrote to the newspapers. 'We who have done real hard work and our duty as we were expected to do should be told frankly that we are not to expect anything from Government. If there is no expectation there will be no disappointment,' appealed one officer stationed in Bangalore.[4]

Expectations of freedom were sky high and India was set to become the first part of the empire, beyond the dominions, to win its independence, paving the way for the later decolonisation of other countries in Asia, Africa and elsewhere. At the same time, British civil servants in their isolated outposts throughout the country waited nervously for news that they could take long-overdue leave, and surveyed the political landscape with trepidation while local politicians found ready audiences on soapboxes and in the press. Book sales boomed, papers sold in unprecedented quantities and a sense of imminent change and transformation was palpable in the cities. Congressmen, jailed for the duration of the war, leaped back into the political arena after their release from prison in June 1945, talking more freely and provocatively than ever. 'Independence will be attained soon. It has almost come to us. We have it. None can snatch it away from us', a leading Congressman told the swollen crowds at a political rally in Agra, weeks after his three-year jail sentence had ended. 'Yearnings and hunger for independence have so much increased that anyone who obstructs or comes in the way will be burnt to ashes.'[5] Abstract notions of freedom and fine British sentiments would no longer do; the people were determined to have independence and to experience it for themselves.

After two centuries of imperial rule the British had become confused, equivocal imperialists in India, at best. The state had postponed, or simply abandoned, many of the other projects which might have warranted attention in peacetime and resorted to a simplistic form of basic imperialism during the war: keeping the peace and extracting the necessary resources to fight the war. The bureaucracy itself, the notorious 'steel frame', was creaking under the weight of the new duties that it had assumed during wartime. Indians now outnumbered Europeans in the civil service and a deliberate policy of gradually Indianising the services had been greatly accelerated. It was becoming practically impossible to recruit young British men to staff the Raj and by 1943 Indian Civil Service recruitment in Britain had effectively dried up. By 1946, many of the British men who had enlisted during the Second World War were attracted by the business opportunities of the post-war world, and were not inclined to travel four thousand miles to manage a fading empire. High-ranking British policemen in India started casting around for openings elsewhere in the empire or even beyond: 'this consulate alone has already been approached by three of the higher ranking officials who have been interested in the possibilities of obtaining positions in the United States,' reported the American Vice-Consul in Karachi.[6]

Grainy photographs of the Partition era sometimes hint that it was a 'medieval' horror that occurred in a poor and undeveloped landscape, but this is a manipulation of the truth; urban India was in the midst of rapid change by 1946, change which had been greatly accelerated by the industrial spurt caused by war, and although it is unwise to generalise about such a vast and variegated economy – which ranged from gritty industrial centres such as Jamshedpur (home to the largest single steelworks in the British empire pioneered by the entrepreneurial Tata family) to remote and extremely poor villages entirely dependent on agricultural crops – Partition took place in the mid-twentieth century. The battle over India and Pakistan was fought in towns and cities that would be instantly recognisable today.

Giant metropolises – Bombay, Madras, Delhi and Calcutta – differed from the smaller towns founded on government service and small-scale production, such as Karachi, Lucknow, Dacca or Lahore, yet by the 1940s all these towns and cities had richly complex civic lives, with numerous banks, schools, hospitals, chambers of commerce, temples and mosques, densely packed roads, bazaars and alleyways. Colleges and universities swarmed with well-read, politicised students who awaited the start of a new era. Many wealthy landowners and members of princely elites failed to notice, or mistakenly ignored, the winds of change blowing through society and persisted with their annual rounds of balls, parties and dances.

Among the middle classes, the buzz was about new poets, fashion magazines and pulp fiction. Eating out was becoming more popular, and there was a sudden rash of new restaurants and coffee-houses. Standing on the fringes of the middle class, city dwellers with jobs, perhaps as petty clerks or schoolteachers, could buy new types of consumer goods for the first time in the 1940s. They packed the cinema halls and took the opportunity to travel more than their forefathers, either by bicycle or train. New attitudes percolated through society: in Punjab women were increasingly going without the veil and favouring high heels and synthetic saris. Tea-drinking from ceramic cups was becoming more commonplace and smoking leaf tobacco was catching on. Markets selling brightly patterned cloth, gold jewellery and sweets would have looked entirely familiar. The towns, typically based on small trading businesses, petty shopkeeping and service trades, were, and are, disproportionately powerful in relation to a vast agricultural sector. 'No favorite wife could have been treated with more favor than the town', noted one observer, and provincial towns such as Amritsar, Lucknow, Lahore, Dacca and Karachi were the nerve centres of political life.[7]

For those without money, the cities were darker and more dangerous places. Many landless agriculturalists were compelled to seek work and the overcrowding of the greatest cities had been greatly exacerbated by the wartime boom. 'Nowhere in the world today', wrote one eminent economic historian and well-travelled contemporary commentator, 'are there slums worse than the single-story *bustees* of Calcutta or the multistory *chawls* of Bombay.'[8] Cities such as the northern manufacturing metropolis Kanpur exploded during the war owing to the escalating demands for cotton, wool, jute and sugar and the population of the city, overwhelmed by migrant labour, nearly doubled between 1941 and 1951. At the end of the war, when much of this production contracted, labourers faced unemployment. Thousands of workers returned to their wives and children in their home villages, and tried to revive livelihoods as cultivators. Others remained as casual workers, or carved out a life on the margins of the city, living among other caste and community members, taking part in union politics, local clubs or *akharas*. In the 1940s, 40 per cent of the debt-ridden peasantry neither owned nor rented any land at all and were entirely dependent on casual, seasonal employment.[9] Too many were barefoot, poorly dressed, sick or suffering, barely surviving on one meal a day. 'It was market day,' wrote a journalist from Bihar. 'We were surrounded by starving people and in the whole of the market except for *sag* [spinach] and *mahuwa* [edible seeds and flowers] we found nothing else. For three months, rice had not been selling in the bazaar and the people were living on *sag*.'[10] The empire had not delivered much in the way of development to its poorest members. Unstoppable waves of sometimes seasonal, sometimes permanent, migration to the ballooning cities persisted, despite the post-war depression, and have continued ever since.

For most Indians, especially town dwellers, life revolved around getting hold of daily essentials, especially bread. Wheat, grain, cloth, and kerosene were all in desperately short supply. In a classic Hindi novel of the time, *Adha Gaon*, Phunnan Miyan, the father of a soldier serving abroad in the army, anxious because he hasn't heard any news from his boy, is asked to donate money to a war fund towards the end of the war, and promptly retorts: 'You can't get cloth. Eh, *Bhai*, everything to eat has disappeared from the bazaar. I couldn't get sugar to make offerings. Kerosene has become like the water of paradise. Only certain special people get it. I'm not giving an *anna* to the war fund. Do whatever you like.'[11]

This depth of feeling opened a window of opportunity for the politicians as perilous food shortages and hunger, the threat of hunger, and anxiety about food supply were running sores in 1946. India had been living 'hand to mouth for the past three years,' admitted the Secretary of the Food Department. A devastating cyclone destroyed crops in the west of the country and the monsoon failed in the south. Nearly half the Indian population was subject to rationing. In the early months of 1946, the Viceroy was preoccupied by the food issue, which, in his own words, 'threatened calamity'.[12] Farmers were tempted to dodge fixed-price government procurement, keep back their rice, wheat and vegetables and to sell their produce on the black market. 'One way to defeat the food law-breaker is to report him to the authorities. Another is to hound him out of society,' instructed a government-sponsored newspaper advert. 'Hound him out!'[13] Despite the adverts, selling on the black market became commonplace and the government itself admitted that food could be bought for nearly three times its ration price in the small towns.

Understandably, resistance to forced requisitioning broke out as the poor and ravenous rebelled. In a Gujarati town, hungry labourers refused to load bags of wheat on to lorries and a sympathetic crowd gathered to join their protest, tearing at the sacks with their hands.[14] The very poorest were worst hit as they were compelled to make do with the paltry, leftover rations doled out by the state. At the close of the war large painted hoardings in Calcutta could still be seen, sponsored by the biscuit-maker Britannia, which depicted smiling, uniformed soldiers. The slogan in neat letters accompanying the picture spelt out the wartime food equation with stunning brevity: 'Their needs come first!' A shocking lesson that Calcutta had come to feel only too painfully. In the Bengal famine of 1943 the Bengali public had been left starving to death, and perhaps as many as three million died because of shoddy government food allocation and skewed political priorities.

It is not easy to say, then, where wartime politics ended and the politics of partitioning began. Partition took place in a society only partially emerging from long years of war. Two-and-a-half million Indian soldiers served in the Second World War, over 24,000 were killed and 64,000 wounded. This, the largest volunteer army in history, which had served in theatres from Greece to Burma, was now in the process of a euphoric and disruptive demobilisation. It was only a fortnight after Victory Week in Delhi, when huge processions of soldiers, brass and pipe bands with regimental flags rolled through the centre of the city to celebrate the end of the war, that the members of the British delegation sent to negotiate a constitutional settlement for India, and to plan its disengagement from empire, arrived in the capital. Partition emerged from a cauldron of social disorder. The Indian economy, which had been completely geared towards feeding soldiers and supporting the war effort, now shifted in a new direction. The Second World War and Partition bled into each other. Indian society, like the British, was undergoing widespread readjustment and demobilisation from 1946–7 and this determined the lines upon which the state fractured.[15] Indians stood on the threshold of change and revolution but, as yet, the shape of this change was unknown and frighteningly uncertain.

A religious divide?

How and when the British should leave India, and who they should leave power to, were the vital questions dominating all facets of Indian political life by 1946. The Indian National Congress and the All India Muslim League were unquestionably the frontrunners in the race to acquire official sanction as 'leaders' by the mid-1940s. Indian imperialism had long operated through a careful balance between the forced coercion and the assistance of Indians who had entered into public life in India, both in cooperation with, and in resistance to, the political and administrative structures erected by the Raj.

The most successful party, the Indian National Congress, created in 1885, would have been unrecognisable to its founders by 1946. Under the leadership of Gandhi an elite, patriarchal group of lawyers had, since the 1920s, transformed itself from a polite pressure group into a mass nationalist party, with over four-and-a-half million members and many more sympathisers. The League, in contrast, was far more of a latecomer to the political scene. Although it was founded in 1909 the League had only caught on among South Asian Muslims during the Second World War. The party had expanded astonishingly rapidly and was claiming over two million members by the early 1940s, an unimaginable result for what had been previously thought of as just one of numerous pressure groups and small but insignificant parties.[16] By the late 1940s the League and the Congress had impressed on the British their own visions of a free future for Indian people. These visions appeared, on the surface, to be incompatible as one, articulated by the Congress, rested on the idea of a united, plural India as a home for all Indians and the other, spelt out by the League, rested on the foundation of Muslim nationalism and the carving out of a separate Muslim homeland. Yet, things were far more finely nuanced than these simple equations between the League as the-party-of-the-Muslims and the Congress as the-party-for-everyone-else would suggest, especially as both parties continued to vacillate about the future nature of a free India, and its constitutional division of powers.

Evidently, in the run up to Partition something had gone badly wrong between Indian Sikhs, Hindus and Muslims. The nature of this breakdown has remained mysterious and unfathomable even to some of those who experienced it or who were caught in the middle of it. As a civil supplies officer, A.S. Bakshi, a turbaned, Sikh civil supplies officer from the fertile district of Jullundur later puzzled, 'we used to be together . . . for days and nights, all of a sudden they lost confidence in us . . . at that time there were only two things . . . Muslims, and non-Muslims'. These feelings run to dismay as well as bitter-

ness: 'we have lost the best of our friends, the people whom we loved, the places
. . . so much of us was embedded in every brick where we'd stayed for generations'.[17] The sorrow at the centre of numerous Partition stories – and the lack
of reconciliation with Partition among so many people – hints at the lack of
legitimacy in the division, the wider feeling that good social relationships had
been ruptured by a settlement forcefully imposed from on high.

Most histories of Partition necessarily cast back in time, to the 1920s or
earlier, to find the answer to this dark question at the heart of Indian nationalism, to understand why Hindus, Sikhs and Muslims grew apart, and debate
whether this schism and sense of division were actually widespread. In the
three decades preceding Partition a self-conscious awareness of religious
ethnicity – and conflict based on this – had undoubtedly escalated in intensity
and was becoming more flagrant. Riots, which had been breaking out on religious festivals such as the festival of colour, *Holi*, or in connection with the
slaughtering of sacred cows or when Hindu religious music was piped too
loudly in front of mosques during prayer time, broke out after increasingly
shortened intervals, and with more frightening ferocity, from the end of the
First World War onwards. Groups working for religious education and
conversion were becoming ever more adept at winning followers and were
powerfully entrenched by the 1940s. Reformist groups such as the Tablighi
Jamaat, Arya Samaj, and Jam 'at-i Islami became richer, stronger, more
dogmatic and more persuasive. They blended, in different ways, politics and
religious symbolism, the internal personal quest with an external missionary
zeal. Inevitably, perhaps, they also clashed doctrinally and politically with each
other. The most important storm centres of this new type of conflict tended
to be the cities and towns of north and west India and the newly minted
identities were strongest in the educated, middle-class urban milieux of the
burgeoning cities.

By the end of the war, many people were revelling in new and simplistic
expressions of religion. There was nothing ancient or predestined about these
politicised manifestations of identity. The experience of colonial rule had
doubtless stirred up these divisions and added to a sense of separation, especially among elites. Reminders of religious 'difference' were built into the
brickwork of the colonial state; a Muslim traveller would be directed to the
'Mohammedan refreshment room' at a train station and drinking taps on
railway platforms were labelled 'Hindu water' or 'Muslim water'. Religious
holidays were factored into the official working calendar and government
statistics, maps, gazetteers, routine instructions, laws and, above all, the
census, all operated on the premise that highly distinct communities, of

Muslims, Sikhs and Hindus resided in the subcontinent. 'A stranger travelling in Indian trains may well have a painful shock when he hears at railway stations for the first time in his life ridiculous sounds about *pani* [water], tea and the like being either Hindu or Muslim,' lamented Gandhi in 1946. 'It would be repulsive [for this to continue] ... it is to be hoped that we shall soon have the last of the shame that is peculiarly Indian.'[18]

Generations of European administrators, travellers and scholars fore-grounded the 'spiritual' in all their interpretations of India and, in their eyes, Hindus, Muslims and Sikhs were inescapably separate and mutually incompatible. As a result of this short-sightedness and an inability to see the finely grained distinctions and differences within, and between, these peoples, all sorts of misguided imperial interventions on behalf of 'communities' were put in place. Well-intentioned policies intended to show British fair play and even-handedness could end up encouraging co-religionists to bond more tightly together. The most important of these moves was the decision to give separate electorates to different religious communities from 1909 so that they were represented by their 'own' politicians.[19] Religious groups acquired stronger voices and more visible spokesmen. New types of association and organisation could link up together, using the railways and the power of the printing press. All this backfired catastrophically as religious boundaries, both more porous and less sharply defined in an earlier age, now hardened.

So the experience of empire exacerbated religious difference. Of course, taboos about purity and pollution, especially about eating, drinking and inter-marrying, did have a far longer pedigree and much older historical precedent; internecine warfare *had* taken place in the past. Yet Partition and its build-up was something entirely new in India and directly related to the ending of empire. Soldiers in the wars of the pre-European era would have considered their religious affiliations in much more localised and less universal ways. They would not necessarily have identified with other co-religionists in other parts of the region, let alone the country or even the world. These earlier wars did, though, provide twentieth-century Hindus, Muslims and Sikhs with a full-blooded stock of superheroes, myths and stories, in which one righteous spiritual community pitted itself against another, from which to draw during their own struggles.[20] The exclusionary politics of Partition, the scale of the killings and the grouping along religious lines were new. Even non-believers or self-proclaimed atheists were labelled as members of a 'community' because of the group that they happened to be born into – not what they believed. Such rigid classifications were novel and completely different from any battles of the preceding centuries.[21]

Professor Mohammad Mujeeb would have meditated on this, and would undoubtedly have been familiar with the heroes and villains of the old stories of Mughal rule and Indian dynasties before the British conquest of the eighteenth century. He was an eminent scholar and educationalist, in his mid-forties at the time of Partition and Vice-Chancellor at the influential Jamia Millia University in Delhi. As a leading nationalist, from a family of staunch Congress supporters, he had a rich social circle of friends and colleagues in the urban literati, which crossed all religions. It was not untypical for Muslims such as Mujeeb to support the Congress and to oppose the League, and he was close to many prominent national politicians. And yet, despite all this, and his great personal friendship with Nehru, his account of shopping in Delhi's markets in the years leading up to Partition is highly revealing. 'For a few years under the influence of the idea that the Muslim consumer should support the Muslim trader,' he remembered, 'I made it a point to buy what I needed in Muslim shops in Old Delhi.' Among educated nationalists during these years, a sense of separateness and self-conscious awareness of difference had set in. Yet this was not the end of the story. Making such straightforward connections between co-religionists was not so easy. Whenever he went shopping, the harsh, practical realities of the situation quickly came home to Mujeeb. 'There were good and bad salesmen,' irrespective of religion and the shops of the good salesmen – with their stacks of sweets, silver pots and pans, or bundles of cloth – 'were always crowded, and Muslim customers were an insignificant part of the crowd'. When the professor tried to get the women in his family to take up his scheme of 'buying Muslim', he was rebuffed with undisguised scorn; practical housewives would shop where the produce was good and where they were given courteous service, they told him, not on the basis of some simplistic, abstract notion.[22]

Mohammad Mujeeb's tale is instructive. On the threshold of Partition, Hindus, Muslims and Sikhs – especially those in the highest political circles – lived with an awareness of difference. This was not grounded on how often someone prayed or went to the temple; it transcended individual levels of piety. It was a strongly felt kinship with others of the same faith that was preserved and promoted through intermarrying (and the strict censure of those who dared to marry outside the group), shared histories and myths, and the instillation of customs, habits and superstitions from an early age. But it was pragmatic. It was not easy to hook together co-religionists in political allegiances across great expanses of territory; there was no such thing as one Muslim, Hindu or Sikh community in South Asia, as numerous demagogues found to their peril. For one thing, linguistic and cultural differences zigzagged across the country and for another, there was little common ground between people with such divergent incomes.

On the eve of Partition, even in the places where there was a heightened sense of difference, there were many countervailing forces. Mercantile and manufacturing communities from sari weavers to tea planters depended on pragmatic co-operation for their livelihoods, while festivals and holidays were flamboyantly celebrated across the board. Class, as ever, acted as a social gel and rich Hindus, Sikhs and Muslims of the same social standing partied together in gilded hotels, irrespective of religion; university friends of various backgrounds attended the same classes; and poor agriculturalists relaxed together on *charpois* at the end of a day's work. Above all, it was a very long jump from a sense of difference, or lack of social cohesion, to mass slaughter and rape. There was nothing 'inevitable' about Partition and nobody could have predicted, at the end of the Second World War, that half a million people or more were going to die because of these differences.

2

Changing Regime

On 14 June 1945, a little over a month after Germany surrendered to the Allies, Nehru and the other leading members of the Congress stepped out of jail. They were free men, released from prison for the final time.

In the absence of the Congress leadership from national political life, however, the political tableaux in which they acted had changed drastically. As the party president at the time, A.K. Azad later claimed, in prison he had been 'completely cut off from the outside world', even denied his trusty transistor radio, 'and did not know what was happening outside'. On their release, the leadership was 'thrown into a new world'.[1] Indians ecstatically greeted their pantheon of heroes but Nehru and the others had fallen out of step with the popular politics of the moment. Gandhi had been freed earlier in 1944 but seemed a figure from the past, removed from the mood of anti-European populism with its roots in labour protest and peasant radicalism. Now, there was little popular regard for the ideology of non-violence and Subhas Chandra Bose, the Indian National Army chief was the hero of the hour. Even more importantly, the Muslim League had been able to exploit the gaps in public leadership exposed by the removal of Congressmen from the limelight, building up a vast groundswell of support that was fatally underestimated by the Congress leadership when it returned to the negotiating table. The Congress message had become more muted in the interim years. It was not clear that the Congress leadership would be able to lead and control popular outbursts as it had done in the past.

By this point, the Congress Party was a bulky organisation, much changed since its heyday of mass public protest against British rule in the 1920s and 1930s. It was a victim of its own success, as it had become a gargantuan umbrella party, housing all manner of political thinkers, politicians, idealists and unscrupulous opportunists. Gandhi famously suggested that the Congress should be disbanded after Independence, as it would have exhausted its stated purpose since 1929 of delivering *purna swaraj*, or full independence, from British rule, but his suggestion was conveniently overlooked as the Congress transformed itself from liberation movement to ruling party. Even if desirable, it was impossible to enforce one pure ideological line. Within the Congress broad church jostled committed Gandhians, liberals, socialists, politicians with narrow regional or local agendas and Hindu nationalists who drew on religious symbolism and history to define their vision of a free united India. Defections took place from smaller parties as the Congress's omnipotence became inescapable. 'I have joined the Congress,' said Maheshwar Dayal Seth, former president of the United Provinces Provincial Hindu Sabha, in a statement. 'I have not joined the Congress for the loaves of office but for service through sacrifice and suffering.'[2] Despite the protestations, it seemed more likely that many jumped on the Congress bandwagon because they knew it was hurtling towards the finishing line; it was obvious the Congress would be the party of power.

The Congress hierarchy was racked with anxiety both about these ideological divisions and about the splinters surfacing in the organisational capacity of the party. National leaders and rank-and-file supporters disagreed vehemently among themselves on all sorts of matters: the basis on which nationalism should be agreed, the ideological policy of the new state, in particular the place that religious symbolism would play in it, and about the meanings of freedom for ordinary South Asians. 'The system of enrolling indiscriminately four *anna* members,' complained the General Secretaries of the party about the quarter of a rupee subscription fee, 'has led unfortunately to many forms of corruption and malpractices disfiguring our political life.'[3] The leadership, which had been attracted by Gandhi's visionary call in their twenties, and drawn to his deceptively simple message of non-violence and self-rule, now approached old age. Nehru was fifty-seven, Vallabhbhai Patel, second in command to Nehru and soon to be Indian Deputy Prime Minister, was seventy-one, Gandhi himself was seventy-seven. They were still engaged in the same protracted, wearisome tug-of-war with the British rulers. Unsurprisingly, differences of opinion among the hierarchy were also transparent by 1946. Gandhi's continued emphasis on spiritual development, self-sufficiency and the foundation of village republics was viewed with barely concealed scepticism by Nehru, despite his personal love and profound respect for the Mahatma, while Nehru's own intellectual spadework and prolific writings paved the way for a liberal, industrial and plural state.

Without anchorage in Gandhian non-violence the nationalist movement was a much more volatile and dangerous proposition, as the leaders themselves were only too aware. To be sure, Gandhi's own concern about this may have been controlling and innately conservative. 'A great many things seem to be slipping out of the hands of the Congress,' he protested to Vallabhbhai Patel. 'The [striking] postmen do not listen to it, nor does Ahmedabad [where a Hindu–Muslim riot had occurred], nor do *Harijans*, nor Muslims. This is a strange situation indeed.' Gandhi was far too astute not to realise that the Congress was only just managing to stay loosely in control of a much larger, more volatile and diverse collection of political movements.[4]

It is little wonder, then, that the Congress tried uneasily to latch on to the popular movements that were breaking out all over India at the end of the Second World War. In particular, Congressmen teamed up with men returning from the Indian National Army. After tedious waits for demobilisation, many soldiers were recruited into military and civil police units and others became ideal recruits for the new defence groups and volunteer bodies springing up across North India. 'Our boys cannot forget politics,' Nehru boldly asserted, 'and work as mere mercenary automatons of a foreign government' and many of the soldiers had indeed developed their own appraisal of the political situation, had high hopes of the meaning of freedom and were passionately nationalistic. In the emboldened words of a Pathan soldier who had fought in North Africa and Italy to Malcolm Darling on his tour in the winter of 1946, 'We suffered in the war but you didn't . . . we bore with this that we might be free.'[5] Disgruntled former soldiers were not going to sit by quietly and wait for concessions from the British: they were armed with a new appreciation of the desperateness, and the injustice, of colonial rule.

The political 'isms' of the post-war world – communism, socialism, fascism and nationalism – could no longer be regarded as abstract philosophies but were deeply felt as matters of life and death. Wartime had created new opportunities while exhausting older ways of doing political business, beefing up the economic and social power of India's cities and, even more importantly, changing the ways in which people thought of politics. Conditions had irreversibly changed. As 1945 drew to a close, India was rocked by rebellions and revolts on an unprecedented scale.

The ending of an era

'I am not very much looking forward to 1946,' the British Viceroy, Wavell, wrote sombrely in his diary on New Year's Day, 'and shall be surprised and very pleased if we get through without serious trouble.'[6] His pessimism proved to be well founded and soon ships in Bombay harbour, where fireworks for New Year's Eve had boomed weeks earlier, turned their guns against British authority, and trained them on those venerable institutions of imperial life: the Taj Hotel, the Yacht Club and the other neo-Gothic buildings that lined the Bombay shore. The naval mutiny was just one of numerous popular rebellions in the early months of 1946. B.C. Dutt, a ringleader of the strike, later remembered the scene on Bombay's shoreline during those tense but festival-like days, when Indian sympathisers fearlessly came to deliver food and water to the mutineers under the full gaze of British officials:

> From every walk of life they came and crowded the seafront around the Gateway of India, with packets of food and pails of water. The restaurant keepers were seen requesting people to carry whatever food they could to the beleaguered ratings. Even some street beggars, it was reported in the press, were seen carrying tiny food packets for the ratings. The harbour front presented a strange spectacle. The whole area was patrolled by armed Indian soldiers. British forces were kept ready at a distance. Indian soldiers with rifles slung across their backs helped to load the food packets brought by the public on boats sent from the ships in the harbour. The British officers were helpless spectators.[7]

It is difficult to exaggerate the turmoil that India was experiencing at the close of the Second World War and the sense of entitlement and hope that had fired the imagination of the people. This was in stark contrast to the situation the average British colonial official found himself in: disliked, overburdened and heavily constrained by a fiscally cautious regime.

Strikes were incessant and held by everybody from tram drivers and press workers to postmen and industrial workers in cotton mills, potteries and factories.[8] In 1946 there were 1,629 industrial disputes involving almost two million workers and a loss of over twelve million man-days.[9] An All India railway strike, which would, of course, have brought gridlock to the country, was threatened in the summer of 1946 and was only narrowly avoided. In Bihar in March 1946 a very serious police mutiny, during which policemen broke open a central armoury, and rampaged through a handful of major towns, was brought under control by the firing of the military. A copycat incident in Delhi involved the mutiny of over 300 policemen.[10] In addition to nationwide anti-British protest movements in retaliation for the firings on the naval mutineers in Bombay, Karachi and Madras, peasant movements, or *kisan sabhas*, attempted to seize control of food committees, resist the control of richer food-hoarders and protest against ration cuts.

The newest aspect of 1946 was the fusion of so many different movements, some urban and some rural, some violent and some law-abiding, many of which were explicitly directed against the British while others, led by rebels, targeted exploitative Indian landlords, loan sharks, autocratic princes and existing social dynamics more broadly. The one thing in common was a feeling of resistance to the status quo. Many of these movements sliced across the neat chronological parameters of Independence and Partition. The armed clashes of the colossal Telengana uprising spread to three to four thousand villages in the Telugu-speaking regions of Hyderabad where peasants armed themselves and seized land.[11] This rebellion, stretching from July 1946 to October 1951 was an interconnected series of armed reprisals for excessive rents, extortion, oppression and the pitiful living conditions in lands ruthlessly controlled by the Nizam of Hyderabad and his landed oligarchy. Radicalised by communist leadership, peasants attempted to liberate their village hinterlands, to redistribute land, and to establish a more equitable society, and even after Independence, once the Nizam had been removed from power by the violent intervention of Indian troops, rebels continued in their struggle against the Indian state itself well into the earliest years of Independence.

Elite Indo-British relationships endured and for the select few the rounds of tea parties, shoots and open houses, attended by rich Indians and Europeans alike, continued unabated. On the streets of major cities, though, a definite streak of anti-Europeanism started to mar relationships, with western ties and hats forcibly removed from Europeans in Bombay, Calcutta and Karachi, the Punjab Governor's car stoned by student demonstrators on the Mall in Lahore and Europeans thrown from their bicycles, while some British tommies about to be shipped home chalked 'cheer, wogs, we are quitting India!' on railway carriages.[12] 'I am bound to say that I cannot recollect any period,' wrote the anguished British Governor of the Central Provinces and Berar to the Viceroy in 1945, reflecting on the charged political rhetoric of the times, 'in which there have been such venomous and unbridled attacks against Government and Government officers.'[13] The 1946 Victory Day parade, a grand spectacle that would have been utilised, in the old order, to express imperial might and to celebrate Indian and British connections, was boycotted by nearly all the major political parties and accompanied by anti-imperial rioting in New Delhi. Mills, schools, shops and colleges were closed, black protest flags were draped from windows, and European-owned cars smouldered while police used fire and tear gas to control crowds. As the procession passed through Connaught Circus, Delhi's commercial hub, crowds cheered the men of the Royal Indian Navy, which had recently mutinied in Bombay, but other units were jeered as they passed through.[14] The popular mood had changed to one where anti-imperial feeling could be aired freely and without fear.

Ultimately, European civilians were not harmed during the violence of 1946, or in the Partition conflict that followed, and some even commented on the ease with which they were able to move around afflicted cities: 'the start of a street fight was delayed to allow my wife to cross the road,' one British newspaper editor bemusedly recalled.[15] Yet it was not self-evident that this would be the outcome and there was mounting anxiety about the safety of Europeans as the Raj went into terminal decline. As an alarmist intelligence report, forwarded by Wavell to the Governor-General, recorded, 'In Delhi, large handwritten posters in red ink recently appeared threatening death for "twenty English dogs" for every INA man executed.'[16] Ultimately, during the Partition that ensued, Indians turned against each other rather than against Europeans, but it was not immediately apparent that this would be the case.

Power was slipping out of British hands and morale in the civil service, especially among European officers, reached its nadir. 'Many of them are feeling the reaction from the strain of the war years here, and see little prospect of constructive or pleasant work,' reported the Governor of Assam on the anxious atmosphere among his civil service cadre. 'Among subordinates there is an increasing uneasiness and feeling that it might be wise to ally oneself with the winning side', while among British military officers there was an itchy impatience to return home. From Bombay, by the beginning of the following year, the assessment was that 70 per cent of the European civil service officers were 'in a mood to go this year'.[17] The anti-imperial rhetoric became ever more grandiloquent and nationalist leaders deftly fused the post-war economic strains, the memory of the Bengal famine and the suppression of the 1942 movement into a powerful invective against British rule.

The stout, mustachioed leader Pandit Pant, an influential Congressman and linchpin of the party in the United Provinces, looked out at a packed crowd of faces in a village in the district of Benaras, in the plains of the River Ganges. Like many others, he had abandoned a promising legal career in the 1920s and had dedicated his life to the Congress. He had been beaten and left disfigured in *lathi* charges, and had spent years in prisons, sharing a cell with Nehru who had become a close ally. On the raised platform, garlanded with heavy strings of flowers, he saw around him villagers who eagerly anticipated freedom, or *swaraj*. Two members of this village had died in 1942 during clashes with the British during the Quit India movement. Now Pandit Pant did not curb his words. 'These days poor women cannot afford to buy cloth to cover their bodies,' he told his listeners. 'Bribery is so much rampant that nothing is available without greasing the palms of officers. In Bengal, *lakhs* of people died and nobody knows even their names. But they all have become martyrs and their matyrdom will be recorded in history in letters of gold. Now we can no longer tolerate the misbehaviour of officials. We have to finish the present Government and throw it away in the sea.'[18]

Congress politicians, trying to keep abreast of the popular mood, did not rein in their words as they might have done in the past. The ruthlessness with which the Quit India agitation had been suppressed was fresh in the memory of Congress supporters, and British officials were starting to resort once again to the degrading suppression of political agitation; the Whipping Act was being applied in cases of rioting in Bombay. As in so many other cases, authoritarian violence was a product of a government in a position of weakness rather than flowing from a position of strength.

Things went from bad to worse for the imperial state when a dynamic outburst greeted the British attempt to prosecute three officers of the Indian National Army at the end of the war. The officers were leaders of the break-away force that had been recruited from Indian army prisoners of war, after the Malayan campaign and the fall of Singapore, and had, under the command of Subhas Chandra Bose, fought with the Japanese in an attempt to dislodge British imperialism from the subcontinent. Soldiers captured while fighting for the INA had been court-martialled in 1943 and 1944 but the Indian public's sympathy for the rebellious army was subdued until the British decided to hold public trials of several hundred INA prisoners, seven thousand of whom had been dismissed from service and detained without trial.[19] Three officers, Prem Kumar Seghal, Shahnawaz Khan and Gurbaksh Dillon, were tried for treason by the colonial state in the ill-chosen and highly symbolic venue of Delhi's Red Fort – Shah Jahan's sandstone fortress from which pre-colonial, Mughal power had emanated. The INA case also became a flashpoint for a more generalised anti-British and anti-imperial feeling, which was quickly outrunning the tempo set by the Congress's political leadership.

Congressmen could not hope to monopolise the protests but rather rode a wave of popular feeling, at times riding in front of it, at other times being wiped aside by more radical leadership. 'There has seldom been a matter that has attracted so much Indian public interest and, it is safe to say, sympathy,' wrote a vexed British intelligence officer and it was reported that politicians were compelled to talk about the INA in appreciative terms during the central assembly election campaign in order to grab – and keep – the interest of their listeners. [20] INA men were garlanded with flowers wherever they went, invited to speak at public meetings and lent the support of powerful backers, from barristers to businessmen. The Viceroy, who found it personally trying to overlook 'this hero worship of traitors', nevertheless frankly admitted in private that the INA trials were 'embarrassing' and although the trio were found guilty in 1946, the sentences were ultimately quashed. [21] This climb-down by the imperial state marked another notch on the nationalist yardstick, as the ability of the state to enforce law and order appeared distinctly weakened once again. The last refuge and ultimate pillar of the colonial state, its army, was less reliable than at any time since the 1857 uprising and this undoubtedly influenced the British government's decision to hand back the Indian empire to Indians as soon as they possibly could. This victory, and the celebration and drilling of a well-armed military force, enhanced the sense that a revolutionary social upheaval was impending and helped to champion a cult of militarisation among young men.

Voting for freedom

The removal of Churchill from Downing Street, and the Labour Party landslide of the summer of 1945, made British intentions to leave India more concrete and gave the negotiations a fresh injection of realism. 'In accordance with the promises already made to my Indian peoples,' King George declared to the assembled members of Parliament on the green benches of Westminster in 1945, 'my Government will do their utmost to promote, in conjunction with the leaders of Indian opinion, the early realisation of full self-government in India.'[22]

Before anything else could be done, though, there was a more urgent imperative – to work out who the leaders of Indian opinion really were and the political persuasions of, in the words of the British monarch, his 'Indian peoples'. The history of imperial assessments of popular will is a troubled one: how best to find out, at the end of empire, who to hand over power to? Colonial regimes have been notoriously weak, or wilfully manipulative, when identifying and empowering representative leaders. For those engineering the transfer of power, in keeping with the British ideal of democratic decolonisation, the answer was an Indian general election. Some forty one million Indians were eligible to go to the polls in the winter months of 1945–6 or

10 per cent of the general population. The vast size of the country and the logistical difficulties of organising the counts meant that elections were staggered from December 1945 to March 1946.[23]

The purpose of the election was twofold: to form provincial governments in the Indian provinces, and so to draw Indian politicians into the business of running the everyday functions of government from which Congress had been excluded during the Second World War, and to create a central body that would start designing the future constitutional form of a free India. The announcement of the election caused shockwaves that pulsed through British India; this was the first outlet for popular politics sanctioned by the British for almost a decade. All parties accelerated their fund-raising and within days election songs, poetry and campaign propaganda filled the newspapers and the city streets.

While the Congress claimed to speak for all Indians, irrespective of religion, the League claimed to be the mouthpiece of all Muslims. Neither would budge on this fundamental issue. Only a few far-sighted individuals warned of the dangers written on the wall, of the pressing need to address the fractured politics of Hindu and Muslim political communities. The Communist Party of India had built a realistic acknowledgement of Pakistan's popularity into its policy-making, by acknowledging the Muslim right to self-determination in 1942, but the CPI was sidelined from mainstream Congress politics and left-leaning Congressmen were marginalised from the inner workings of the Congress Party by 1945.[24] None of the leading political thinkers in Congress were incorporating a national division into their thinking. Instead, the parties embarked on a concerted bid to rally supporters across the country, by welding economic concerns with religious and emotive symbols into a broad-based, popular appeal.

A flurry of marching songs and poems rang out throughout the country. Printing presses worked overtime producing thin sheets of party information. Party workers pasted up posters and flyers on city walls and telegraph poles. 'The land and nation are our bread and butter,' Muslim Leaguers sang out as they paraded in North India with their distinctive green and white flags. 'But ploughing the nation yields the best crop/ Come to the league, overwhelm all others/ Your people are in anguish/ It's voting day: let's march/ let's march in step, *Mukhiaji* [chief]!'[25]

'Red box for the Congress, cast your vote in the red box of the Congress!' called out a Congress election flyer. 'Gandhiji and Jawaharlal Nehru are awakening us/ *Kisan*! Be awake and know the condition of our country/ There is no food, we can't get cloth/ No oil, it's dark in our house/ All things are controlled [i.e. rationed]/ But sometimes we don't get cloth to put round the dead body/ Vote for the Congress and win our own rule/ Then our country will be happy, *Kisan*!'[26]

These were remarkably similar appeals based on economic hardship and brutal social realities. Before long, though, economic issues were supplanted by a more trenchant issue. The campaigning focal point quickly emerged as Pakistan. Swiftly it became the dominant election issue, and a deadly wedge was driven between the Congress and the League as both parties dug their heels in more defiantly and uncompromisingly. Pakistan was becoming a black and white issue.

Indian leaders had demanded the election, although some criticised the rapidity with which it was thrust upon them, and embraced the opportunity to display their popular power. It was most useful to the British government, which needed to rubber-stamp any future constitutional settlement. This imperative – the need to absolutely ascertain 'Indian will' – meant that the election result had monumental implications that outlived the temporary formation of governments. It was a peculiar mixture of the lofty and the mundane; it was a nation-making referendum with international and permanent implications about state formation. Yet, it was also a vent for far more parochial concerns, at a time of dire economic hardship. Under the diarchal system, which pared off provincial governance, leaving the most critical aspects of the state – defence, budgets and foreign affairs – firmly in British clutches, the provincial legislators elected would be expected to take on jobs overseeing municipal water supply, the school curriculum and road-building. The voters had a double duty: to elect their local party man or woman who would fight their corner in the everyday struggles over resources, but also to express a much more amorphous and nebulous attachment to the idea of 'Indian freedom' or 'Pakistan'. For would-be politicians, appealing to Pakistan, or opposing it tooth and nail, seemed an attractive short cut to winning votes.

The clear connection between the outcome of the election and the likely future shape of the country gave the campaigns an intensely bitter flavour. A.K. Azad observed that it was 'hardly an election in the normally understood meaning of the term'.[27] The electorate was tiny, there was widespread malpractice and fights broke out in constituencies as the election evolved into a plebiscite in favour of, or against, the idea of Pakistan. The League was battling for its life, determined to build a Muslim consensus around the Pakistan demand and to win the strongest possible hand in the constitutional negotiations with the British, which were sure to follow. Nor was the Congress manifesto, which underlined its commitment to secularism, economic development and land reforms, uppermost in the minds of Congress workers whose first duty was to prove that the Congress had universal support and that the population was, therefore, anti-Pakistan.

The central committee of the League studiously avoided publishing a manifesto altogether, and pinned their whole campaign to the demand for Pakistan. As Jinnah clarified to an audience in the North West Frontier Province, this was a winner-takes-all game, a zero sum equation: every vote cast in favour of the League was a vote in favour of Pakistan, every vote against would help create Hindu Raj. 'That is the only choice and the only issue before us.'[28] If this was a referendum, though, the meaning of the question being asked was obscure and could be interpreted in dramatically different ways. With the stakes so high and the number of voters so low, winning seats by fair means or foul was the ultimate end of every party and those who could not vote still participated in the street theatre of the electoral show.

Never before had Indian politicians needed to demonstrate and prove quite so visibly that they had mass support and backing. Ends began to justify means as internal consistency in speech and thought became dispensable. The words 'Pakistan' and 'swaraj', which were already barely defined, began to be used with deliberate impreciseness. People did not just support a political party by this stage – they felt its importance was integral to their sense of self. As the battle to claim the future shape of the Indian state intensified in 1946, politicians wilfully muddied the meanings of freedom and outdid each other in their promises at mass election rallies as they attempted to secure proof of their popularity, to demonstrate their status to the British government, to achieve the right to represent the populace.

It is little wonder that the exaggerated and utopian strand in political rhetoric might be taken at face value; Nehru gave one speech at Sukkur in Sind to a crowd estimated to be 50,000 strong in which he said that, in the free India, 'everybody would be provided with sufficient food, education and all the facilities including a house to live' and that Pakistan was a 'useless idea' which meant 'slavery forever'.[29] During the post-war Indian general election politicians roused their followers with the vocabulary of wartime and articulated their struggle in the global language of alliances and enemies, using the metaphors of battle and blood. 'To vote for the Congress is tantamount to baring one's chest before bullets,' Pandit Pant loftily declared at a public meeting. Jinnah made a direct comparison between his leadership and Churchill's, while Congressmen drew parallels between the Muslim League and the activities of the Nazis.[30] Similarly, a League activist, Zawwar Zaidi, a student who canvassed for the party, later recalled the way in which the idea of Pakistan was propagated during the elections.

> We had a sort of training camp where we were trained . . . what sort of questions might be asked of us, what sort of reply we should give; where and how to contact the voters . . . the message was that we are working for the creation of a new state; sometimes they would not fully understand it and we had to explain this, the idea of a Muslim state, and the slogans that were raised . . . according to the audience that we had, if he was a villager we would say that things would be different, he would have his own state . . . if it was an educated person, and if it was a Congressman then we would adopt a different strategy . . .[31]

The vital importance of the elections as a means of deciding the nature of free India, the speed with which the contests were called and the lack of clarification over what freedom was going to deliver meant that a great many politicians fell back on expedient populism.

The politicisation of religion became the order of the day. Islamic *fatwas* were invoked by all political parties – from the Socialists to the most rabid right-wing nationalists – as they attempted to inject their party image with a quick shot of legitimacy. Put simply, it was not only the League which was manipulating religious feelings in order to gain votes. Congressmen reminded crowds that the Gandhian preference for liquor prohibition was fully in keeping with the Islamic injunction against alcohol. At a speech in support of a candidate it was claimed that at least two Congress measures, alcohol prohibition and curbs on usury, 'virtually translated into practice the commandments of the *Shariat*'.[32] Even the Anglophile Unionist Party leader in Punjab, Khizr Tiwana, stalwart of the privileged Punjabi landlord class and an optimistic advocate of cross-community co-operation, 'garnished his speeches with quotations from the Quran'.[33] The Congress camp too put the icons and networks of Hinduism to practical use to convey the Congress message, by distributing literature at religious *melas* and fairs, encouraging saffron-clad *sadhus* to support the Congress and linking together repellent practices, such as the slaughter of the holy cow, with anti-British and anti-League tirades.[34] Further from the Hindustani-speaking centre of party politics, especially in the Muslim majority provinces, the language of Congress could become unrecognisably twisted by its local allies; in the NWFP allies of the Congress – the Ahrars and Jamiat-ul-Ulema – were endorsing Gandhi and Nehru at Congress meetings yet underpinning this support with

Qur'anic injunctions. Bigotry and bare-faced chauvinism were used to attract voters on all sides and raked the ground for the violent encounters to follow.

For their part, the League played on the motif of exclusionary Islam, tapping into pre-existing chauvinism towards *kafirs* or unbelievers. The language used was prejudiced and bigoted. Little by little the League was able to claim a bedrock of support in the NWFP, a province in which they had failed to win even one seat in the elections of 1937. Flagrant propaganda was used to weld Muslims together and to frighten them into supporting the Pakistani cause. At polling booths the vote was sometimes reduced to a thoroughly misleading question of religion; holding a copy of the Qur'an in one hand and a book of Hindu holy texts in the other, a representative would ask the voter which one they would choose before hustling them inside the polling booth. Elsewhere a respected religious leader, Maulana Shabbir Ahmad Osmani, exhorted his followers to support the League: 'Any man, who gives his vote to the opponents of the Muslim League, must think of the ultimate consequences of his action in terms of the interest of his nation and the answers that he would be called upon to produce on the Day of Judgement.'[35] Even the word 'Pakistan', which literally means 'land of the pure', had multiple resonances. Sayyid Muhammad Ashrafi Jilani, one of the leading speakers at the All-India Sunni Conference in April 1946, said to have been attended by over 200,000 people, gave an address in which he played on the word: 'when a community becomes pure in knowledge, in deed, in disposition, it transforms whichever place it sets foot on into a pure abode'.[36] The emphasis was on restoring order in a world gone awry and on re-establishing local sovereignty.

Not everyone was convinced, of course, by the Pakistan slogan. Different Muslims hailed the League for their own localised, diverse and sometimes contradictory reasons. Some of the most forthright and bloody opposition to the League came from within Muslim communities themselves, especially in the edgy build-up to the elections when some Leaguers and their 'Nationalist Muslim' opponents fought over the same seats, while their supporters fought openly in the streets. Arguments for and against Pakistan took place among members of the same families and the reasons for the division of opinion stretched across the spectrum from piety to agnosticism; some of the most pious *ulema*, or Muslim divines, rejected Pakistan's call because they saw within it the seeds of the delimitation of Islam: the scope and project of Islam would, they felt, be boxed in within artificial national limits. Others were turned off for other ideological reasons or by the upper-crust calibre of the League leadership itself. The president of the Jamiat-ul-Ulema denounced

Jinnah in a *fatwa* of 1945 as the great heathen, Kafir-i-Azam, in a pun on the League leader's popular title, Quaid-e-Azam, great leader.[37]

For many Muslims, Jinnah was most emphatically not their 'Great Leader'. For 'Nationalist Muslims' – as those who stayed loyal to the Congress were called – it was a difficult balancing act. As their label flagged up, they were seen as different from plain 'Nationalists'.[38] 'Nationalist Muslim' politicians had to fight the election in Muslim constituencies and had to go head to head with League candidates for seats. Right on the front line of anti-League politics, these electoral contests became particularly fiery and divisive as they spilled over into street fights and candidates were ostracised by their communities, spat upon or garlanded with humiliating necklaces of shoes. One son complained that his 'Nationalist Muslim' father had been sworn at and 'not allowed to take his prayer in the mosque'.[39] In some cases *fatwas* were passed suggesting that Muslims who opposed Pakistan could not be given a proper Islamic burial. As these Muslims attempted a last ditch attempt to thwart the League, they were ridiculed as traitors or poster boys for the Congress. In the eyes of the League propagandists, these Muslim Congressmen were not real Muslims at all and made good targets for songs and party propaganda. 'Though Muslims in name, in action they are Hindus, Call them half fish, half fowl – if you choose!'[40]

Although money was poured into these constituencies by the Congress Party during the elections (they had become 'almost a bottomless pit'), the battle for popular support had been won long before. 'Mass contact' campaigns initiated by the Congress in the late 1930s to rally Muslims to the Congress side faded away and finally ended in the summer of 1939, unmissed by many in Congress who were consumed by more pressing political and economic issues or feared that the campaign would generate more problems than it solved. 'The Nationalist Muslim,' observed the Socialist leader J.P. Narayan, 'not only finds himself ostracised by his own community but also let down by the Congress itself.'[41] The truth was that the Congress had, ever since the end of the First World War, been establishing an overwhelming base of support in the country and also had some visible, prominent, Muslim supporters. This seemed good enough; ensuring that the party had a soundly representative, plural basis was less urgent in the late 1930s. By the time the Congress leadership emerged from imprisonment at the end of the Second World War it was too late to recover this lost ground and to rally Muslim support. It was even more difficult for the Congress to attract Muslim supporters, especially in North and West India because, for ordinary people, it could seem like a 'Hindu' organisation despite its official open-door policy.

Some Congressmen fused their politics with Hinduism and worked closely alongside *sadhus*, taking advantage of religious holidays and religious iconography to appeal to supporters. Leaguers made the most of this, declaring that Congress was really a cover for a Hindu party and that Indian Islam was under attack or in danger. By the eve of Partition this was a real image problem for the Congress at the grassroots. In practice, if not in theory, the Congress *looked* as if it had long conceded the Muslim vote.

On the election days, shops were firmly shut, clusters of people gathered on street corners waiting for news and party workers travelled through the streets in jeeps or on elephants strung with party flags. In Sind, brightly decorated camels languished outside the polling stations and young children were employed to chant party slogans. Vitriol was poured on opposing parties in pamphlets and through loudspeakers. At the polling booths, people long dead were frequently registered, boxes of ballot papers went missing and women electors wearing veils impersonated other women in order to vote multiple times, in at least one case by changing saris on every occasion.[42]

Despite the affrays, voter-bashing and ballot-rigging, and the Victorian 'franchise', it could be claimed that this was the most democratic exercise ever undertaken in the history of the subcontinent at the time, at least by comparison with the even more tightly restricted franchise used during the elections of 1937. It may have been grossly unrepresentative of India as a whole, yet it was electrifying for the urban middle and lower-middle classes, large segments of which enjoyed their first taste of democratic representation. Millions of those with a little land or a small stake in property could vote: clerks, teachers, landed farmers and stallholders.

Women in particular grasped this opportunity to vote with both hands in 1946 and in countless constituencies the turn-out was high for women. Women League and Congress campaigners explained how to use the ballot paper, accompanied women voters to election meetings and manned the polling stations. 'They went house to house for canvassing, brought ladies to the polling booths and have made a good awakening in women of Delhi.'[43] Photographs show women in *burqas* casting their votes in the provinces. They waited patiently in queues, up to half a mile long in places, and in Bombay, in the midst of a heat wave, several women waiting to vote fainted from heatstroke. Among men, too, the enthusiasm for voting was palpable; in the Netaji Park in Bombay, a sick voter was brought on a stretcher by volunteers, and at least two blind men were assisted into the polling booth.[44] Public fervour, press reports and governmental analysis collided in a moment of collective expectation about the future of the country.

Official interpretations of the electoral results now took on momentous significance. The results showed that the League had become a force to be reckoned with. Massive and polarised support for the League and Congress shocked even those who had expected some degree of division, as it appeared to reflect that Indian society had been pulled apart magnetically along religious lines. The League, which had polled notoriously weakly in the previous elections of 1937, now walked away with a full hand. In the Central Assembly it won every single Muslim seat, and a majority of seats in the provinces. As expected, the Congress swept up the bulk of non-Muslim seats in the provinces and at the centre.[45] It was certainly not a straight fight between the League and the Congress; the revitalised political machinery of the two major players was pitted against older, established regional parties and the Congress fended off local challenges from communists, Hindu Mahasabhites and independent candidates. In Punjab, most significantly of all, some of the landed Muslim stalwarts of the Unionist Party stood their ground, despite growing rifts in the party and the defection of older members to the League, and the Unionists won over 20 per cent of the vote polled. The trouble was that these parties, even if significant on their regional home turf, could not hope to cobble together India-wide support, or to make a great claim to representation in a centralised assembly.[46]

In the short-term, the reversal in the League's dismal electoral fortunes in the North East and North West of undivided India by 1946, and Jinnah's new popularity in these regions, were the indispensable trophy that allowed Jinnah to press ahead confidently with the Pakistan demand. This may appear, at first glance, to be deceptively straightforward: a Muslim party won lots of votes in Muslim-dominated areas. But there was nothing at all inevitable about this and the increase in the League's new popularity broke through the regional barriers that had blocked the expansion of a centralised Muslim party in the past. On a case-by-case basis Jinnah attempted to bring the League's imprimatur to regional politics by making pacts with local politicians, enrolling well-revered *pirs* and spiritual leaders and using the popularity of pre-existing local campaigns. It was a feat of extraordinary political brokerage but also meant bringing together tenuously linked interests and groups. Perhaps the most striking feature is the great differences from place to place among League supporters and the diverse rationales for becoming a Leaguer.

The British watched the results with a view to forging a representative, central body to which it could legitimately pass the baton. From the vantage point of bureaucrats collating results in the imperial capital the results seemed obvious. Any future state would have to take account of the strength of support for the League and Congress and these parties were anointed the legitimate heirs to imperial power. The battle over the precise contours of a free India looked as if it was going to be a two-horse race. As Penderel Moon, a senior government secretary and one of the sharpest political insiders in Delhi at the time, wrote in January 1946, 'It is now abundantly clear that the Pakistan issue has got to be faced fairly and squarely. There is no longer the slightest chance of dodging it.'[47] The League had won its seat at the negotiating table.

In all of this, though, there was a vital element missing: the ideas of freedom and the meanings that people attributed to the intense debates over a future dedicated to *swaraj* or 'Pakistan' (in the most literal interpretation of the word, as life in the land of the pure) had been lost. British administrators unquestioningly accepted that the League and the Congress had become pugilistic and polarised because Islam and Hinduism were such incompatible religious doctrines – and the vitally important reasons why these parties had become so alienated from one another were left unexamined and disregarded as fundamentally uninteresting. The British thought in terms of territory. The grey margins between territorial nationalism and other forms of patriotic, emotive expression – not so easily linked to land – remained imperial blind spots.

Fervent public displays of anti-colonial sentiment in post-war India help to explain the frenzied British scramble to depart from the Indian subcontinent. As the British government began to negotiate its withdrawal from South Asia in late 1945 and the early months of 1946 the political parties – the Congress and the League – that would replace the imperial rulers had been decided, but far less thought had been given to the shape of the state or states that would inherit the empire or to the meaning of the mass support for these parties. Meanwhile, the narrow electorate in the general elections of 1945–6 blocked the participation of millions of Indians from electoral politics and necessarily pushed political demonstrations into the streets and marketplaces where the disenfranchised were determined to have a hearing. The newly installed provincial governments, if they intended to keep in control of this powder keg, evidently would have to enact popular legislation and ensure that they protected the rights – or even the safety – of their constituents. The conditions were ripe for raised expectations of freedom, localised and community interpretations of its meaning, and wildly improbable millenarian dreams. Absent from the official British discussion, and from the League and Congress (which had an interest in keeping their appeal as broad as possible) was any real thought regarding these thousands of divergent expectations and how they might be met in one, single constitutional settlement. This would prove a fateful oversight.

3

The Unravelling Raj

Passing through the lanes of the North Indian city of Aligarh in the spring of 1946 nobody could have been in any doubt about the intensity of feeling over the question of Pakistan. The word 'Pakistan' was daubed on front doors, pictures of Jinnah could be seen pasted on walls, and green and white tinsel and League banners were suspended across the narrow alleyways of the old city, where metalworkers and artisans produced locks, scissors and tools for the rest of the subcontinent in their workshops facing on to the streets. In local mosques and on street corners Muslims heatedly debated the demand for Pakistan while vocal members of groups such as the Jamiat-ul-Ulema's loud rejection of the idea sometimes led to street fights with their co-religionists. The small city, a few hours' drive to the east of Delhi, founded on the site of an old Mughal *qasbah* would have been indistinguishable from many other small cities in the Gangetic plains, sitting squarely in the Hindustani-speaking hinterland where the Pakistan demand was at its most intensely bitter, apart from the fact that, across the railway tracks in the wide open spaces of the civil lines, the soaring rooftops of Aligarh Muslim University could be seen.

Created by Syed Ahmed Khan in the nineteenth century, Aligarh Muslim University was intended as a place to blend Islamic instruction with the demands of the encounter with the western world, an institution that would impart all the manners and educational benefits that an English public school could offer to well-heeled Muslims. Here, enthusiastic support for both the League and the Pakistan demand had been a long-standing feature of university life, dating back to the earliest years of the Second World War. As Jinnah's self-described 'arsenal' of Pakistan, Aligarh University students were at the cutting edge of pro-Pakistan thinking, and they retrospectively claimed the credit for founding the state. In early 1946, the League leadership was energetically courting their support, and when leaders such as Jinnah and Liaquat Ali Khan, a future Prime Minister of Pakistan and university old boy, visited the college they were given rapturous receptions. League leaders were carried aloft on the shoulders of students, who set crackers on the railway lines to welcome them.

The university was well known for having a large Muslim League membership but this was now spreading to the town, where enthusiasm for Pakistan was steadily building. Women organised pro-League meetings and encouraged donations of jewellery for the League's cause while their husbands and sons used printed leaflets, persuasion, processions and placards to bring Pakistan into existence. By the spring of 1946, with the League's victories in the elections confirmed, the whole campus was in a frenzy of Pakistani fever and academic work had been abandoned in favour of political activism. There was consternation and outspoken opposition from some on the campus. At the same time, non-Muslims in the town started to become nervous and looked to their local politicians to protect them from this nebulous and repetitive Pakistan demand.

In Aligarh, in the atmosphere of violent rhetoric, rumours of trouble and the visible drilling of students, suspicion between communities increased. Could Muslim administrators still be trusted? The president of the Aligarh City Congress Committee asked for arrangements to be made for people to register crimes at the local Congress office, rather than the local police station, because the latter was in a 'Muslim part of town'. Political organisations that campaigned for 'Hindu' rights started to attract large numbers, meeting in public places and circulating petitions that called for protection from the university on their doorstep. A retaliatory and accusatory tone crept in. The relationship between 'town' and 'gown' was stretched to breaking point in March 1946. A riot erupted less than a week after noisy celebrations marked 'Pakistan Day' and the League's electoral success in the province. A few Aligarh students buying cloth from a local Hindu cloth merchant quibbled over the price of a bolt of fabric. An altercation broke out, a crowd formed. In the arson attack that swiftly followed at least four people burned to death and the thatched market area of the town was left in ashes.

The Congress government, now in power in the provincial ministry based in Lucknow, lashed back, passing punitive collective fines on numerous local Muslim inhabitants – who said they knew nothing about the whole business – and launching a party-political inquiry into what had taken place. Over time, this became a bitter local dispute between the provincial League and the Congress. Nehru was one of the few politicians who could see the dangers of the alienation of the Congress ministers in the province from the local populace of the city and, after receiving complaints from poor local 'Nationalist Muslims' about the levy, he urged the provincial government to deal with the situation differently in case 'they are driven against their will into the Muslim League'.[1] The risk was, just as Nehru perceived, that Congress and League politicians would start playing up to their core constituents even more, colour their speeches with religious language and stop offering olive branches to the other community. The fines were a direct parody of colonial thinking and simplistic religious assumptions were being made about the multifarious inhabitants of Aligarh. The danger was they could become self-fulfilling. This was, unfortunately, exactly what happened. In the city of Aligarh, a frightening level of polarisation was developing among some of the leading public figures and by the end of the year, the Aligarh University Student Union leader was claiming publicly to have killed Hindus with his own bare hands.

Aligarh had a particularly charged atmosphere in 1946, but some of the changes taking place there, in one small town, offer a window on to the wider breakdown of state power that was occurring that year all over North India. The unexpectedly spectacular victory of the League in the elections had heightened the call for Pakistan. 'Ours is grim determination,' swore Jinnah. 'Nobody should be under any delusion about our stand for the establishment of Pakistan at any cost, whatever the opposition.'[2] The victory emboldened Jinnah's supporters with a new confidence and amplified the demand. Hundreds of the newly elected League legislators gathered together in April in the quadrangle of the Anglo-Arabic hall in Delhi to cheer their success, under the carapace of a green and white tent strung with banners, bunting and flags printed in swirling Urdu and English scripts. One read: 'The road to freedom lies through Pakistan' and the other, 'We are determined to fight till the last ditch for our rights in spite of the British or the Congress.' The world's press were starting to take note and photographers packed the front row. Impassioned speeches followed one after another. Begum Shah Nawaz called for Muslim women to encourage their husbands and sons to take up arms for Pakistan if the British tried to establish a united Hindustan. Telling the story of a visit to a grieving mother in the Punjab whose son had been stabbed to death by a militia group, she claimed that the woman had told her that she was happy to have given her son to the nation. 'Muslim women were prepared for all sacrifices,' the begum announced, 'and were prepared to be put to the test.'[3] The crescendo came with Jinnah's own closing speech: 'Is Britain going to decide the destiny of 100 million Muslims? No. Nobody can. They can obstruct, they can delay for a little while, but they cannot stop us from our goal. Let us, therefore, rise at the conclusion of this historic convention full of hope, courage and faith. Insha'Allah we shall win.' It was rousing stuff but the fine details – and the meanings of this Pakistan for the Muslims of South Asia – had been deliberately and conveniently evaded and ignored.[4]

Nonetheless, League membership figures continued moving steadily upwards. Membership had rocketed from just 1,330 card-carrying Leaguers in 1927 to an official membership of two million claimed by 1944. During the Congress leaders' time behind bars, the League had had the chance to swell and as Jinnah himself admitted, 'The war which nobody welcomed proved to be a blessing in disguise.'[5] The numbers alone do not tell the whole story. By 1946, even taking into account important exceptions, the League had the popular backing of South Asian Muslims in the urban centres and even in large chunks of the countryside: some Punjabi Leaguers were so confident of their support that they called for a universal franchise in 1946.

Jinnah became – as had Gandhi and Nehru – for many of his supporters an ideal type and was hero-worshipped by millions who endowed him with the characteristics of a saviour. Passionate supporters, both men and women, sent him presents and adoring fan mail, including cards, telegrams and letters of congratulation, cigar boxes and attar of roses, different maps of Pakistan carved in wood, and donations ranging from significant lump sums to the pocket money of young children. Stall-holders outside post offices sold post-cards and postal envelopes stamped with Jinnah's portrait and League mottoes. Followers begged him to take the protection of bodyguards. 'Pray let no chance be taken in guarding your person, the greatest single asset of the Muslim nation,' wrote one.[6] Jinnah fuelled this personal adoration and was unassailably 'the sole spokesman' of the League, which was equipped with a remarkably over-centralised and undemocratic internal structure, with budg- etary and decision-making powers firmly in Jinnah's own grip. For many of these Leaguers, Pakistan became much more than the sum of its parts or the territorial outline of a nation state: it meant personal identification with a cause which was increasingly expressed in black and white terms.

Crucially, though, anti-Congress feeling and heartfelt support for Jinnah and the League did not necessarily translate into support for Pakistan as we know it today with its current borders and boundaries. The Lahore Resolution, passed at the annual Muslim League meeting on 23 March 1940 and identified by Pakistanis as the foundation stone for their state, is not much of a guide. It pinpointed the Muslim desire for a more loosely federated state structure, calling for a collection of independent states with autonomy and sovereignty. There was a lack of knowledge or concern about Pakistan's actual territorial limits. Jinnah himself seems to have prevaricated in his understanding of Pakistan as a separate, sovereign nation state distinct from India. It seems more likely, in the early days of the constitutional negotiations, at least, that he was rallying his supporters in order to extract the best possible deal from the British for the League, and would have settled for a federal solution if it guaranteed a firm element of decentralised power in the hands of Muslims.[7] Among Jinnah's supporters, what Pakistan meant was even more opaque. Many did not think primarily of Pakistan as a territorial reality at all, and when they did, they wishfully hoped that large tracts of India would be included in it. The talismanic word 'Pakistan' was used strategically to rally supporters and the League achieved impressive and emphatic endorsement across India. Yet few knew what this Pakistan would mean, and absolutely nobody knew what its construction would really cost.

This ambiguity was convenient. Jinnah was facing the problem of welding together diverse constituents, many of whom read into the Pakistan demands their own local interpretations or seized upon the League as a vehicle for their own regional campaigns. The issue of territory was repeatedly fudged. The town of Aligarh could never have been included in the Pakistani state and today is still a university town in India – many miles from the border with Pakistan. Maps painted on pro-Pakistani propaganda reflect the lack of clarity concerning territory in Pakistani nationalism. In one, the black silhouette of the whole of the Indian subcontinent is marked uncompromisingly with the words 'Pakistani Empire' – the bold typeface in a diagonal line branding the whole of India and Afghanistan, from the Himalayas to its southern tip at Cape Comorin, as part of this Pakistani realm. Another map, in contrast, shows a fragmented patchwork subcontinent with different provinces marked off as regional 'nations', including Dravidstan, Usmanistan, Rajistan, Pakistan, Balochistan and Bangsamistan. A third map, created around the same time, shows a more easily recognisable outline of Pakistan as we know it today but with the southern Indian princely state of Hyderabad included as part of the Muslim state's natural limits.[8] Pakistan was an imaginary, nationalistic dream as well as a cold territorial reality.

Even Muslim Leaguers who believed Pakistan could be a territorial state – distinct from India – had different ideas about where this land would be and what its relationship would be with India. The final shape of the country came as a shock to some of its most fervent supporters. Strolling through Delhi on a sunny afternoon with her family after the elections, the Muslim League leader Begum Ikramullah looked up at the domes of Humayan's tomb, the sixteenth-century red sandstone and white marble masterpiece of Mughal architecture. Her husband reassured her that Delhi would definitely be in

Pakistan when the country came into being. 'The frontiers of Pakistan had not been defined and it never entered our heads that Delhi would not be within it.'[9] There were a small handful of far-sighted individuals who saw the dangers of a two-state solution to the constitutional problem. Two Congress workers from North India suggested that the weakness in the League's strategy, and its failure to outline Pakistan's proposed territory, should be exposed. They wrote asking the Congress to paste up posters and flyers around the streets with a suggested map of Pakistan under the caption 'Are you ready to leave your house, land, property and everything and go to Pakistan?'[10] But this was a rare appeal. Nobody knew what this map was – and nobody was contemplating migrating in 1946, let alone the mass movement of twelve million people only one year later.

Getting ready to rule

On 28 March 1946, the provincial governors formally returned the election results from their provinces. Ministry-making could begin in earnest. Congress ministries started governing in Bombay, Madras, UP, Bihar, Central Provinces, Orissa, Assam and North West Frontier Province, while a League government ran Sind and, propped up by third parties, started to govern Bengal. There was only one real coalition: in Punjab. Here, the League was kept in abeyance, waiting at the door of power, and the Unionists, led by Khizr Tiwana, joined up with Congress and the Panthic Sikhs. Soon the corridors of power in the regional capital cities buzzed with politicians and their supporters. 'The change which came over the Secretariat was almost unbelievable,' wrote an Oxford-educated civil servant of the old guard, Rajeshwar Dayal, who was rather perturbed by the new order and by the change in his secretariat. 'The orderly and silent corridors with officers and staff moving silently about their business were transformed into babels of noise.'[11] For others, this was the beginning of the transition to democracy and marked the start of real popular participation in political institutions.

As Indian politicians and their staff took over the offices of British officials, moving in crates of papers and sometimes surreptitiously taking down pictures of the King-Emperor and the Union Jack, the power of the imperial state broke down. All eyes were naturally fixed on Delhi. Talk on the streets and in the press was about the main negotiations, and focused on when and how power would be passed at the centre. Yet the drawn-out, painful process of decolonisation in South Asia was already well under way. Provincial governments were already setting the agenda. Their coming to power in early

1946 drew the sting out of anti-British sentiment in India. Politicians made the difficult transition from opposition to government. 'The new government came in a rather belligerent mood determined to stretch the constitution to the limit and beyond, and to show the remaining British officials their place in the new order of things,' remembered Rajeshwar Dayal.[12] Struggles still endured in Delhi's political heartland over central powers, yet in the provinces the imperial endgame was over. The problem was that Leaguers and Congressmen remained fundamentally unreconciled and nobody could see how their differences might be patched up. While some blithely wished these differences away, others hardened their opposition.

The new ministries were inaugurated with a fanfare. The ministers had to swear their allegiance to the King-Emperor but many whispered hoarsely as they did so. People clambered up to see the first day of the new assemblies, packed viewing galleries, and press and photographers were out in force. For those who were on the losing side, however, the feeling grew that these politicians in power could act with impunity and that they were not representative of *all* Indians. Dress became important. Congressmen sat on the benches in white homespun dhotis, worn with sandals and Gandhi caps – the same outfit still worn by many Indian politicians today. Jinnah's fur cap was becoming a style icon and Muslims wore kurta pyjamas with a cap or fez while Sikhs retained their distinctive turbans. This exuberant new order alienated those who felt on the wrong side of it or left out from its culture and symbolism. Mohammad Mujeeb later remembered the hubbub when he watched the United Provinces assembly from a viewing gallery for the first time:

> It was, I believe, the inaugural session. There were crowds of people in the visitors' galleries and the hall, but hardly a face that was known to me. I was simple-minded enough to ask a man standing next to me where the chief minister was, and I got in reply a reproachful look and the remark, 'Can't you see he is sitting there?' I felt extremely uncomfortable. I could not spot anyone dressed like me, the language spoken around me was not the Urdu which I thought was the language of Lucknow . . . I left the assembly building with a feeling of mingled panic and disgust.[13]

Now League and Congress politicians roamed freely, devised and imposed laws, spread propaganda and built up their political assets as never before. 'We are inaugurating this regime of popular government after nearly six and a half years of administration under section 93 of the Government of India Act. Naturally people will expect all the hardships and evils they have been suffering from to be removed immediately,' declared the new Prime Minister of Bombay, A.G. Kher, at his inauguration, urging patience while announcing a radical programme of alcohol prohibition and the unconditional release of hundreds of political prisoners.[14] Party workers had established networks of supporters but had rarely been able to deliver much in the way of meaningful favours in the past. The moment ministries were sworn in, these party workers and the politicians they worked for were plugged into the main power source. The whole balance of power was reconfigured. In provinces where Congress or Muslim League ministries were in power, these networks were skewed in favour of those who were well connected to the provincial ruling party.

After years in limbo, local power was suddenly palpable. Ideological commitments to the improved governance of India were muddled together with personal profiteering and local rivalries. Provincial governments assumed responsibility for policing, public health, road-building, irrigation, education and food-licensing. In Madras, it was the local Congressman who could now help his supporter to obtain a liquor permit, if he wished to establish a small kiosk. In Sind it was the local Leaguers who might help someone who wanted to escape the attention of the police because of a petty theft. In the North West Frontier Province, where a Congress ministry had come to power, 'all with an axe to grind turn to the Ministers where in the old days they would have gone to the Deputy Commissioner and, if necessary, waited hours to see him'. When one Muslim revenue official was asked whether the people minded this sea change in the nature of the administration on the frontier he pithily replied, 'Whose the stick, his the buffalo.'[15]

Acquiring a permit to sell food or other essential goods was a difficult business, complicated by red tape, and competition for these permits became ferocious. The black market was thriving. Accusations of foul play chimed with the grievances of small traders and stallholders. District food and supply committees – which had the right to distribute permits and supplies – often divided along party-political, religious and caste lines, and competition for seats became intense. Casually used phrases like 'Hindu Raj' or stories of Muslim oppression could start to resonate even when the material evidence was patchy or scant. Now that Congress and League provincial ministries had come to power, if people could not get hold of resources, it was all too easy to attribute blame to the party in power. A culture of complaint emerged in Congress provinces that 'It is the followers of Congress who get the wheat and the sugar, the paraffin and the matches' whereas in League-run provinces it was the reverse story.[16] The smallest things could become decisive. 'Look at this,' said a Pathan interviewed by Malcolm Darling during his tour, drawing a box of matches out of the folds of his garment, 'yesterday I had to pay four *annas* for this, and the controlled price is two *pice*.' So many people were complaining about the cost of matches to Malcolm Darling that he concluded: 'Matches have, indeed, become almost a battle-cry between the two parties.'[17] Where Congressmen presided over the system, the Muslim League made hay with the idea that the Muslim public were being discriminated against and, as one Congress supporter recalled, 'accused us of theft, saying that we were misusing our full access to the government machinery. They incited people saying that we were depriving people of cloth for *kafans* [funeral shrouds].'[18] Even in New Delhi this vital question became sharply politicised and Wavell's efforts to set up some form of food advisory committee buckled under the pressure of party politics. Access to rations was not a marginal issue and dominated hungry people's waking thoughts.

In effect, a great deal of power had already been transferred from the bottom up; culturally, economically and politically, the provincial governments set the tone. Those enjoying access to power, often for the first time, wanted to push forward as much legislation as possible before it was stripped back by a new constitution, and rushed to pass bills enforcing new school curricula or official state languages. Wrongs committed by the imperialists were promptly righted; political prisoners emerged from prison, bans on proscribed literature were lifted and journalists wrote with a new sense of freedom. More problematically, the new ministries naturally started to try and influence the – highly uncertain – vision of a future independent India.

The Indian politicians now controlled access to information, ministers authored and edited reports from the provinces, the local presses wrote with vitriol about the remnants of the British administration still *in situ*, and attempts by British provincial governors to direct or shape policy (which was constitutionally still their technical right) had lost all moral sanction. In regions where support for the wartime Quit India movement had been deep-seated, blatant friction between the British governors and their ministries now occurred. There was little support from London for British administrators still dealing with the intricacies of routine local politics, as Wavell tried to steer an uncertain course between a British 'scuttle' and 'repression'. As he wrote to the King-Emperor in July, 'We are in fact conducting a retreat, and in very difficult circumstances.'[19] British control at the provincial level was both blunted by the South Asian leaders-in-waiting and wilfully withdrawn by an imperilled British administration.

The British cut their losses. It was a classic imperial response. By mid-1946, the British government was reluctant to invest a penny more in India's administrative infrastructure. Intelligence units were run down and reports reaching district officers, magistrates, policemen and Criminal Investigation Departments suffered in quality. This would become deadly in time. 'Police intelligence in Bombay City is said to be poor,' the Governor reported, 'with the result that the Government are not in full possession of information as regards the leaders of miscreants.'[20] In 1946, the government disbanded Information Films of India, which produced black and white newsreels and propaganda films shown in cinema halls. The ailing colonial machinery could not even produce a figure when asked to say how many Europeans were living in India. The figure of 97,000 was settled upon somewhat arbitrarily when an initial educated guess of 44,000 was considered to be too low. At exactly the time when clear information was most in demand it became a scarce commodity. The last British census in India was a slender volume compared to its decennial predecessors and much of the information collected for the census still had not been collated by the end of British rule. As W.H. Auden accurately pointed out in his poem 'Partition', the census returns were 'almost certainly incorrect' and the calculations of 'minority' and 'majority' Muslim populations, which were so indispensable to the political debates, were based on out-of-date information.

Access to information meant power. Recognising in which direction the wind was blowing, some Indian civil servants and other government employees started showing their political colours more openly now that the end of the Raj appeared to be imminent, and forged relationships with the Indian politicians-in-waiting. Sympathetic ICS officers were eased into key positions, such as Govind Narain, who became Home Secretary in the United Provinces after Independence, had close family links with the Congress, and had, he later admitted, given the Chief Minister surreptitious assistance when he campaigned in his district during the 1946 elections.[21] The imperial institution in 1946 was a very different-looking beast to its pre-war incarnation. After his release from prison, the Congress President, A.K. Azad, albeit a distinctive figure with his small round glasses and pointed beard, was astonished by his apparent celebrity among policemen and officials – more often perceived as the lackeys of British imperialism, who would have steered clear of openly celebrating a nationalist leader in the past. One afternoon Azad was amazed to find police constables saluting him and shouting political slogans in his favour as he stepped out of his car outside Government House in Calcutta after he had been released from prison. On another occasion when his car was held up in traffic in the city, 'Some police constables recognised me and reported to their barracks which were nearby. In a few minutes a large gathering of constables and head constables surrounded my car. They saluted me and some touched my feet. They all expressed their regard for Congress and said that they would act according to our orders.'[22] Clerks and policemen were making entirely rational and sensible adjustments to the new order and many changed their allegiances long before any formal transfer from the incumbent British had been properly planned. Similarly, supporters of the League inside the secretariats were using office stationery and telephone lines and taking time off work in order to help out with the Pakistan campaign.

Defending the nation

During this terminal breakdown of power in the spring of 1946, in the cities of North India militia groups, extremist parties and armed groups rapidly burgeoned. Their members suddenly became more noticeable in crowded marketplaces, marching in the streets, sometimes with long sticks or *lathis* under their arms, or under banners with lurid slogans. Sometimes they noisily careered around in the back of jeeps. They produced more heat than light, and their activities were casually brushed aside by many as the over-enthusiasm of young men. But students were skipping classes to attend rallies and meetings and strident political opinions crept into their college work. The Ram Sena, a group linked to the Hindu Mahasabha was typical: young students and boys could join up once they had solemnly promised, in front of their fellow members, to 'bear all sacrifices involved cheerfully without any compensation for any kind of loss or injury suffered in the discharge of my duties'.[23] Decked in khaki shorts and shirt, with an orange cap and spear, topped off with the society's flag, they marched through the streets, helped out at political rallies, and in their free time played sports and spent time together. It was both a youth club and a political party, providing an image and a social life into the bargain.

In towns across North India men were collecting together and arming. Month on month, as the temperature climbed from spring to summer, officials returned lines of neat statistics, which showed that membership figures for these groups were moving upwards. In early 1946, it was being reported that a large number of deserters from the United Provinces were still untraced, and that many of them were likely to have firearms.[24] Former soldiers, fired-up students, party activists and opportunist criminals coalesced together in a rag-bag of organisations. Some were entirely amateur. Pre-existing athletic associations, wrestling or football teams were given a political edge and started to participate in patrolling the cities or collecting weapons after their matches.

Such self-defence groups were different in purpose, outlook and levels of structure to more ideologically honed and well-organised armies. These armed bands could be pre-emptive, provocative and defensive, and disentangling which was which was difficult. The strategic picketing and well co-ordinated drills could become overt aggression, and as one colonial official observed, 'a readiness for defence too easily passes into a desire to attack'.[25] From a different viewpoint, these militias could seem reactionary and threatening rather than reassuring.

Other groups were larger, more professionalised and more closely resembled private militias on the offensive, creating and forging ahead with their own pernicious visions of the nation. Kewal Malkani, who was twenty-four years old at the time, was a typical prize recruit for the RSS. Intelligent, well educated and from a respectable Sindi family from the city of Hyderabad, he heard about the RSS from his older brother and started to attend meetings in 1941. The 'clean, uplifting atmosphere' appealed and before long he was inducted as a member into the local *shakha* or branch. Here, standing alongside his new brothers-in-arms, he swore solemn promises to the nation, drilled in formation, and listened to lectures on morality, duty and 'history' – in which exciting, epic battles were waged against Muslim enemies and an inventive panorama of Hindu gods and national heroes fought to save the Motherland. He later remembered the emphasis on 'character, on discipline . . . a certain element of Puritanism'. For Malkani, and thousands like him, the attraction was in the simplicity of the organisation's call. It rode roughshod over India's linguistic, religious and regional melting-pot.[26] Militant groups provided easy answers to complex questions.

The dark underbelly of these organisations was their exclusive, rigid, right-wing ideologies. These 'nationalistic' visions were flagrantly at odds with the way in which Indian freedom was being envisaged in Delhi and London. Other militia groups with clearly defined histories and ideologies included the Khaksars, the Ahrars, the Muslim League National Guards and the Akali Fauj. All used a heady combination of bombastic rhetoric, militaristic boot-camps and sexually charged appeals which often drew on religious imagery and stripped down ideas of 'religious identity' to its barest essentials. The 'shadows of the swastika' were not only cast by the RSS. Across North India other private armies and militia movements blossomed on the student campuses and in the comfortable living rooms of middle-class urban India.[27] The Khaksars, founded in Punjab in 1930, wore khaki uniforms, carried spades or trowels and were preoccupied with an intoxicating creed of violent action. For the Khaksars, Islamic ideas played a supporting role, but the core tenets were 'unity' and 'discipline'. Khaksars kept themselves busy with daily parades, between evening and night prayers, compulsory tasks such as street-cleaning, roll calls and collecting subscriptions. Lord Baden-Powell's Scouting movement had been an inspiration.

Prior to Partition, the similarities of these bodies – whether affiliated to the 'Muslim' or the 'Hindu' cause – far outweighed their differences. The imprint of western fascism is clear and these armed groups had distinctly modern precedents; the Khaksars' leader acknowledged the example of Hitler, reading *Mein Kampf* and modelling his forces on the SA and the SS. 'Freedom can be secured only in the field of battle,' the Khaksar leader commanded, 'therefore for the field of battle prepare only military strength . . . . Against one who uses violence, non-violence, civil disobedience, imprisonment, *ahimsa*, humbleness, and the philosophy of getting freedom by begging is absolutely wrong.'[28] M.S. Golwalkar, leader of the RSS, wrote warmly of the Third Reich. 'To keep the purity of the Race and its culture, Germany shocked the world by her purging the country of the Semitic Races – the Jews,' he wrote in *We, or Our Nationhood Defined*, 'Race pride at its highest has been manifested here. Germany has also shown how well-nigh impossible it is for Races and cultures, having differences going to the root to be assimilated into one united whole, a good lesson for us in Hindusthan to learn and profit by.'[29] Similar batches of young men, often bachelor students, the educated unemployed or those let loose from the army, found that these ideas resonated with their own lives and concerns.

During the summer of 1946, at the same time, more people were enthusiastically signing up for membership of the Congress and League's own cadres. Various groups of volunteers cleaned the gutters of dirty cities, offered first-aid services or dug gardens, filling the vacuum in services that the skeletal colonial state was not able to offer. Others stood guard as night-watchmen, or helped control the crowds at Congress or League demonstrations. The novel *Tamas*, set in Punjab in the months leading up to Partition, opens with the scene of a band of Congressmen dressed in distinctive homespun cloth – some cheerfully, some rather more grudgingly – sweeping and washing the narrow lanes in a poor Muslim part of town.

> Most of the houses in the locality were small single storeyed houses, built in two parallel lines on either side of a spacious courtyard. Gunny-cloth curtains hung over the front doors of most of them. The lanes were not paved. Only one of the lanes had a *kachcha* drain, the other one had no drain at all. In some lanes, cattle were tied. From the houses, now and then,

women emerged with earthen pitchers on their heads to fetch water. A small boy was collecting dung from under a buffalo . . . Mehtaji and Master Ram Das picked a *tasla* each and went to work in the yard. Shankar and Kashmiri Lal, armed with shovels headed for the drain, while Sher Khan, Des Raj and Bakhshiji began sweeping the courtyard with brooms. The residents of the locality watched them, puzzled.'[30]

Volunteerism was an essential part of being an Indian nationalist, and had longer antecedents in Gandhian spinning and *swadeshi* campaigns.

Many provincial politicians went further, rejecting conventional forms of policing, and looked to their own volunteer bodies, nationalist training groups and assorted gangs of volunteers and helpers who, they argued, were more imbued with the 'nationalist' spirit. The Muslim League National Guard was an integral part of the League's armoury. By March, F.K. Khan Durrani, a correspondent living in Lahore, was seeing the writing on the wall. His warnings are even more striking because he was a loyal Leaguer and friend of Jinnah. While pledging his loyalty to the 'Muslim Nation' he was warning that the activities of the Muslim Leaguers were getting out of hand. 'At present one must shout with the crowd or get lynched by the crowd, and the feeling has been created that one who is not a Leaguer is worse than a kafir and should be hanged like a dog forthwith.'[31] There was a great danger, he correctly foresaw, of militias going into battle against each other.

Congress politicians similarly continued broadening their vote-banks and built up disciplined bands of followers. One of the first jobs carried out by the newly installed Congress ministry in the Central Provinces was to hire a retired army officer to recruit 'young, well-built and able-bodied people', to give them 'basic military training' and to coach them 'in the art of self-defence'.[32] 'I want every boy and girl to become a soldier in the cause of the independence of the country. By soldier I mean a disciplined and honest worker who will serve the country and maintain the honour and prestige of the motherland,' Nehru told a crowded audience of Congress volunteers in 1946 and, six weeks later, 'There is no doubt that our organisation has non violence as its creed yet unless the discipline of the army and the spirit of the volunteer are blended together, we cannot have a good organisation.'[33] These workers, it was claimed, were completely different and were working towards a true, peaceful unsullied version of nationalism. For some, the coming of Independence meant a total overhaul of the old administration and displacing the police – the old stooges of imperialism – with new forms of order and social control.

There was an obvious danger here. By the spring of 1946, Gandhian non-violence, or *ahimsa*, had become a weak currency among sections of the Congress Party. During the long years of non-cooperation and civil disobedience of the 1920s and 1930s, there had been numerous lapses and peaceful protests against the British had been frequently punctured by violence, such as the arson attack on a police station in Chauri Chaura in 1922. Notwithstanding this, during these earlier years the moral high ground created by *ahimsa* was held firmly by the Congress Party and there was a widespread belief in the efficacy of non-violence among Congressmen from the cities to the smallest towns and villages of India. By the end of the war Gandhi's ability to enforce this non-negotiable pillar of his belief, even within his own organisation, was terminally weakened. Fears of Muslim League assertiveness, uncertainty about the future and, in many cases, the sheer *size* of the Congress Party which embraced so many of the politically active across the country by 1947, irrespective of the nuances of their thinking, undermined the policy of non-violence.

Gandhi's coherent ideology, which he regarded as timeless and universal, had been utilised by many in a temporal and limited way to fight British imperialism. By 1946, with freedom from the imperial masters already conceded, however, the rules of the game had changed so that Gandhian non-violence was eschewed by many as a spent force. By the spring of 1946 volunteer wings and militarised groups could charm new recruits and justify their violence on the grounds of self-defence. Their presence speaks of the lack of faith in the traditional state apparatus and the grinding down of trust in the usual ways of policing the towns. Even the epitome of Gandhian forbearance, the peaceful Red Shirts of the North West Frontier Province who had used non-violence for over two decades and swore heartfelt allegiance to peaceful means, splintered in the political tension; in defiance of the leadership a popular youth wing, the Young Pathans, or Zilme Pukhtun, renounced non-violence, and its members added ominous black stripes to the collars and cuffs of their scarlet uniforms.[34] As the Congress leader in the mountainous borderland with Afghanistan, Abdul Ghaffar Khan, ruefully admitted, 'While I was away from my frontier land for three and a half months in Bihar my people got much agitated over the violent League movement and themselves began to harbour violence in their hearts.'[35] Sorrowfully, those who had faithfully followed Gandhi since the agitations of the 1920s watched the belief in non-violence that they had carefully nurtured break down.

In the prelude to Partition, therefore, the Congress Party itself might become implicated in violent action, just like the League, even when this had not been officially sanctioned by the upper echelons of the party. Nehru, although an impeccable pluralist and desperate for peace (personally risking his own life in order to break up fighting when he witnessed it in the streets of Delhi), wavered on the issue of violence in the heightened tension of 1946; could and should the Congress organise for self-defence if the Muslim League were the aggressors? Nehru spoke out against violence and suggested that people collect together in their *mohallas* for protection, and trust their local police force. He gave a frank, and pained, assessment to one correspondent: 'You ask me about non-violence in these circumstances. I do not know what I would do if I was there [in Calcutta, during the riots of 1946] but I imagine that I would react violently. I have no doubt whatever that violence in self-defence is preferable to cowardly non-violence.'[36]

In the polarised atmosphere of 1946, the words used by numerous politicians became overtly incendiary and coasted perilously close to incitement to violence. Some now talked openly of civil war. It was widely reported that one of the foremost Congressmen, Vallabhbhai Patel, had declared, 'Pakistan is not in the hands of the British government. If Pakistan is to be achieved the Hindus and Muslims will have to fight. There will be a civil war.' A prominent Leaguer, Liaquat Ali Khan, echoed this inflammatory tone: 'the Muslims are not afraid of a civil war,' he told his listeners. Others invoked earthquakes, volcanoes, blood and fire to describe the revolution that was approaching.[37]

Last push for peace

'The triumvirate of Cabinet Ministers cannot realise with what hopes and misgivings their coming is awaited in this country,' wrote the Punjabi physicist and chemist Ruchi Ram Sahni, in March 1946. Sahni was eighty-two years old at the time and approaching his last days in Lahore. He had seen India transformed since his birth in 1863 and had played his own part in this transformation by popularising science, setting up educational institutions and a library and, in his youth, giving incredibly popular scientific lectures in Punjabi to ordinary crowds of people gathered in parks, gurdwaras and in open stages, on topics from electricity to soap-making. Now, though, his mind was firmly turned to politics. 'Attlee's own words inspire the hope that a heavy weight may soon be lifted from India's breast and that we may at last have a chance to stand erect like self-respecting men. For England no less than for other great nations of today it is a time of serious searching of the heart.' Sahni's appeal was to three men, Lord Pethick-Lawrence, Secretary of State for India, Sir Stafford Cripps, President of the Board of Trade and

Mr A.V. Alexander, First Lord of the Admiralty, collectively known as the Cabinet Mission, or, in Wavell's words, 'the three magi'. They had come to India to try and forge a compromise, to create a constitutional package for one united India and to plan the British handover of power.

The three British men had arrived in India on 25 March 1946, just as the temperature was starting to climb, charged with the task of trying to resolve the constitutional deadlock which India faced. This was, as everybody was aware, the last push for peace and the best chance of achieving the agreement between the different parties that was vital if Britain were to relinquish its imperial control. Under the arresting title, 'Friends! This is for you,' Ruchi Ram Sahni sent his article to the head of the delegation by registered post. 'I appeal to you,' he wrote, 'to approach your great task in the spirit of ministering angels to the good of India and to humanity at large.' Over the preceding weeks, which rolled into months, as the Cabinet Mission repeatedly extended the length of its stay in India, Ruchi Ram Sahni wrote seven more open letters which he posted one by one to the delegation. In them, it is possible to trace the steady deterioration of hope and expectation which accompanied the mission's arrival and the steady descent into gloom and pessimism about the future among the Indian populace. At the end of three months of negotiations between the political parties, the mission went home empty handed, and the question of apportioning power in a fair constitutional settlement remained unresolved. 'I am pained to bring to a close this long series of articles on a note of hopelessness suddenly turned into one of disappointment,' Sahni was writing by June, although not, he added, one 'of helplessness'.[38]

Sahni was one of hundreds of correspondents, of a myriad political persuasions, to write addresses, memos and appeals; the Cabinet Mission was overwhelmed by the weight of correspondence during its stay. In Britain and India all eyes were turned to the delegation; in Britain the Archbishop of Canterbury led prayers for the success of the negotiations. Administrators and soldiers in the Indian provinces looked on, and gave portentous warnings of the risk of failure. 'If the situation arises in which the Muslim League are bypassed,' reported one army major, 'I think they will be able to mobilise violent resistance on a large scale. In the Punjab they are busy contacting and training demobilised soldiers and are even training women to use arms.'[39] Adding to the confusion were reasonable doubts – based on past disappointments – about the British intention finally to relinquish its Indian empire after two centuries. Back in Britain, over a thousand Indians in Bradford, mostly seamen and industrial workers, waited nervously and planned a mass fast. A sit-down demonstration in front of the House of Commons was attended by Indian delegates from London, Manchester, Birmingham, Glasgow, Wolverhampton and Coventry in support of the mission's success. 'They doubt the sincerity of the Cabinet Mission and are making preparations for demonstrations in case it fails.' In early 1946, doubts about whether the British were really genuine in their desire to relinquish their Indian empire were still heartfelt.[40]

Despite all this pressure from home and abroad, after weeks of initial wrangling in Delhi, attempts at negotiation between the parties failed to achieve any concrete results. The Cabinet Mission persisted with its task of trying to arrange an interim government and a smooth handover of power to a representative government and in early May the leading politicians of the League and Congress were invited to Simla to resume talks. Over a hundred journalists accompanied them, crammed into the hotels and restaurants of the sleepy hill station perched in the Himalayan foothills. The town was packed with politicians, while the streets hummed with political conjecture about the shape of the agreement. The Indian public, though, despite its intense interest in the negotiations, remained in the dark about what was happening behind the closed doors of the viceregal summer lodge.

In contrast to previous negotiations, the politicians and administrators remained tight-lipped, and leaks were studiously avoided. 'We realise that the public is entitled to a report of what has happened,' announced the Congress President, appealing on the steps outside to the press to avoid speculation, 'but in view of all the circumstances we hope that for a brief period our reticence will be understood and appreciated.'[41] Outsiders were kept guessing about developments inside this tightly knit, secretive inner circle. When it was finally announced that these talks had also failed, politics spilled on to the streets and Muslim League and Congress supporters paraded Simla's central Mall shouting slogans at each other. Armed police were called to keep the crowds apart.[42] Politicians, who had been remarkably accessible and unprotected in the past, were allocated bodyguards. The tension of the failure to patch up an agreement at the centre had immediate resonances in the anxious networks of supporters and crowds backing the parties.

The cabinet delegation had decided to try an entirely different approach. Rather than persist with fruitless negotiations they opted to present a *fait accompli* to the Indian population. On 16 May 1946 word circulated that there would soon be an important radio announcement. People tuned in or gathered in the streets to hear the clipped tones of Lord Pethick-Lawrence's broadcast at 8.45 in the evening. 'The words which I shall speak to you are concerned with the future of a great people – the people of India,' he began. 'There is a passionate desire in the hearts of Indians expressed by the leaders of all their political parties for independence. His Majesty's Government and the British people as a whole are full ready to accord this independence whether within or without the British Commonwealth and hope that out of it will spring a lasting and friendly association between our two peoples on a footing of complete equality. . .' And so it went on, for over fifteen minutes, a long, complicated constitutional proposal in English.[43]

In essence, the mission presented the parties with a complete proposal for a future constitutional settlement. They could choose either to accept or to reject the plan in its entirety. The plan was intended to circumvent the main objections and anxieties of all the leading players. It was designed to deliver Pakistan in spirit if not in letter by devolving power to Muslims within a united India. India would be governed by a three-layered federation in which a central government would take charge of portfolios such as defence and foreign affairs. Provinces would have autonomy on some matters but, crucially, would be grouped together to deal with other questions of their choosing collectively. If agreed, large Muslim blocs would be able to act in concert within the Indian Union, in order to preserve or defend their own welfare. As one newspaper headline put it, this was a straightforward decision, a 'Choice between peace and civil strife'. Both parties did – at moments and with reservations – agree to the Cabinet Mission plan and this has given it poignant fascination. There was a moment of great optimism and relief, which was quickly dashed. If successful, it would have meant that Pakistan as we know it today would never have come into existence.

Reactions to the plan in India's towns and cities were mixed and uncertain. The elderly, maverick Urdu poet Hasrat Mohani, a recent convert to the League, was on his summer holidays, visting Sufi pilgrimage sights in the historic town of Rudauli. He had been taking part in the celebrations of a Sufi saint when he returned to his lodgings and heard the Cabinet Mission proposals announced on the radio. Mohani was a latecomer to the League but had recently secured a seat in the elections. He was delighted with the news of the Cabinet Mission plan. The future looked bright; he was planning to perform the hajj by air. For many Muslims living in the provinces where they were a minority, this version of 'Pakistan' was good enough. There would be a form of devolution, Jinnah had extracted some major concessions from the talks and the Congress and the League could move towards power-sharing at the centre. The information 'from Muslim quarters', among the elites of North India, was that Muslim leaders were 'pressing Jinnah to accept the scheme'.[44]

Depending on political persuasion and regional location, there were lots of good reasons for Muslims to accept the plan.

Interpretations of the plan mattered, though. As the press was itself already polarised, and journalists were often party members, the interpretations of the mission plan were frequently at odds with its 'real' meaning. In Sind, banner headlines in League papers proclaimed 'Pakistan rejected' and many Muslims felt dejected by the idea that Pakistan had somehow been 'lost', a feeling confirmed by the decisive rejection of a 'sovereign Pakistan' in the mission statement's preamble. Among many Muslims the lack of clarity about the meaning of Pakistan, and its double usage, both as shorthand for a millenarian aspiration and as the title of a new country, muddied the waters. Was the mission plan delivering Pakistan or not? Could it, or could it not, be celebrated as a victory by the League? Popular hype and expectations of freedom which had taken on euphoric qualities in some places could barely be assuaged by the complex and conciliatory Cabinet Mission plan.

Conversely, there were many on the lower rungs of the Congress Party who felt aggrieved by the suggestion that there had been any concession to the Pakistan demand at all, and fully exploited this in the post-war vocabulary of 'Nazi appeasement'. In their eyes, the Cabinet Mission plan was as good as granting Pakistan, and made a travesty of *swaraj*. In the solidly Congress provinces, where Muslims made up a sliver of the population and the League presence was weak, such as the Central Provinces, it seemed that the British were bowing to League pressure and granting unnecessary concessions. The agreement looked a step too far: it meant caving in to local opponents for no apparently good reason. For these reasons, Gandhi, never a fan of the English language in any case, told listeners at his prayer meetings to study the fine details of the plan in their own language, rather than in English, to make up their own minds about its meaning and not to borrow their opinions from newspapers.[45]

From their perspective, mill-owners and mighty Indian industrialists, men such as G.D. Birla, saw in the plan all their dreams for a strong, centralised India leaking away. Birla, like many, was hoping for a powerful central government in free India, footing the bill for capital-intensive projects, paving the roads and pumping the power and water supplies that India desperately lacked. The Cabinet Mission plan seemed a cruel watering down of all these plans.[46] Similarly, some regional Congress politicians believed they had little to gain by making sentimental or generous concessions to Muslim interests when Independence, and their own power in a national parliament, was frustratingly within reach. 'The Congress premiers of Bombay, UP, Bihar, Central Provinces and Orissa pressed for the establishment of a strong centre and said that the Muslims had been given far more concessions than they were entitled to,' recorded the Viceroy in his diary.[47] Elsewhere, regional sensitivities took precedence. In Assam, where local leaders feared being swamped by their arbitrary grouping together with Bengalis in the proposed scheme, opposition was instantaneous and vociferous.

To add to the complexities, many Sikhs felt that they had been entirely overlooked. The proposed settlement threatened to put their own regional interests in the hands of the Muslim League. The president of the Sikh Party, the Akali Dal, said the plan was adding insult to injury and appealed for a united Panth and for Sikhs to prepare to 'stake their all'; the Sikh Panthic Conference resolved that the mission's recommendations 'liquidated the position of the Sikhs in their homeland'; while Sardar Sarmukh Singh Chamak told worshippers at the shimmering Golden Temple, the holiest place for the community, that the British were 'trying to atom bomb the Sikhs'.[48]

In short, there were doves and hawks in all communities. Needless to say, in the end, the plan failed. It became obvious by June that both the plans for a federal solution and even attempts to put into place some form of provisional, interim government had come to nothing. The Cabinet Mission represents a galling missed opportunity and exactly *why* the Cabinet Mission failed so spectacularly has long been the stuff of nuanced debate about the intentions and motives at the top level of negotiations. The bottom line was a failure of trust, with both Congress and the League unwilling to take the leap into an unknown future without cast-iron guarantees that the plan would be interpreted in precisely the same way by all parties once the British had departed.

Very many Indians across the social spectrum were deeply disappointed by the failure. But it was a boon for the most vocal, well-organised nationalist hardliners. The uncertainties and hesitancies in the politicised grassroots of the League and Congress about the meanings of *swaraj* and Pakistan, and about how these hopes were going to be fulfilled, played a supporting role. 'There was absolutely nothing settled about what would be the shape of things in India once Independence was achieved,' reflected the writer Nasim Ansari, still casting his mind back four decades later and trying to unravel what had gone wrong in the build-up to Partition. 'The urge for freedom was common to both Hindus and Muslims but no one had any clear idea of what should follow independence. So misunderstandings grew, and developed to such an extent that such fraternal unity, as existed earlier, was never seen again.'[49] It was an onward march towards an uncertain destination. Old ways of life were crumbling, and the nervous anticipation of a settlement ratcheted up a sense of both insecurity and exhilaration.

By the time the dejected Cabinet Mission boarded their aeroplane for their return to Britain on 29 June the power that they thought they were trying to broker had already slipped out of British hands in the towns and cities of provincial India. Partition was closely entwined with this slow, protracted passage of decolonisation, which has been masked by the pedantic language of the transfer of power. Cumulative, minor cracks were building all over the Indian urban landscape. Even more ominously, the loud, omnipresent calls for Pakistan or for *swaraj* had been taken up by militias and strongmen, middle-class students and their urban supporters. These calls were being made more urgently and repeatedly than ever, and were shattering the peace of the cities where smaller groups were being pushed to the political margins. British responsibility for control, at the provincial level, already seemed to have been abandoned. As one governor reported: 'I spoke to Pant [the Congress premier of United Provinces] sometime back about communal organisations, the Rashtriya Swayam Sevak Sangh [RSS] and the Muslim National Guard. I told him that there was a whirlwind coming which some-body would have to reap. It probably wouldn't be me, for I would be gone.'[50] In the logistical calculations of British withdrawal, armed groups which posed no direct challenge to British interests proved neither especially interesting nor especially threatening to the government.

'In Karachi the other day the accidental dropping of an onion from a verandah by a child nearly started a communal fracas.'[51] An exaggeration, perhaps. But by the second half of 1946, the British administration knew, after the failure of the Cabinet Mission's attempt to forge a settlement, that the state was cracking. Wavell's personal diary, in which the Viceroy scribbled his musings, was verging on the apocalyptic. There had been tension in the past and this had sometimes resulted in major riots between Hindus, Sikhs and Muslims. Small riots when they occurred had caused deaths in the tens, though rarely in the hundreds and never in the thousands. They had tended to be set pieces, predictably coinciding with religious festivals. Now the violence, when it broke out, seemed stranger and less manageable. In July 1946 there was rioting in the Gujarati city of Ahmedabad and random stabbing attacks started to occur in the city. From the middle of the year, urban riots between bands of political activists broke out in city streets, as processions clashed and men fought pitched battles, throwing stones and brickbats. As soon as the Cabinet Mission plan failed, urban scraps and stabbings intensified in frequency.

The big names at the top of the party hierarchies were finding it harder and harder to intervene and to control events. Vallabhbhai Patel, second in command to Nehru in the Congress, didn't go and visit Ahmedabad, a city of fellow Gujaratis, when riots and sporadic stabbings started there in July as his offer to visit was rejected by local leaders. Party activists started snubbing leaders who urged quiescence and calm. That month, two Gandhian workers who tried to intervene to halt riots there succumbed to the knives of rioters. Near to the very place where Gandhi had grown up and had started his experiments in non-violence, Gandhian workers were being murdered: the despair of peace workers and faithful followers of Gandhi is visceral. They appealed to Gandhi for help: 'Two of our Congress workers, Shri Vasant Rao and Shri Raja Bali, went out in such a quest and fell a prey to the *goonda's* knife,' wrote their co-workers. 'They laid down their lives in pursuit of an ideal and they deserve all praise. But no one else had the courage to follow in their footsteps. They have not the same self-confidence. If they had it, there would be no riots, and even if riots broke out, they would never assume the proportions and the form that the present day riots do.'[52] As old certainties broke down, Gandhian workers – and even Gandhi himself – seemed to be losing moral authority.

The impartiality of Indian policemen, administrators and politicians was also coming under public suspicion and intense scrutiny. Militias snowballed in size as news of the rejection of the Cabinet Mission plan spread. This paved the way for the breaking of trust which was already well under way, but reached a crisis with the events which took place in Calcutta in August 1946. This would be swiftly followed by devastating attacks in Noakhali in East Bengal and in Bihar from October, followed by Garhmukhteshwar in the United Provinces in November. All occurred outside Punjab, where worse was yet to come. In all these places, the nature of the killing would become brutal, sadistic and grisly; women and children were attacked, and rapists worked alongside the killers. Everywhere, there was an element of planning and organisation involved and a sense of immunity from the governing provincial party – whether League or Congress. By the end of 1946, there was a collapse of faith between the parties, largely because of the graphic news of these attacks. Most ominously of all, when people asked for, or resisted, the idea of Pakistan, or clamoured for *swaraj*, it was without any clear idea at all of what the real costs of this were going to be for the Indian state and its people.

4

The Collapse of Trust

The streets of Calcutta were eerily empty on the morning of 16 August 1946. The Muslim League provincial government had called a public holiday to mark Direct Action day. Three days later at least 4,000 of Calcutta's residents lay dead and over 10,000 were injured. The streets were deserted once again. Now the scene was one of carnage, buildings reduced to rubble, rubbish uncollected from the streets, telephone and power lines severed. Schools, courts, mills and shops stayed closed. A British official groped for an analogy, describing the landscape as a cross between the worst of London air raids and the Great Plague.[1] In the intervening days, the worst riots between Hindus and Muslims ever remembered in India broke out. What had once been violent, but almost theatrical, encounters between politicised militias and activists, had burst their limits and had become targeted attacks on innocent civilians, including women, children and the elderly.

Although there had been riots in Calcutta in the past, the violence of August 1946 was distinctive in its scale and intensity. Vastly different social groups and sections of the city amassed along religious lines. Jinnah's call for a day of direct action on which a complete *hartal* would be utilised to demonstrate support for Pakistan undoubtedly triggered the violence. Jinnah ratcheted up the oratory, speaking of Congress as a 'Fascist Grand Council'. The day of direct action was clearly a strategic manoeuvre. Jinnah needed to strengthen his own hand of cards in the unfolding dispute over the membership of the interim government which was taking place in New Delhi, and to show just how ardent the demand for Muslim representation really was. Jinnah called on his followers 'to conduct themselves peacefully and in a disciplined manner' although his own usually precise and legalistic prose was vague enough to allow for violent reinterpretation.[2]

A few days before Direct Action day, the Calcutta district League set out its own plans; there would be a complete strike of Muslim workers in shops and factories, then numerous processions accompanied by musical bands and drums would converge from all over greater Calcutta – from Howrah, Hooghly, Matiaburz and elsewhere – ending in a mass rally. Leaguers were told to go out to the mosques, where they should tell people about the plans, hand out pamphlets and say special prayers for 'the freedom of Muslim India, the Islamic world and the peoples of India and the East in general'. Older networks of mullahs, mosques and *pirs* were put to work, to spread the call for direct action in Bengal.

On the morning of 16 August League supporters opened their newspapers to find large printed advertisements inside them:

Today is Direct Action Day
Today Muslims of India dedicate their lives and all they possess to the cause of freedom
Today let every Muslim swear in the name of Allah to resist aggression
Direct action is now their only course
Because they offered peace but peace was spurned
They honoured their word but they were betrayed
They claimed Liberty but were offered Thraldom
Now Might alone can secure their Right[3]

What 'direct action' meant, though, was wide open to speculation and distortion. During the build-up, handbills and fly posters using religious language urged Muslims to act and linked the earliest Muslims with the contemporary situation, announcing that, 'In this holy month of Ramzan, Mecca was conquered from the infidels and in this month again a Jehad for the establishment of Pakistan has been declared.'[4] This kind of Islamic populism drew on older myths and stories, reworking history and compressing time. The Mayor of Calcutta himself commanded: 'We Muslims have had the crown and have ruled. Do not lose heart, be ready and take swords. Oh Kafir! Your doom is not far and the greater massacre will come.'[5]

On the morning of the 16th, thousands of Muslims, many of them armed with *lathis* and brickbats, processed to a mammoth meeting at the Ochterlony Monument in Calcutta to hear speeches made by Husseyn Suhrawardy, the Provincial League Chief Minister, who, if he did not explicitly incite violence, certainly gave the crowds the impression that they could act with impunity, that neither the police nor the military would be called out and that the ministry would turn a blind eye to any action that they unleashed in the city. Whether he anticipated the carnage that followed is a different matter, and whether the Calcutta riots were a product of questionable political naïvety or a calculated pogrom is still a moot point.

Eyewitness accounts of what took place in the aftermath of the dispersal of the mass meeting are chilling. Jugal Chandra Ghosh was running an *akhara* at the time, a gymnasium which also served to drill squads of young men. He later admitted his own role in organising retaliation on the streets of Calcutta, remembering 'a place where four trucks were standing, all with dead bodies, at least three feet high; like molasses in sacks, they were stacked on the trucks, and blood and brain was oozing out . . . the whole sight of it, it had a tremendous effect on me.'[6] It was no longer warring political groups who were involved in the battle over India's future. Ordinary people going about their daily business were targeted, from tea-shop owners and rickshaw drivers to stallholders who had been dragged out, beaten and burned or had their property looted. Hindu-owned shops and homes were looted and smashed by those in cahoots with League activists. In Calcutta, people were outraged not just by the events themselves, but also by the way in which political leaders, especially Suhrawardy, failed to deploy the military and police quickly. A definite impression was gaining ground that the state's resources had been exploited by the murderers with the League's blessing; rioters used state-owned trucks and had mysteriously accessed extra petrol coupons.

'People showed signs of being intoxicated, whether with alcohol or with enthusiasm,' remembered Syed Nazimuddin Hashim, a student at Presidency College at the time, and in this strange, nationalistic euphoria Leaguers went off as if into battle. Huge portraits of Jinnah riding on a white horse and brandishing a scimitar were carried through the city.[7] The involvement of politicians granted the violence legitimacy in the eyes of the rioters who believed that they fought for ill-formed and simplistic notions of 'freedom' 'space' and 'history' which hardly tallied with demanding the territorial nation state that came into being.

There were undoubtedly well-prepared Hindu militias ready for the moment, too. On both sides, the violence was anticipated – at least a week prior to the riot inhabitants of *bustees* were sharpening daggers and making weapons from railings uprooted from public parks, and political leaders along with local hard men instigated and carried out much of the violence. Members of Hindu militia organisations – ranging from more professionalised volunteer bands such as the Bharat Sevashram Sangha to local football and gymnasium club members – were equally prepared to fight.

That autumn, Gopal 'Patha' Mukherjee – Gopal the goat – was stirred to action. He had acquired his nickname because his family ran a meat shop in Calcutta. Like several of the major gang leaders in Calcutta, he had a background in the wrestling pits and gymnasiums of the city where he had built up a reputation for toughness and daring on the streets. Young men looked up to him and they called him other nicknames too: 'brave' and 'strongarm'. The local police knew who he was, and probably kept a watchful eye on him. Once the riots started, Gopal was more than ready for them. He could summon at least a few hundred men, perhaps more. 'It was a very critical time for the country,' Gopal remembered: 'we thought if the whole area became Pakistan, there would be more torture and repression. So I called all my boys together and said it was time to retaliate.' He considered it his patriotic duty. 'Why should we kill an ordinary rickshawwallah or hawker, they were not part of the politics . . . basically people who attacked us . . . we fought them and killed them . . . we prepared some country bombs, we'd also secured some grenades from the army . . . to camouflage myself . . . I grew a beard and long hair.' This was preparation for war in the name of nationalism.

The links between local strongmen and politicians were blatant and well remembered by one of the perpetrators. 'I had a club, an *akhara,*' he says. 'I was a wrestler, and I trained my boys, and they carried out my instructions. There was this Congress Party leader. He took me round Calcutta in his jeep. I saw many dead bodies, Hindu dead bodies. I told him, "Yes, there will be retaliation".'[8] As one student at the time recalled on College Street there were lots of small Muslim booksellers: 'when we went there . . . we saw dead bodies piled up on both sides, men, women, children, and all the books on the road, burnt, gutted . . .'[9] Rioters, as always, sought political legitimacy wherever they could find it, imagining blessings from omniscient national leaders and seeking the green light to kill from members of local party hierarchies.

The political purposes of the riots are not in doubt. The Calcutta killings reinforced, in a graphic way, the *idea* that Hindus and Muslims were incompatible, and planted this seed in the minds of British and Indian policymakers. Violence and injustice were not unfamiliar in the largest Indian city where unemployed mill-hands suffered the stagnation of the post-war slump, and squalor and overcrowding badly affected a city still reeling from devastating famine. This level of violence was something entirely new, however, in a metropolis which also had a strong tradition of regional patriotism and coalition governance and where robust trade unions and anti-imperial organisations cut across religious lines.

Intense feelings had been aroused around the notions of freedom and oppression, independence and tyranny but nobody had come any closer to envisaging the final shape of a settlement, or spelt out emphatically what either *swaraj* or Pakistan would mean to the Indian people in reality. At the grass-roots, then, these ideas of Pakistan and *swaraj* could both be glossed with a different set of dreams and priorities: euphoria, millenarianism, the idea of a freedom, which would not only deliver a territorial state to govern but also open the door to a new kind of world order. Many terms used by the imperialists and the colonised were lost in translation; British 'Raj', used in Indian languages to mean 'rule' or 'kingdom', was to be replaced, in the rendering of different Congressmen with *swaraj* (self-rule), *Hindu raj* (the rule of Hindus), *Ram-rajya* (the regime of the god Lord Ram), *gram raj* (village rule) or *kisan mazdoor raj* (peasant and worker autonomy). The various terms available for 'state' in Hindustani at the time – *raj, sarkar, hukumat, riyasat,* and *mulk* – carried different connotations to the British reading of the word and similarly clouded the possibilities of what form Independence could take.[10] As one member of the public, identifying himself only as 'V.K.J.', wrote to a leading newspaper, 'The thinking public have different visions of future India. The idea of Rama Rajya is one such vision which is sponsored by Mahatma Gandhi. The other day one of your readers proposed Dharma Rajya and I offer another conception of the future state of India . . . Kalyana Raj . . . in which the future head of state will be an elected president and not a hereditary king.'[11] People inevitably filled in gaps in their understanding with their own experiences of oppression, their own hopes and expectations.

Pakistan, then, meant myriad things to different people. The call for Pakistan could be equated with all manner of ambiguous hopes and dreams. Conversely, for many of those who supported the Congress, Pakistan was perceived as a total and sweeping threat which risked shattering the whole of Mother India, rather than as a question of territorial self-determination in a specific part of the subcontinent. It was feared that Pakistan, if granted, would mean alien rule, even for those who resided in Hindu 'majority' provinces as hard-hitting editorials in Hindi newspapers reflected. In one North Indian Hindi newspaper during the late 1940s 'Pakistan was understood as an all-encompassing catastrophe about to befall India' and as a 'death-wish'.[12] Allowing Pakistan to be created was akin to dismantling the promise of a free India altogether, and risked opening the floodgates to further national disintegration and secessionist movements. As a commentary in the paper *Vartman* put it during the pre-Partition debate, Saumya Gupta notes, 'Giving in to the Pakistan demand would only lead to endless partitions. We will not be able to sit peacefully . . . All minorities would ask for the right to self-determination. How would we then stop them? Even women . . . would one day demand a separate *Jananistan* [land for women].'[13] By the late 1940s, 'Partition' and 'Pakistan' had meanings far in excess of paring off two rather small and poorly industrialised corners of the Indian subcontinent. Pakistan had come to signify anti-freedom for many non-Muslims and a utopian future for many Muslims, and political propaganda nourished such ideas.

The Calcutta killings marked – and continue to mark – a psychic break between many South Asians and the idea of Pakistan. Neutrality or political indifference was fast becoming an unrealistic and untenable option in the face of this activity and the killings hardened the nationalist lines as other, older and overlapping ideas about identity were stripped back to more simplistic badges of allegiance to either the 'Hindu' or the 'Muslim' cause. Whereas in the previous months these allegiances, when they had existed, had been along *party* lines they now reworked themselves and became more sinisterly along *religious* lines.

Calcutta also marks a watershed. It was followed by the first major series of Partition massacres that spanned the northern flank of the subcontinent and in which, again, both Muslims and Hindus suffered. On 15 October 1946, only weeks after the Calcutta riots, and as the city was still returning to normality, workers in the Bengal Congress Office received a shocking telegram from their colleagues in the East Bengali district of Noakhali nearly 200 miles away:

HOUSES BURNT ON MASS SCALE HUNDREDS BURNT TO DEATH HUNDREDS KILLED OTHERWISE LARGE NUMBER HINDU GIRLS FORCIBLY MARRIED TO MOSLEMS AND ABDUCTED ALL HINDU TEMPLES AND IMAGES DESECRATED HELPLESS REFUGEES COMING TO TIPPERA DISTRICT GOLAM SARWAR LEADER INCITING MOSLEMS TO EXTERMINATE HINDUS FROM NOAKHALI . . .[14]

The telegram was a call for help and the Congress workers dispatched a delegation to investigate immediately. But by this time it was too late. A programme of well-planned ethnic cleansing had been augmented in Noakhali and its neighbouring district of Tippera and perhaps five thousand people had perished. In addition there had been public conversion ceremonies to Islam where Hindus were forced to consume beef, cows were sacrificed in public spaces, shops were looted, temples and idols desecrated.

As the historian Suranjan Das has suggested, 'The fact that 1800 troops, 600 armed police, 130 unarmed police, and Royal Air Force Planes had to be mobilized indicates the magnitude of the crisis.'[15] Much of rural Noakhali, which is in present-day Bangladesh, is a watery area of paddy fields intersected by lakes and canals connected by bamboo bridges. It is a very different place to Calcutta and the way in which violence occurred in this quiet and poor backwater was especially frightening. There were old grievances among poor Muslim peasants against the Hindus who tended to be more prosperous landowners and dominated trade in the region but the main cause of the violence was a systematic and political pogrom organised by one man, Golam Sarwar, an elected politician and his henchmen, some of whom came from outside the region and were former military men or members of the Muslim League National Guard. They primed local Muslims through incendiary speeches and deliberate provocation, telling terrible tales of atrocities in Calcutta and meshing this with a millenarian command that the world was coming to an end and that all non-Muslims should be converted.

The violence in Noakhali and Tippera was defined by clear strategic organisation (roads in and out of the almost inaccessible region were cordoned off), systematic destruction of Hindu-owned property, temples and homes, and mass killings. This marks the terrible beginnings of an era when women became the repositories of national identities and their bodies were used to demarcate possession of land and space. Religious 'conversions' which ranged from perfunctory recitations of the *Kalma* to fully-fledged conversion processes involving regular prayer, re-education programmes and ritualised beef-eating, were frequently followed up by the rape of women. The bodies of 'the other' were to be completely controlled, both figuratively and literally, as in Punjab the following year, when mass violence against women became commonplace. 'All our efforts in Noakhali came to naught,' lamented one peace worker. 'It broke our hearts. If the land was to be divided, then who belonged to whom and where? Who would listen to our words of unity and peaceful cohabitation?'[16]

Gandhi arrived in Noakhali on 6 November and remained in Bengal until March the following year, far detached from the political machinations in Delhi. His train was fitted with a special microphone; pulling up at small stations along the way, he would preach peace to as many people as possible. Gandhi had to practise negotiating the rickety bridges which linked together the district and went walking for long days at a time, sometimes barefoot, with his band of workers, holding prayer meetings in villages, consoling victims, trying to instil the spirit of unity. Just to catch a glimpse of Gandhi was a privilege; children and young men clambered on to the roofs of trains and women lined his route with palms clasped together in respectful greeting. Others looked on silently and inquisitively. 'In the beginning there was some resistance,' remembered a journalist and peace worker, Sailen Chatterjee, who accompanied Gandhi during his stay: 'they were not coming to his prayer meeting, they [Muslims] were not coming to meet him . . . slowly they began to realise here is a man who is not that type of Hindu or anything, so they began to come . . .' Indeed, it was the most taxing and dispiriting mission Gandhi had ever undertaken. His own life was at risk and he had an armed police guard at times, despite his resistance to the idea. His frustration and unhappiness was clear. 'Oldest friendships have snapped,' he wrote in one report. 'Truth and *ahimsa* by which I swear and which have, to my knowledge, sustained me for sixty years, seem to fail to show the attributes I have ascribed to them.' A fellow companion, Nirmal Kumar Bose, wrote later of hearing the Mahatma mutter to himself, '*Main kya karun?*' or 'What can I do?'[17]

Gandhi was not walking alone. Other peace workers also spread his message, often leaving their families in the face of incredulity, and travelling many hundreds of miles to follow in the footsteps of their leader. Amtus Salaam was one such woman, born into a landowning Muslim family in Patiala in the Punjab. A slight young figure, with thick dark hair and thick-rimmed glasses, in the winter of 1946 she arrived in Noakhali to play her part in the peace mission. Amtus Salaam, dismayed by the scenes in Noakhali, fasted for twenty-four days to try and convey the message of Hindu–Muslim unity. By the time that Gandhi came to visit her, she was verging on starvation and was too weak to speak. She sat up a little, cloaked in pale homespun blankets, and took some orange juice to end the fast. There were still faithful groups of Gandhian believers in India at the end of 1946, trying to counteract the spirit of the age and to carry out his teachings. The waves of terror brought by the massacres, however, meant that their work was more difficult than it had ever been.

A web of fear

In late October and November, the violence spread rapidly westward. On Bihar's seemingly endless, flat Gangetic plains, the poor in villages and towns suffered some of the worst poverty in India. Troubled by an inequitable landholding system and the domination of landlords, during the preceding years more people had become increasingly poor and landless. Little by little those with even a small plot of land had been forced in the post-war years to sell up, much against their will. Congress had long built its Bihari support on the bedrock of protests by farm labourers and left-wing activists. It was not really considered a danger zone for Hindu–Muslim conflict. In October, though, the same patterns of violence raged in Bihar; thousands of Muslims were killed and perhaps 400,000 Muslims were affected – by mass migrations, upheaval and brutality – in Patna, Chapra, Monghyr, Bhagalpur and Gaya in both the towns and the countryside. National jubilation and expectations of freedom had become muddled and entwined with the 'othering' of Muslims. Slogans, symbols and songs were utilised to rally the rioters. Nehru was shocked to see that 'In the main bazaar as well as elsewhere every Hindu house and shop had Jai Hind or some other slogans [including 'Hindus, beware of Muslims'] written in Hindi on the wall' and was devastated by what he saw. 'These two days here [in Bihar] have been so full of horror for me that I find it difficult to believe in the reality of things I must believe in.' He upbraided the crowds who came to see their future Prime Minister: 'Is this a picture of Swaraj for which you have been fighting?' and 'All of you are shouting Jai Hind and "Long Live Revolution" but what kind of country do you want to build up?' The Congress message of freedom and liberty had been reworked and manipulated in new and frightening ways.[18]

Among the ministers and party workers in Bihar, as in Bengal, a deep streak of party-political bias was apparent. In some villages in Monghyr, Congress workers did not turn up to investigate for three or four days after the 'riots' had taken place – signalling their lack of concern. Sultan Ahmed, a Congress Muslim of Bihar complained to the leaders in Delhi about the lack of arrests and the impunity of the attackers. 'The house searches are also very few and stolen jewellery and grains are being transferred from place to place and being sold freely without fear of conviction.'[19] Little news came out of Bihar about what was taking place, and the Congress-controlled provincial papers kept the lid on the story. League activists, for their part, rushed to the spot to protect and help 'their' people and Leaguers running camps for homeless Biharis manned the doors and would not allow other people or government officials to enter.

In November, further west again in Meerut district, near the small market town of Garhmukhteshwar, closer to Delhi, violence started during a local religious fair. The next day the killings continued in Garhmukhteshwar town itself, three miles away, and the Muslim quarter was ruined. Perhaps some 350 people were murdered. Property and livelihoods were destroyed, and several young girls were abducted. The violence fanned out into other parts of the district.[20] There was general agreement that this attack had been well planned and organised, and in the memory of one Congress minister who witnessed the scene, 'The RSS had carefully laid the plot, marked all Muslim shops which after dusk were burnt according to a plan without doing the least injury to the neighbouring Hindu shops.'[21] During arson attacks in nearby Hapur, the local Indian Superintendent of Police concluded that most of the gangs 'are in the pay of *banias* of Hapur' and that the responsibility of rich Hindus 'cannot be ignored'.[22]

Violence was being carried out in the name of freedom. In some places, such as the western coastline of Gujarat and Bombay, freedom appears to have chimed with hopes of a new moral purity, and Gandhian-inspired attempts to ban alcohol, foreign cloth, prostitution and salacious films were attempted as Independence dawned.[23] In the provinces of the south, with small minority populations and very different political economies, the 'Muslim problem' seemed further away and the challenges of Independence were to direct and shape the place of regional languages and caste within a free India. In other places though, especially in the northern Hindi belt, popular expectations of freedom had a pronounced Hindu colouring and the overlap between the consolidation of nationalism and the 'othering' of the Muslim could not be escaped; Hindu extremists – and Congressmen on the right of the party – mixed their politics with support for religious mendicants, championed the abolition of cow slaughter, the restoration of temples, and the purging of Arabic and Persian words from the Hindi language. It was not irrational, then, that the Congress should be seen as threatening to Muslim traditions and customs and this boosted the League's polling power, giving the sheen of authenticity to the crass cries of 'Hindu Raj'.

Fear of or involvement in violence hastened this process and consolidated new sorts of relationships; for instance, between rich and poor co-religionists. People who may never have had much in common in the past were thrown together by virtue of their faith: Begum Ikramullah remembered how poor Muslims from nearby slums shared their paltry rations of eggs and vegetables with her household during the difficult days of the riots when the markets were closed and food became scarce under curfew conditions.[24] Businessmen took sides by paying out to protection rackets, lending their vehicles to political parties or making hefty donations. Unbidden, Punjabi League volunteers escorted their distressed co-religionists in Bihar from their disturbed homeland to their new 'home' in Punjab, hundreds of miles away. This evacuation, if infused with humanitarian impulses, could not be anything except politically provocative (as well as bewildering for the refugees themselves) in the context of the time, as the refugees became living symbols of a generalised 'Hindu' brutality and useful propaganda objects.

Fatima Begum, an Urdu journalist who had begun her career as a municipal inspector of Urdu girls' schools in Lahore, and became a faithful League activist, travelled to Bihar in a medical relief party organised by members of the Provincial Women's Subcommittee in 1946 and ushered at least two hundred women back to Lahore.[25] Similarly, a Pakistani politician, Abdul Qaiyum Khan, later remembered that 'Pathan volunteers who were sent as relief workers into Bihar came back entirely disillusioned after witnessing the harrowing details of the treatment meted out to the Muslims.'[26] In the process new ideas about who was inside and outside the community were established and activists could invest in idealised, if short-lived, forms of pan-Islamic religious community.

Many humanitarian activists said that relief work opened their eyes to the ways in which their fellow Hindus or Muslims in faraway parts of South Asia or in neighbouring, but previously unvisited, *mohallas* lived. Offended by the dire poverty that they saw, relief workers became imbued with the philanthropic but condescending urge to reform the poor, to improve them through education and instil better hygiene. Participation in relief work often coloured the assertion of ethno-religious identity with this improving mission: cosseted middle-class women had never realised before how poor, or uneducated, some of 'their people' were. Involvement in relief work also energised groups by giving them a sense of energy, direction and usefulness; in some ways it gave meaning to existence altogether. Groups such as the Mahasabha, RSS, the League and Jam 'at-i Islami stepped into the shoes of the government and filled the critical need for nursing, food handouts, shelter and rudimentary counselling that the state was too overburdened to provide.

On the other side of the country, in Lahore, exaggerated accounts of events in West Bengal were being circulated in the press and political leaders called for 'blood for blood'. A Noakhali day was marked in October and processions of students and lecturers from local colleges drew attention to the brutal violence that had occurred against poor Hindu peasants in rural Bengal.[27] In Bombay city, similarly, a sudden rise in tension, the closure of the stock market and the hasty pulling down of shutters in the bazaar were attributed directly to news of events in Noakhali combined with a trenchant rumour that Nehru had been shot and injured on his visit to the frontier.[28] (Nehru had in fact been pelted with a rock but was not badly injured.) In the past it had been much more difficult for political provocateurs to persuade people that their religious identity needed to be defended and that they had shared kinship with Hindus or Muslims living elsewhere. Now, though, as people worried about distant relatives and heard anxious rumours, the task of linking religion and politics became easier.

For many of the Bengali elite, or *bhadralok*, the partition of Bengal began to appear a solution and a way out – both to resolve the crisis and to protect their own business interests – and a pro-partition movement gained momentum as petitions and telegrams from landowners and merchants, tea planters and white-collar workers flooded into Congress and government offices demanding partition of the province.[29] For the extremists of both communities, the memory of the Calcutta killings also became an important weapon in the propaganda war fought across the country and retellings of the 16 August stories, in lurid poems, newspapers and stories, were systematically disseminated (even being used in a schoolchildren's poetry recital competition) and fully exploited to provoke further violence in Noakhali and Bihar in the following weeks.[30] In this atmosphere, circles of allegiance rippled outwards, particularly in the cities and towns.

Paranoia and intense fearfulness had become part of the fabric of everyday life by 1946 in Punjab and larger parts of North India. Polarisation depended upon a linear and totalising experience of complete isolation and faith only in a one-dimensional form of political identity – 'If you are not with us you are against us' – and a sense that retaliation and preparedness for aggressive assault was all that any rational person could engage in.[31] What is more, the doomsayers and political voices controlling the press and the public discourse at the time of Partition wilfully manipulated senses of space and time, moving backwards and forwards across historical stories and future portents of Armageddon-like destruction to fill their listeners and readers with a sense of immediate terror. Hindus would be subject to collective extermination, ushering in an era akin to the centuries of supposed Mughal domination, while Muslims were reminded of times of former glory and both the real and imaginary humiliations that had followed.

Explicit pamphlets on historical heroes, mythic figures and episodes from history, including the rebellion of 1857 (and its brutal British backlash), were printed, circulated and gossiped about so that history itself became a crucial part of the tool kit of the most fascistic elements in the country.[32] Fears of domination and subjugation in the minds of Hindus and Sikhs, if Pakistan was brought into existence, or in the minds of Muslims if Pakistan failed to materialise, far outstripped the bounds of conventional politics as they had become so closely tied to the ability of individuals to govern their own existence, to have autonomy over their own bodies and families, to express their own religious faith. In the British conceptualisation of politics, reliant on straightforward statistics and the routine calculations of democratic politics, these fears and paranoia were entirely irrational and hence were grievously underestimated.

Disciplinary measures intended to punish and bring order to the situation unfortunately exacerbated it. Collective fines were used to punish rioters in many places. After a bout of serious rioting, the authorities would impose fines on all the members of 'the guilty' religious group who lived within a certain radius of events. In Varanasi, local officials, in the manner of town criers, announced by beating a drum that locals would have to pay a fine whenever anybody was stabbed.[33] Extorting money from all adult males in an area *en masse*, irrespective of whether or not they had been guilty of violence, created resentment and forged a new coherence between co-religionists. 'Why this anti-Hindu policy?' the pamphlets of the Hapur Hindu Defence Committee complained after a collective fine of 200,000 rupees was obtained from a portion of the town's community after a spate of bloody killings there.[34] The state, yet again, was treating Muslims, Hindus and Sikhs as undifferentiated groups. Indian and Pakistani ministries continued this practice of imposing collective fines in a way reminiscent of their colonial predecessors.

Extremists exploited loopholes and misunderstandings in this habitual use of 'fines'. Ideally, collective fines were meant to be used as compensation for the victims of riots but this policy had inherent risks. In Noakhali, League activists forcibly levied a 'charity fund' on Hindus in order to compensate Muslim victims of the Calcutta riots who resided hundreds of miles away. Local officials turned a blind eye as this money was extorted.[35] This kind of illegal activity parroted the logic of the colonial state as co-religionists were assumed to have a natural affinity with one another that stretched across time and space. In the turbulent Kolaba district of Bombay, a group of Muslims was compelled by activists to sign written denunciations of events in Noakhali, to denounce the idea of Pakistan and to put on Gandhi caps.[36] It was not too much of a stretch from this to using violence to 'avenge' riots in one part of the country in another completely different place. The vast differences between Hindus and Muslims – in class, language and local culture – were conveniently overlooked and political provocateurs set out deliberately to link together chains of riots in different parts of the country, by defending their actions in the language of revenge, retribution and compensation.

Even in peaceful, undisturbed areas with much stronger regional cohesion and little tendency to inter-religious conflict, the presence of refugees from

outside the limits of the province, political rhetoric and deliberate provocation combined with a dearth of reliable information could act to poison the
relations between harmonious communities. By the end of 1946, approximately 25,000 refugees from Noakhali had taken shelter in the mountainous
region of Assam and there were recurrent bouts of false alarms and rumours
of violence in the province. Government reports were replete with trivial, yet
momentous, detail: 'Some families left Sukchar for Dhubri but are being
persuaded to return. The movement of a lorry load of tea garden labourers on
the way home from a festive event in Karimganj subdivision led to newspaper
reports about secret journeys of lorry loads of Pathans. On occurrence of a
rumour in Kamrup that poisoned *biris* [cigarettes] were in circulation stocks
of *biris* are reported to have been burnt . . .'[37] In Assam, as elsewhere, the
chastity and protection of women was a touchpaper for anxiety; there was a
lot of talk of abducted women being brought into the area from Bengal, under
the cover of *burqas*.

People started to move in with their relatives, or considered selling up and
shifting to a different part of town. It was not unusual for one community to
predominate in a city quarter, but this was not a clear divide and the outer
edges of enclaves shaded together. Now in affected towns, co-religionists
moved closer together, advised to do so by local leaders, and numerous alleyways lost their rich ethnic complexity. Sometimes these moves were temporary but sometimes they were the first stop in a longer chain of unsettling
moves and homelessness. Crossing the lines became increasingly difficult and
the assumption was that the enemy lurked in 'other' settlements even in times
of calm; it was not right, an upper-caste Hindi newspaper in Kanpur
complained in its editorial, that 'the Hindus of the ward Patkapur have to
cross three Muslim *bastis* in order to reach the ration shop and are greatly
inconvenienced'.[38]

The economy was also starting to suffer. Influential business magnates such
as G.D. Birla – who bankrolled the Congress – felt frustrated and worried.
Birla was impatient to get on with building the India of his dreams, and
complained about the mayhem that was affecting production at his own
factories. 'It is hardly necessary for me to draw your attention to the economic
consequences of the disturbed conditions,' he told the Congress leaders.

> If I do so it is only to emphasize the danger and I hope that our Govern-
> ment may be able to take timely steps to prevent the catastrophe which is
> hanging on our head . . . in provinces like Bengal, Bihar UP, production is
> seriously affected. Today you can't even build a house . . . serious labour

shortages, coal shortages, no bricks, Muslim *mistries* [workmen] don't come in Hindu areas and Hindu labour don't [*sic*] enter Muslim areas.[39]

In the minds of some influential individuals such as Birla, the seed of an idea had been growing for a long time: that a rapid and decisive solution to India's constitutional stalemate had to be found.

Populist governments were not expected to take action against their 'own' people. When the party in power *did* pursue the perpetrators and strove to dissociate itself from the violence, and when the administrative scramble to halt and restrain rioters began, in late 1946 and early 1947, as the devastating risks of the violence spreading became evident, nonplussed supporters grew angry, having thought they would be shrouded in protection by their political connection to the governing party. These massacres were not just the random, violent background noise to the constitutional decision-making process but were designed purposefully to influence and shape its outcome by enforcing a mono-religious state and purging the land of 'the other' – whether Hindu or Muslim. By the autumn of 1946, fear for personal safety was spreading in much of North India and cleavages between previously amicable communities had widened. Towards the end of December, Penderel Moon found a member of the Amritsar municipality busily repairing the municipal hose-pipes. 'The city will soon be in flames,' he reportedly explained with exceptional prescience. 'I'm making such preparations as I can.'[40]

In the autumn months of 1946, whenever the potential for a compromise between the different parties seemed likely, it was knocked off the front pages by news of the atrocities occurring in the provinces. In Delhi, League politicians finally decided to join the interim government and were sworn in on 26 October. They would work alongside their Congress colleagues at least in the day-to-day running of India, if not in the formulation of a constitution. But news of this positive move barely caused a stir in Bombay where it was 'swamped completely' by the impact of tales of atrocities from Noakhali.[41]

Placing the blame

In late 1946, A.P. Hume, a British district magistrate stationed in Varanasi – India's most holy city for Hindus where the dead are cremated on *ghats* lining the banks of the Ganges – surveyed the scene around him with mounting trepidation. A forty-two-year-old Methodist and conservative, Hume felt morose about relinquishing Britain's hold on the empire. '[It is] most painful and depressing,' he wrote to his parents, wife and young children back in England, 'to assist in the passing of a great empire.' Derogatory about Muslims and Hindus, convinced of western moral superiority and condescending in the extreme about India's readiness for democracy, Hume bore all the hallmarks of an unreconstructed imperialist at the high noon of empire. He kept a copy of the New Testament open on his desk in the hope of inspiring his Indian visitors. The scene unfolding in India, was, in his eyes, predestined because of the depravity of Islam and Hinduism.

'I ask myself whether it is worth the while even trying to stem the onrush of decadence and decay,' he wrote, anticipating the prospect of violence between the local communities in Varanasi, and weeks later, 'No matter what Wavell, Nehru and Jinnah may patch up temporarily Hindu and Muslims will fly at each other's throats sooner or later.' This fatalism and expectation of disorder cloaked all his attempts to carry out his duties in the district with a dark pessimism and fatalistic despair, 'I should think it quite likely,' he was soon saying, 'that Benaras eventually will be burnt down.' As refugees arrived in Varanasi from Bihar, Hindu Mahasabha representatives toured the city with loudspeakers spreading news of killings – both real and imagined – and in November sporadic stabbings started to occur almost nightly in the city's poorly lit streets. Hume was active in trying to bring a semblance of order to the city but was even more concerned with getting out of India. He began making inquiries with the United Nations about possible positions and sharing his feelings with other British district magistrates who felt similarly moribund; a neighbouring Collector and friend he described as 'thoroughly disgusted' and thinking 'only of getting out of India for good'.[42]

Hume was an extreme case and represents the worst of the British in India. Others were doubtless more astute and more liberal. Some stayed on. Some worked hard to stem the violence. Yet Hume's letters open a vista on the state of North India and the collapse of the administration as the British withdrew both their manpower and the moral will to continue the Raj. At the chalk face of empire, as 1946 drew to a close, men such as Hume were disgruntled by the orders of their superiors – he had been rebuffed when he asked the British Governor about the possibility of retirement and was told it was his 'moral duty to stay on'. Hume was also cynical about the Governor's fine words: 'he talked with what was intended to be reassurance of the steps being taken promptly to prepare for disturbances which might arise in the near future'. As India approached the moment of freedom, British officials such as Hume looked on with a detached and diluted sense of responsibility – 'I observe all that is going on around me as if from a distant safe place' – and eyed their Indian successors with suspicion. Those who had become accustomed to ruling by personal fiat in their districts disliked consulting the Indian politicians who motored in from the provincial capital when riots took place. Right until his final days in India, against the backdrop of the mayhem that was unfolding, Hume went on camps, shooting parties and summer holidays in the Himalayan hills. His closest encounter with violence was when telephone reports came into the magistrate's bungalow of stabbings, interrupting his dinner and causing him to carry out late night tours of the city. The pressures of an imperial ending meant that some British colonial officials absolved themselves of responsibility for the crisis on their watch. In the New Year of 1947, with relief, Hume filed his own application to leave India.

The Indian political classes were in a state of shock by the closing weeks of 1946. Trust had been broken between the major parties and the violence was directly affecting the decisions and attitude of politicians. 'You would realise how difficult it is for an Indian Home Member,' Patel told the British negotiator, Stafford Cripps, 'to sit in his office quietly day by day, when innumerable piteous appeals and complaints are received for some kind of help which could give these unfortunate and helpless victims some protection.' Official inquiries into the riots became saturated with political posturing. Older procedures now went to the wall. In the aftermath of the Garhmukhteshwar massacre an official inquiry was announced, but it was indefinitely postponed and the Governor admitted feeling 'lukewarm on the subject'. Similarly, the Muslim League was asked to drop their demand for an inquiry into violence in Bihar by Mountbatten because of the risk of embitterment.[43] An inquiry into Calcutta's disturbances was set up but, once it became obvious that it would never reach a conclusion, it was quietly dropped six months later. Impartial adjudication, or even the semblance of impartial adjudication, was impossible.

Nobody could see a way out. 'We are not yet in the midst of a civil war. But we are nearing it,' Gandhi warned simply in his paper, *Harijan*, and analysing the Indian scene at the end of 1946, the distinguished Canadian writer and critic of empire Wilfred Cantwell Smith wrote, 'Of late the situation in the country has deteriorated menacingly . . . Instead of an India with freedom for all, united in friendly communal partnership, there have been signs pointing to, at best, a stagnant India of intense mutual bickering, on problems of constitutions and of problems of daily bread, within an atmosphere of moral degradation and of riots; and at worst, an India of civil war.'[44] Others – of many political persuasions – started advocating a partition, and the separation of territory, as the best solution. They erroneously believed it would bring an end to the problem, not foreseeing that it would, in fact, mark the beginning of new calamities.

5

From Breakdown to Breakdown

The wheat-growing tracts of the Punjab – the land of the five rivers – had long been a special, and specially treated, part of India. A vast military recruiting ground for the British army, it was also renowned as a prosperous, cultivated land, studded with trading towns. It had its own distinctive culture and its own strategic importance, and was both the birthplace of Sikhism and home to a closely knitted Punjabi-speaking population of Hindus, Sikhs and Muslims. The Punjab had been a valuable jewel in the Raj's crown ever since its conquest in 1849 and the imperial rulers had bent over backwards to please and sustain the landlords and army families who propped up this vital backbone of empire. If it was a divided society in 1947, this was most dramatically apparent in terms of class. A core of elite Indian administrators, businessmen and senior military men and their wives patronised the renowned artists, writers and musicians in the twin cities of Amritsar and Lahore, sometimes described as the 'Paris of the East'. Memories of Lahore before 1947 sparkle with nostalgia and a good dose of idealisation, of its courtesan quarter which 'came to life at night with reverberating sounds and glittering sights, when fun-loving Lahorias would flock to it for entertainment' and of its food, architecture and poetry. Around the major cities lay hundreds of miles of countryside cultivated by peasants and yeoman farmers, raising wheat, rice and pulses with ox-driven ploughs.[1]

By the New Year of 1947, though, the frivolities and pleasures of life in the Punjabi cities were already fading from memory. Drawing immense strength from the large student population, the Muslim League National Guard and the RSS had been recruiting and arming for months. This was the eye of the storm; the ready availability of weapons (a British policeman remembered 'continually finding dumps of live grenades' in the countryside left by soldiers who had brought back 'souvenirs' from the Second World War),[2] the large highly politicised middle class and the complicated religious make-up of the state made for a combustible mixture. All sorts of smaller armed gangs and bands proliferated.

The League, bypassed by coalition-building in the Punjabi assembly, waged an insistent, daily street campaign against the ministry of Khizr Tiwana, attempting to bring it to the point of collapse. Well-off Muslim women and students found a new liberation from the constraints of domesticity, marching in huge demonstrations against the ministry, fighting their way up buildings and hoisting flags made from their green scarves, courting arrest and putting up resistance to police when they came to arrest their husbands and sons. When the Punjabi government dared to try and restrict the activities of these militias and banned them on 24 January 1947 there was uproar. The circle of protesters widened, as shopkeepers, artisans and butchers pulled down their shutters and joined the crowds with placards and ready slogans against the ban. The ban on the RSS and Muslim League National Guard was lifted before the end of the week. The government had signalled its weakness. A League newspaper headline was printed within hours, telling the activists to 'Smash the Ministry'.

All this deeply affected daily life in the cities. Specific political contests between elite members of the League and the Congress were transmuted into a more amorphous sense of Muslim versus Hindu. This was plain to see. Some Hindu women took to wearing the *tilak* on their foreheads. Sales of the Jinnah cap boomed. Hindus who may have casually wished their neighbours hello or goodbye with a Persianised '*adab*' or '*Khuda Hafiz*' abandoned these greetings while Muslims jealously guarded 'their' phrases. It was suggested in a Punjabi newspaper that Anglo-Indians and Christians in Punjab should wear a cross as a marker of their identity, presumably to ward off the risk of accidental involvement in riots. The newspaper *Dawn*, mouthpiece of the League, started printing quotations from the Qur'an on its front page. More than in the past, household servants were recruited by their co-religionists and job advertisements started to specify communities: 'Wanted Muslim or Christian steno-typist and an accountant.' Gentlemanly League leaders, who were usually more likely to be found in the clubhouse or on the croquet lawn than in the mosque, started to pray ostentatiously. Even the rulers of princely states, generally better known for their profane, secular excesses and their eclectic admixture of pomp and ceremony, did not escape these pressures to display religious affiliation publicly; the ruler of Jind declared in 1947 that his pious New Year's resolution was to grow his beard and hair.[3] People bought arms and kept them in their houses for 'self-defence'. All the dangerous signs that had preceded violence in other parts of

India were here in full force in the Punjab – weak and partial government machinery, armed gangs and militias and an anxious population with heightened expectations of freedom and terror of domination by the 'other'.

In Delhi, meanwhile, the constitutional negotiations were pushed forward by priorities and deadlines set far away from India. In London, daily life in Punjab was far from the mind of the policy-makers. Concerns were about the frosty Cold War climate, the health of British balance sheets, the safety of British civilians in India, Britain's international reputation in the global press and the risk of British involvement in civil strife in Palestine and Greece which could end up badly overstretching the capabilities of the British army.[4] These priorities were evidently now quite at odds with domestic considerations about the safety or security of Indians: London's aim was to cut British losses, by leaving a united India if possible, a divided India if not, a view far detached from the intricate community politics of the subcontinent. At every turn the British government now accelerated the speed of events, and the Indian public was stunned by Attlee's statement on 20 February 1947 that the British intended to pull out from the subcontinent no later than June 1948. 'This announcement meant Partition,' remembered Penderel Moon, 'and Partition within the next seventeen months. Whatever London might think, everyone in Delhi knew that the Cabinet Mission's proposals were as dead as mutton.'[5] This, of course, only intensified the bombastic rhetoric in Punjab, added to the size of the crowds, and boosted the exaggerations and outright lies printed in the papers. The resignation of Khizr as premier of Punjab on 2 March and the collapse of his fated ministry was the final straw and marked the Punjab's descent into civil war.

Punjab on fire

By the end of the first week of March, within days of the collapse of the ministry, quarters of most of the major cities in Punjab were burning: Lahore, Amritsar, Jullundur, Rawalpindi, Multan and Sialkot all had sections gutted. Gangs roamed the streets, some wearing steel or tin helmets, setting shops and houses on fire (the government quickly restricted the sale of diesel and petrol), firing weapons and throwing heavy rocks and glass soda bottles. 'I was living in an area that was predominantly Muslim but every night we were afraid that there'd be an attack on us; so we used to be on house tops all night, watching whether an attack was coming or not, that was a perpetual feeling ... we thought an attack could come at any time,' later recalled the journalist Amjad Husain who was a young man in Lahore at the time.[6] On

20 March Standard General, a major Punjabi insurance company, placed a large advertisement cancelling all its new riot protection policies, of which it had been doing brisk sales. Throughout March and April markets and shops could only open for brief intervals and essential services fell into a state of decay. These riots went on for weeks. In April, H.K. Basu, the postmaster of Amritsar, dismayed at the mountains of undelivered mail at the central sorting office, personally went around the city in a van from house to house, trying to entice his postmen back to work. Some did go with him to the GPO to sort the mail but not one could be persuaded to deliver the letters on the streets of the city. It was simply too dangerous. Municipal revenues suffered too; in Amritsar the municipality claimed it had lost 70,000 rupees from tax receipts. No electricity or water rates had been paid for months, not least because it was impossible to send out the bills.[7]

Depressing features of Partition in other parts of the subcontinent were taken to new extremes in Punjab. In Bombay in March 1947, even during lulls between episodic stabbings, people were nervous about crossing into each other's 'zones'. League National Guards escorted Muslims back from cinemas. Visitors to Calcutta reported that residential streets were being divided up along 'communal' lines.[8] In Punjab, this was occurring on a new level. Barricades and gates were erected while protection racketeers and vigilantes stalked the streets, and in the worst affected areas the religion of all those entering the *mohalla* would be solemnly checked. It was easy to cloister off the dense overhanging *mohallas* in the old parts of cities such as Lahore but this practice spread to the more open and wide-avenued middle-class colonies. 'May I bring to the notice of the Amritsar local authorities,' wrote one anxious Punjabi, 'that the people belonging to the various communities are losing confidence in each other because, among other things, of the big iron gates by which the people are blocking their streets.'[9] As the evocative novel *Tamas* reflects, 'Overnight dividing lines had been drawn among the residential colonies and at the entrance to the lanes and at road crossings, small groups of people sat hidden from view, their faces half-covered, holding lances, knives and *lathis* in their hands.'[10]

Security was the paramount need of the hour. Anxious families acquired basic arms or barricaded in their allies but this had an escalating effect as it made other neighbouring communities feel more insecure. Crucially, local politicians, who often had far more authority in their own districts than Gandhi or Jinnah, made the call to arms. Master Tara Singh who had already warned that Sikhs must be prepared to die for their cause, called for the formation of an Akali Fauj, or Sikh army, and stood defiantly brandishing his unsheathed kirpan on 3 March 1947 on the steps of the Lahore legislative building, vowing, 'We may be cut to pieces but we will never concede Pakistan.' Extremist groups swelled as moderates who used to belong to the Congress, or Unionist parties, lost their political influence. As one former Punjabi Congressman says to his colleague in the novel, *Tamas*, 'will you come to save my life when a riot breaks out? . . . The entire area on the other side of the ditch is inhabited by Muslims, and my house is on the edge of it. In the event of a riot, will you come to save my life? Will Bapu [Gandhi] come to save my life? In a situation like this I can only rely on the Hindus of the locality. The fellow who comes with a big knife to attack me will not ask me whether I was a member of the Congress or of the Hindu sabha . . .'[11] Politicised elites stoked stereotypes and the delay during the implementation of the Partition plan gave armed brigades exactly the time they needed to circulate rumours, stockpile weapons and prepare ambush plans. Lulls in the episodic violence were frequently illusory as at these precise moments plans were being laid while defensive organisations honed their techniques.[12]

The decision to Partition

As a desperate response to the disaster unfolding, Congressmen in the highest echelons started to use the vocabulary of 'Partition'. Some Sikhs called loudly and provocatively for the division of the Punjab. Nehru himself started to imagine Partition as a possible way out. As Jinnah continually vetoed the vision of one strong united India, it emerged that the price of a strong central government was the division of the country. 'The truth', Nehru admitted in an interview in 1960, 'is that we were tired men and we were getting on in years . . . The plan for partition offered a way out and we took it.'[13] If these quarrels continued unabated in one bitterly divided Constituent Assembly, the whole economic future of the country could be undermined. Freedom was being painfully postponed. 'It is better to pass onto freedom even through chaotic transition than to be under the foreign yoke. Even a parrot would prefer to live half-starved but free rather than to remain in a golden cage, getting all the time raisins and dry fruits,' mused the quixotic industrialist Seth Ramkrishna Dalmia.[14] On paper, the division of the provinces of Bengal and Punjab looked like a solution, of sorts. The Congress Working Committee – the party's innermost circle – accepted the division of the Punjab as a possible solution on 8 March 1947. 'These tragic events have demonstrated that there can be no settlement of the problem by violence and coercion, and that no arrangement based on coercion can last,' the leaders regretfully acknowledged. 'Therefore it is necessary to find a way out which involves the least amount of compulsion . . .This would necessitate a division of the two provinces so that the predominantly Muslim part may be separated from the predominantly non-Muslim part.'[15] The heinous crimes of the preceding year forced the politicians to rush forward the decision to partition. Few were thinking about the line as a real or permanent fixture and the precise meanings of a partition were still inconsistent and unclear. It seemed to offer a way of attaining freedom and a compromise.

For other politicians who dreamed of infusing national iconography and policies with a more ostentatiously explicit 'Hindu' flavour, and remained less convinced by Nehru's insistence on pluralism, Partition might also relieve them of accommodating Muslim opinion altogether. They rejected Partition in the loudest voices, yet, in private, could also see its benefits. In July 1947, within weeks of Partition's acceptance, the Education Minister of United Provinces, a former schoolteacher named Dr Sampurnanand met with the sectarian Hindu Mahasabha and was told that, 'for the first time since the age of Prithwiraj [a twelfth century Rajput ruler], we had received the opportunity to develop the country according to what could broadly be called Hindu ideals. Whatever our choice of words, the culture of this part of India could not be otherwise than predominantly Hindu.'[16] Partition, for politicians of different ideological hues, was a painful blow to their original conceptions of freedom, but also had some practical utility. Partition would clear the decks for nation-building by the Congress, in whatever form that might take, and in the final analysis a Balkanised or fragmentary Indian state with extensive regional autonomy was of little value to the Congress Party.

The words on most of the Indian public's lips, though, remained *swaraj* and Pakistan. The word 'Partition' came a very poor third. What people most wanted was freedom and sovereignty over their own communities. The colonial leadership and its heirs were at a remove from the intensity of these patriotic and non-territorial demands. The idea of *partitioning* ancient homelands was barely contemplated or understood. As the power of the state to deliver law and order visibly collapsed, other regional aspirations came bubbling to the surface and all sorts of groups made violent bids for their own portion of land, their own community's sovereignty. There was still no inevitable or pre-ordained final shape to the subcontinental settlement and with the euphoria of an imperial ending surged the hope for self-rule and the will to power among princes, caste leaders, spiritual *pirs* and clusters of ethnic minorities. In short, the plan itself had far too little popular legitimacy and few had asked for it or even fully debated its consequences.

A few weeks later Mountbatten flew in with his own posse of hand-picked private staff to take up his post as the last Viceroy of India. The new viceroyalty, which started on 24 March 1947, two days after the Mountbattens landed in India, was strikingly different to any earlier regime in New Delhi. Mountbatten had visited India several times and had been the Supreme Allied Commander for South East Asia during the war. Mountbatten and his colleagues, though, had not loyally worked their way up through the pecking order of the British Raj, from district to imperial capital, and his enthusiastic band of advisers and press secretaries had little insight into the machinations of local Indian politics, or the implications of severe rioting. His predecessor, Wavell, who had spent his childhood in India and also served as Commander-in-Chief of the Indian army, appears to have been more hamstrung by sensitivity to the problematic political scene that was unfolding in India and aware of the interconnected difficulties that any kind of settlement could fuel, rather than ease. This left him struggling to take concrete steps whereas Mountbatten was less plagued by worries about regional, and bloody, repercussions. When a group of British provincial governors, exhausted and deeply anxious about the likelihood of violence in their provinces, arrived in Delhi for a meeting shortly after Mountbatten's arrival they were greeted by a buoyant and optimistic new regime.[17]

Once halving the contested provinces of Punjab and Bengal was accepted by the careworn Nehru and other Congress leaders as a viable option, as a pathway out of the interminable political morass, it was only a matter of time before the creation of two separate states took on momentum in the thinking of the Viceroy and his advisers. Mountbatten denied having arrived in India with any prepared plan, although he was rapidly reconciled to the idea of Partition once he was exposed to the political intransigence of the different parties. Within a month, and before he had even toured outside Delhi, he was starting to think that Pakistan was inevitable and that he had arrived on the scene too late to alter the course of events fundamentally. As K.M. Panikkar, the historian and diplomat who was advising the princely state of Bikaner, put it, 'Hindustan is the elephant . . . and Pakistan the two ears. The elephant can live without the ears.'[18] Mountbatten liked to describe the Viceroy's vast house as a small town, in which he presided as mayor. From this highly insulated perspective he was perfectly suited to his remit, which was to chart the making of nation states and the settlement of a constitutional solution. He achieved a much-coveted agreement between the League and the Congress by refusing to dwell on the implications of his actions, instead emphasising the practical aspects and stressing the expediency of finding a constitutional settlement.

On 18 May, less than two months after being sworn in as Viceroy, Mountbatten departed for London clutching the papers which sketched the Partition plan, ready to persuade the Cabinet that it was a workable scheme and hopeful of finishing the job on his return to the subcontinent. Only the fine-tuning remained: Punjabi and Bengali legislators would have the opportunity to vote on a potential split of the provinces, and a plebiscite for or against joining Pakistan would be necessary in the NWFP, where a Congress ministry, territorially far detached from the rest of India but strongly in favour of a united India, posed a particularly delicate problem. The paper plan, however, based on territorial and statistical maps, was entirely dislocated from the regional nuances of political life in India, and a top-down conceptualisation of state-centred politics would be imposed directly from London on the subcontinent. Furthermore, the plan was tragically un-concerned with human safety and popular protection. It did not even begin to examine the fear and apprehension of Indians, or to build in suitable safeguards to assuage these fears of domination.

The elite bartering and the final decision to partition was in the hands of a small cabal of British and Indian politicians and was staged theatrically in the classical buildings of Lutyens's New Delhi. By the spring months of 1947 negotiations had left provincial politicians and their followers far behind. The final settlement outran popular will in these localities, and the diverse political struggles taking place nationwide were scarcely factored into the simplistic plan to cut the Raj in two. It is this dislocation between New Delhi and its vast hinterland which has made Partition seem such an unwanted, alien imposition. In some ways, the final settlement was a true compromise, splitting land, resources and people between two entities, yet it satisfied no one. The League was handed a scarcely viable, 'moth-eaten' state to run, the Punjab and Bengal (ironically perhaps the two Indian provinces with the most distinctive regional cultures and interwoven populations) would be wrenched apart, and even Jinnah, who had at least achieved his Pakistan, admitted to a journalist in a letter, 'It is very difficult for me to understand what led His Majesty's Government to come to the conclusion of parti-tioning Punjab and Bengal. In my opinion it is a mistake and I quite agree with you. But now we have accepted the plan as a whole and I feel confident that we shall make a good job of it.'[19] His optimism, despite all the flaws in the plan, seemed justified. In the eyes of the politicians a conclusive settle-ment had finally been reached; freedom would arrive and almost one year earlier than anybody had ever expected. Perhaps this was the path to a peaceful settlement?

Stepping into the unknown

On 3 June, the plan was broadcast to a nervous and expectant population. In the lush green hills of Assam, in the north-eastern corner of India, the local Congress politicians heard of the plan to divide up the country in the British Governor's own living room, where there was, at least, a working radio. The paper copies of the 3 June plan did not arrive, as the post had been hampered by strikes and heavy sheets of monsoon rain. The Governor himself, Andrew Clow, was emotional at the momentousness of the occasion and the announcement that power was now going to be transferred. 'Leaving India is a big wrench,' he wrote to Mountbatten, 'particularly as I shall, in my own country, be rather a stranger in a strange land.' For many of empire's repatriated administrators, returning to the British 'homeland' would not be straightforward and Clow had been in India since 1914. For all his experience of the Raj, though, Clow's reading of the 3 June plan was that it was not permanent. 'I am very sorry that . . . the unity of India has *at least for some time to come* been broken,' he wrote. Like very many others his impression was of an expedient settlement rather than a permanent border. Imagining the transition from empire to free nations was complex and uncertain even for those in the imperial inner circle.

The Muslim League had won its Pakistan. But there was no firm line between winners and losers. Endemic confusion and disorientation followed the announcement, which sliced horizontally through all communities. One does not have to look far to find signs of the utter confusion which greeted the 3 June plan. The plan, which was such a relief to the British government, was foisted on a population entirely uninformed about its details and implications. Local understandings of 'freedom' and 'Pakistan', inspired by millenarianism, fear and heightened anticipation of revolutionary change, suddenly had to be squared with the creation of full-blown modern nation states. The country was to be divided – that much was clear – but would populations be expected to move? Where would the boundaries lie? What would be incorporated in Pakistan and what would not? None of these questions were satisfactorily answered by either the British or Indian political leadership. In the Indian army, on Mountbatten's own admission, 'Many of the troops had not, ten days after the announcement, yet realised the full implications of the plan.'[20] On the question of the princely states, a day after the announcement of the plan a government source suggested the British would 'begin to think' about entering into new relationships with over five hundred Indian states, home to 24 per cent of undivided India's population.[21]

Some Pakistan supporters ecstatically celebrated the victory that they had longed for and, for those in the vanguard of promoting a modern territorial state for Muslims, the news was an irreproachable triumph. 'When a few years ago, some of us, students at Cambridge, began to dream of an independent Muslim State in India and called it "Pakistan",' wrote I.H. Quraishi, a well-known historian at Delhi University in an emotional letter to Jinnah, 'even in our wildest dreams we were not so hopeful as to think that our cherished goal was so near at hand.'[22] For those who had consciously fought for a Pakistani territorial nation state it was a day of jubilation: sweets were distributed, songs sung, flags paraded. Leaguers celebrated the achievement of bringing a new country into being as a homeland for Indian Muslims; one thousand Muslim women gathered at Jinnah's house in Bombay to give him a standing ovation; and after saying their prayers in Agra's central mosque, Muslims celebrated the creation of Pakistan and collected donations for the new state.[23]

Jinnah made an appeal for funds in mid-June with which to build up the nascent Pakistan. He was inundated with donations and letters which came, in the main, from Delhi, Lahore and the North Indian urban areas where the League had always gained most vocal backing. The receipts for donations offer a fleeting insight into the enthusiastic support for Pakistan, especially from landlords, small businessmen and officials. The Railway Board Employees' Association in Delhi collected 250 rupees, and the Muslim employees of the Press Information Bureau in Delhi proffered a cheque for 80. 'Decent Leather Works' in Kanpur gave 25 rupees and twenty-three divisional sepoys from Madras offered 337 rupees from their wages. Women gave as well as men, and supposedly 'neutral' civil servants and officials dug into their pockets. The wealthy tenants of Razia Begum, who lived in her *haveli*, or traditional white-washed house around an open courtyard in Delhi, gave the princely sum of 500 rupees in their landlady's name. 'I venture to send a very petty amount I have saved out of my monthly pocket money received from my parents and pray you, respected Sir, to very kindly accept this humble offer,' implored Athar Shafi Alavi, a young student living in the old quarter of the railway junction town of Bareilly in the United Provinces, who wrote directly to the League leader. Pakistan was still managing, as an ideal, to capture the imagination of a segment of South Asian Muslim society.

The Partition plan, however, was a 'bitter pill' for Jinnah. For his supporters who now found themselves marooned, sometimes hundreds of miles from the real Pakistan, it was even tougher medicine.[24] In the midst of the celebrations nagging doubts emerged about the nature of the prize. As Begum Ikramullah put it, 'even though we may have wished for it and I, in a small way had worked for it, it was a bit frightening now that it was actually going to take place'.[25] What would happen to the leadership of the Muslims left in India? Should they migrate to the new country? In the provinces where Muslims were in a minority, the shock was for those who had constructed Pakistan as a fictive, imaginary counter-nationalism to the Congress, or had dreamed of a more capacious Pakistan, who were left with the cold realisation that Pakistan was not going to include their home areas. This affected leadership and masses alike. Z.H. Lari, a lawyer, had campaigned energetically for the League. When the final form of Pakistan was announced, however, he was bitterly disappointed with the result, and gave an emotional speech in which he said that if the plan was accepted it would be 'a major catastrophe' as 'the Pakistan which is being offered to us will be from every point of view so weak that we will find ourselves in serious difficulties'.[26]

The crushing fact, from the League's viewpoint, was that Pakistan's limits would be marked by two half-provinces, not the whole of Punjab and Bengal, and more expansive dreams of Pakistan's future had to be promptly reined in. Professor I.H. Quraishi, who had lavished praise on Jinnah's successful establishment of Pakistan just six days earlier, now wrote to him again. He had had time to examine the terms and conditions of Partition, the reality of the settlement had sunk in and he urged his leader to create a committee, 'to study and prepare the Muslim case for increased territories in Eastern Punjab and Western Bengal'.[27] He pressed the urgency of the situation on Jinnah. 'You have perhaps read a news item in today's paper saying that the Hindus and Sikhs will advance considerations other than population for demanding certain areas. I think that we should also prepare a case on the basis of history, strategic considerations, irrigation and a feasible customs barrier.' Minds turned to squeezing the settlement for the best possible deal. In Jinnah's own words the plan was 'titanic, unknown, unparalleled'.[28]

Among those who had vocally supported the Pakistan demand without giving much detailed thought to its potential territorial implications at all, and who had pinned their hopes and dreams on religious revival or revitalised power, there was more unhappiness. In the United Provinces, elation about achieving Pakistan 'got moderated by the realization among the more sober elements . . . of its logical implications for Muslims outside Pakistan'.[29] Some members of the League continued to hope that the boundaries of the new Pakistani state would include the Mughal heartlands of North India, in the

face of all the demographic evidence to the contrary, and even after the declaration that the Punjab and Bengal were to be divided, a circular was issued by
some members of the provincial League trying to popularise the idea of
'Pakistan pockets' in the province.[30] A hastily convened provincial League
committee in Bombay demanded the establishment of a 'homeland or homelands for the Muslims in Bombay province'.[31] Firoz Khan Noon, a Punjabi
League leader and later Prime Minister of Pakistan, responded to the 3 June
plan by suggesting that the Sikhs should be incorporated as members of the
new Pakistani Constituent Assembly, or that the Punjab's boundaries should
be redrawn on a linguistic basis, while in Amritsar a former newspaper editor
started a campaign for a united Punjab.[32]

Other Muslim groups, with different political attachments, felt aghast at
the prospect of the new state. On the Afghan frontier, the Muslim Congress
supporters felt an immediate sense of betrayal and Abdul Ghaffar Khan said,
'the idea that we could be dominated by outsiders is beyond my compre-
hension'.[33] The militant Muslim Khaksars violently rejected the plan,
demanded the whole of Punjab and Bengal and ransacked the stately
Imperial Hotel in Delhi, smashing glass and wreaking havoc, as nearly five
hundred League legislators met to ratify the plan. One hundred or more
were arrested as they tried to storm the hotel's staircase and the police fired
tear gas to quell them.

Accompanying the shocked reactions to the Partition plan, there was also
the new date to be contemplated; freedom had been advanced from a vague
time in 1948 to the definitive date of 15 August 1947. 'Necessity for Speed'
was, in case anyone was in any doubt, one of the subheadings of the 3 June
plan. The diary of Shahid Hamid, private secretary to Auchinleck at the time
and later a major-general of the Pakistan army, reveals little ambivalence
about the *idea* of Pakistan but total outrage at the manner with which the 3
June plan was delivered and the urgency with which freedom was granted:
'It was a bombshell! I wonder what brought this last minute change? Does
he [Mountbatten] realize its consequences? Why this hurry? Why this shock
treatment? . . . Why is he bulldozing everything and leaving no time for an
organized handover . . .'[34] He also acknowledged that there was confusion
about the plan in the army, even among commanding officers, and that
some suspected that 'the plan is some sort of trap'.[35] Haji Moula Bux, a
member of the Sindi Legislative Assembly who had stood against the
League, reassured his followers in Karachi that a reunion of the two countries was absolutely inevitable within two years, 'as sure as day follows
night'.[36]

Muslim Leaguers' thoughts now turned to what sort of country they wanted to build up. One Abul Quasem, a junior judge or *munsif* from Bengal, sent Jinnah his 'Thoughts on Pakistan'. 'To my mind it appears that we have not only not achieved Pakistan but our journey to the achievement of Pakistan has only begun and the way is full of dangers and pitfalls . . .' he wrote.

> If Pakistan means majority rule of the Muslims, I would not much care or labour to have it as it was almost in our grip if we accepted the A.B.C. plan [i.e. the Cabinet Mission plan] with right of succession from the Centre . . . Thus let us not mistake what we are for. If Pakistan means a homeland for the Muslims to develop their manhood to the fullest stature according to Islamic ideals, traditions and cultures, I must give my all to achieve it and here would come the question of my vision, sacrifice and labour.[37]

In not so many words, he was asking, what role will Islam play in the new state? Immediately Pakistan was declared a reality, the convenient ambiguities which had been used to glue the League together – hazy idealism and imaginative aspiration towards Islamic statehood – started to haunt the new country's leadership.

Among non-Muslims, too, the same questions were in circulation. Was this a temporary or a lasting settlement? Even as it reluctantly accepted the partition, the All India Congress Committee simultaneously kept alive the older idea of the indivisible Mother India. 'Geography and the mountains and the seas fashioned India as she is and no human agency can change that shape or come in the way of her final destiny,' resolved the Congress at an emotional meeting where it accepted the Partition plan in June 1947. 'The picture of India we have learnt to cherish will remain in our minds and hearts.'[38] From the standpoint of many Congress-supporting Indians it was unthinkable that those parts of the country in the north-east and the north-west which became Pakistan should be cut away, and the nationalistic imaginings of India, as part religious goddess, part mother figure, meant this was a debate about more than territory.

'I have lived and worked for freedom of India as a whole for the last 40 years,' declared Dr Chothi Ram Gidwani, president of the Sind Provincial Congress Committee, 'and today when [a] great many portions of India are as good as liberated, apart from other harmful effects of partition which need not be enumerated here, I cannot reconcile myself to the very conception of a divided India in which I become an alien in a great part of my own beloved motherland, and a citizen of a new Muslim theocratic state created overnight.'[39] His speech in reaction to news of the 3 June plan typifies the horrified reaction among many Indian nationalists.

All of this involved psychological adjustment. The nationalist map of 'India' – with territory reaching as far north as Afghanistan and as far south as Sri Lanka – was lodged firmly in the middle-class mind. This was a vast, sweeping picture of India as a continent rather than a country. Companies advertised by picturing their products against the silhouettes of Indian maps: they featured on everything ranging from lamps and tobacco to wristwatches. The black outline of India's shape was printed on letterheads and books. Furthermore, the idea of India had become, for many, personified in the shape of Bharat Mata or Mother India, who was both a goddess and geographical entity. Not just cold cartography, she embodied a real, warm, all-embracing mother figure. Her distinctive figure, in red flowing sari and often holding a flag, had many incarnations, ranging from ferocious Goddess Kali to demure housewife.[40] The goddess, Mother India, and the map were entwined together. A temple to Bharat Mata in Varanasi had been opened by Gandhi himself in the 1930s where worshippers could gaze on a vast marble depiction of the subcontinent. It was difficult to give up this idea and this dream. For this reason, Partition was (and is) often described in India using medical imagery, such as the severing of limbs, the hacking off of body parts.

It was a stirring, potential assault on the psyche of Indian nationalism. So there was vociferous denunciation of Mountbatten's Partition plan by the various parties gathered under the Hindu nationalist umbrella. The Hindu Mahasabha attempted to organise black flag days and passed indignant resolutions that Mother India's body could never be ripped asunder. On 3 July an anti-Pakistan day was marked with considerable success in Bombay, especially in Marathi-speaking districts, where almost all factories, shops and schools remained closed in protest and several effigies of Jinnah toured in funereal processions, one garlanded with a degrading necklace of shoes.[41]

Away from such certitudes, the predominant feeling was one of intense confusion, angst and anxiety about the future from all sections of society. Days after the plan had been formally announced, it was reported from Bengal by an American diplomat that 'The significance of the British decision substantially to complete transference of power by August 15, 1947 still seems not to be fully comprehended by most of the provincial politicians. A number with whom I have talked during recent days continue to feel that they will have the protection of British authority and military power at least until June

1948.'[42] The confusion and fear is palpable in the archives, diaries and letters of the time. If this plan brought an end to violence and delivered the long-awaited freedom might it not in reality be a positive development? The optimists were pitted against the pessimists, who perceived the logistical nightmare which lay ahead. Socialist Party members expressed 'disapproval and grief', generally seeing in the plan the seeds of British neo-colonialism and denouncing it as an international conspiracy to weaken Asia and prolong British economic and military might in India. As the Socialist Party leader confidently asserted, 'It should be realized that the plan is a stop-gap arrangement of a defined duration.'[43]

Others called for the separation of major South Asian cities as city states: just a fortnight prior to Independence Day, Sardar Sardul Singh Caveeshar, a Punjabi politician and president of the All India Forward Bloc, suggested that Calcutta, Delhi, Karachi and Lahore be singled out as city states, ruled independently by elected governors.[44] Countless politicians announced that there was every chance that the subcontinent would be reunited within a decade. 'I have not lost faith in an undivided India. I believe no man can divide what God has created as one,' declared the first President of India, Rajendra Prasad, on the day the plan was made public.[45] New and belated schemes were rushed out to try and change the fate of the subcontinent. In Bengal, as the historian Joya Chatterji has depicted, a last-ditch campaign was launched to try and keep Bengal united by regional politicians, includ- ing Sarat Chandra Bose and Suhrawardy, for which, Gandhi lamented, 'money (was) being spent like water' although of course this was to no avail in the face of the finalised plan which was being hurriedly rolled out from the Indian capital.[46]

'I am being flooded with telegrams,' Gandhi told his followers at his prayer meeting in June. 'I cannot say I am the only one to receive telegrams.' Just as some of Jinnah's supporters turned to thinking about the role of Islam in Pakistan, thousands of Congress supporters made appeals for the banning of cow slaughter which, for them, was integral to the meaning of true freedom; local understandings of what nationalism meant could be quite different to the conception of national political leaders. As the Bareilly Goshala Society put it, 'the British regime in which cows were slaughtered has ended and self-government has been set up'. Wasn't banning the killing of the sacred cow an essential part of *real* freedom? 'Rajendra Babu tells me,' Gandhi said, referring to his fellow Congressman, 'that he has received some 50,000 post- cards, between 25,000 and 30,000 letters and many thousands of telegrams demanding a ban on cow slaughter . . . why this flood of telegrams and letters?' He was continually telling people to stop the tide of telegrams; it was 'not proper to spend money on them'.[47]

Today we are accustomed to the fixed boundaries of the Indian and Pakistani states and their ideological orientation. In 1947, however, very different outcomes were contemplated with seriousness by the leading politicians of the day. The existence of such ideas, and their support among supposedly well-informed regional politicians and intellectuals, suggests the dislocation that had occurred between centralised constitution-making and provincial politics in India in 1947. Profound confusion, both about the precise boundaries, and about the meaning of 'freedom' and 'Pakistan', was part of the cause of the mass movement of people and stoked the ethnic violence that followed. Among poor agriculturalists there was little clarity about what Pakistan would be and where it would lie, even if there was an understanding about the manner in which the empire had been brought to its end. As one peasant farmer told a friend of Malcolm Darling, 'The English have flung away their Raj like a bundle of old straw and we have been chopped in pieces like butcher's meat.'[48]

The division of the Indian army was surrounded by so much uncertainty and lack of clarity that the *Daily Telegraph* headline in Britain only hesitatingly proclaimed on 4 June 1947 that 'Army may be split into two parts.' As with so many aspects of the Partition plan, national leaders publicly countenanced this part of the scheme only *after* the decision to partition had been announced. Even the highest ranks displayed bemusement about the real implications of Partition and the Indian army's division came as 'a great surprise to all' (except Field Marshal Auchinleck, who had been part of the confidential inner circle) when the top brass of the military establishment dined at the Viceroy's house the evening before the plan was announced to the world. In Bombay public opinion was aghast at the prospect of the army's division, 'as it seemed to destroy even the remote hope of India and Pakistan uniting again in the future'.[49] The complicated untangling of soldiers reduced the strength of the army just as it was needed more than ever to ward off militants. The sudden cracking in two of the army – and the creation of a new rival – coexisted with a broader feeling of disbelief about the reality of Partition and opposition to change within the military ranks. The deliberately vague wording of the Partition documents which spoke of 'reconstituting' rather than 'partitioning' the massive and intricately organised army into two parts further obscured the real meaning and permanence of the initiative.

There was some fierce resistance within the institution itself to breaking up the army and those Sandhurst-educated Indian officers, including some who would come to play decisive roles in Pakistan's future after 1947, pointed to the military's aloofness from local political control, and to distinguished regimental histories and military fraternity as they tried to avoid the inevitable division. The British Commander-in-Chief, Auchinleck, stubbornly refused to countenance division of his hallowed army into two halves when the idea was first tentatively raised by the League in a Defence Committee meeting in April 1947 and his attachment to the unity of the Indian army complicated the situation further as the terms of reference for the division were only placed on the table in July. Beneath this high-level wrangling, day by day the situation in Punjab was becoming more anarchic and bloody.

The most stunned and frightened reactions to the plan naturally came from Punjab. People living alongside the proposed Punjabi borderline, settled for generations on the fertile farmlands, could not, and would not, accept that they might become aliens, minorities or subjects in a state ruled by another religious group. The guesswork of newspaper artists who sketchily traced the provisional border on hastily constructed maps did not help. The border itself would not be finalised until mid-August and, preposterously, would remain a secret in the hands of an elite cabal headed by the Viceroy until Independence Day had passed. Caught in a horrible double bind, those Sikh leaders who had miscalculated and urged Mountbatten to divide the Punjab, in order to limit Pakistan's extent and to save the whole province from Pakistani domination, now faced the unimaginable prospect of a severed community, with one half in India and the other half in Pakistan. The regions around Lahore, Multan and Rawalpindi were dominated numerically by Muslims but home to over half a million Sikhs, and the holiest Sikh pilgrimage sites, including Guru Nanak's birthplace, fell squarely in territory which was now labelled Pakistani. Any farmer worth his salt knew that the prosperity of the region rested on a complex interlocking set of canals which now risked separation under the terms of the plan. Fissiparous arguments broke out among Sikhs about the best course of action and for many the emerging consensus was that the best tactic was to force the boundary westwards, either by appeals to the boundary commission or through violent tactics, pushing the limits of Pakistan back beyond Sikh heartlands to the Chenab River.

Adding to these conceptual confusions about what the newly independent India and Pakistan would look like was the entirely precarious position of the princely states. The future of the princes was relegated to a secondary problem by Mountbatten, to be picked up again in June only after the League–Congress deadlock had been broken and the Partition plan agreed. Some princes had taken up the offer of seats in the Constituent Assembly, while others resisted participating, but the absorption of the states by the Indian and Pakistani territories and their democratisation still seemed unlikely in mid-1947. Some European states, including France, reassured the princes of their status by signalling that they would open diplomatic ties with independent princely states. The rulers of extensive lands such as Bhopal and Hyderabad, which had potential as viable states, manoeuvred themselves towards an independent future.[50]

In the weeks before Independence, the majority of the princely states yielded to Indian pressure, granting the right to the new national government to intervene in matters of defence, foreign affairs and communications. At this moment, though, the continuation of local princely power was not a pipe dream. Patel told the princes in July 1947 that it was 'not the desire of Congress to interfere in any manner whatever in the domestic affairs of the states'.[51] When pressure to accede and merge was ratcheted up by the new governments in the summer, it caused explosive situations and armed resistance in the princely states of Kashmir and Hyderabad, where national allegiances were not clear-cut and were complicated by diverse populations. Hyderabad was only resolved in 1948 when Nehru resorted to force and ordered the annexation of the state. Up to the present day, Kashmir has not been decided to the satisfaction of all parties and remains one of the longest running disputes in the world. But aside from these more infamous cases, numerous smaller states faced troubled internal strife and determined popular and princely resistance to being subsumed into the all-encompassing Indo-Pakistani framework. There was a popular revolt in the tiny isolated North Indian state of Rampur in August 1947, an Indo-Pakistani scuffle over the accession of Junagadh perched on the tip of the Kathiawar peninsula (a state still claimed on Pakistani maps today) and, further north, the princely states of Bahawalpur and Kalat made overt bids for freedom from Pakistani control; the *New York Times* printed a map of Kalat as an independent state two days before Independence Day in August 1947.[52]

The extensive territories of the princely states alone, covering well over a third of India's total territory, meant that these territories, their wealth and populations, mattered to the future of the subcontinent even if the leaders of the Congress and the League only came to recognise their real importance late in the day. The lack of resolution of the princely state question by the time that the Partition plan was decided added immensely to the confused interpretations of Indian and Pakistani statehood and, ultimately, to the scale of Partition violence. Some decided to hold out and retain their old borders and try for independence while others hoped to reconfigure, merge and link up with kinsmen to create new states. In present-day Rajasthan, the Maharaja of Alwar had hopes of expanding his territory and creating a kingdom infused with the imagined warrior spirit of the Kshatriya caste, while the ruler of Bharatpur believed in the possibility of an independent land for his fellow Jat caste members. In Punjab, it seems that the Sikh princes of Patiala and Faridkot had set their hearts on the possibility of carving out a separate, independent Sikh kingdom under their own leadership. In their eyes, there was still everything to play for.[53] Seeing the confusion around them, the princes rallied their own bodyguards and small armies which were capable of serious military manoeuvres. These armies proved more than just royal playthings – the Maharaja of Bahawalpur kept three infantry battalions and some other units, including a few platoons of Gurkhas, and his force included local men as well as soldiers recruited in the frontier.[54] Kings harked back to the days of their family's former glory before the British arrived in India. Some imagined defending or even expanding their own territories.

Even the descendants of the erstwhile and long-disbanded princely state of Oudh, which was merged into Indian territory before the 1857 uprising, threw their hats into the ring and claimed their pre-treaty rights as heirs to the land. Some, with a view to the future, realised the likely territorial outcomes and quickly acceded to India while others believed that independence, continued autonomy or alternative federal arrangements could be arranged. Given the treaty history of these states – which had been created or ruined at the whim of British officials in the eighteenth and nineteenth centuries – and the long memories of these princely families, their suspicions about the final shape of independent India are not as bizarre as they sound. War was not an idle threat, as princes with personal treasuries, armed guards and significant power to marshal their local populations prepared for violent clashes. In some cases, the delusions of grandeur of the princely rulers meant that they decided to fight out an alternative scheme, use the force of arms and secure their own slice of Indian territory. Elsewhere, popular revolts ensued. The most notorious cases, Hyderabad and Kashmir, resulted in violent showdowns but, arguably, they were no more than symptoms of the broader malaise caused by the imperial breakdown.

Of course, nobody, as yet, had properly defined Pakistan's territory and some League leaders clung to the prospect of linking up with Muslim-ruled states such as Bhopal and Hyderabad, although they sat squarely in India, or even achieving the accession of the tiny states lacing the deserts along the Rann of Cutch on India's western flank. Well-tended myths and histories in these states reminded people that their communities had prospered through war. If well-educated Indian princes and maharajas, who had the ear of Mountbatten and open invitations to Delhi's political drawing rooms, genuinely, if quixotically, aspired to radically different visions of South Asia's future, then it is little wonder that the ordinary people living within these princely states were confused about Independence and regarded preparations for self-defence as a rational proposition.

On the precipice of Partition

Journalists bombarded Mountbatten with questions in press conferences in the days after the 3 June plan was announced and pressed him for information about procedural details, India's membership of the Commonwealth and the timing of the British departure, but only one thought to ask what would, in retrospect, turn out to be the most vital question of all. 'Do you foresee any mass transfer of population?' 'Personally I don't see it,' the Viceroy replied. 'There are many physical and practical difficulties involved. Some measure of transfer will come about in a natural way . . . perhaps Governments will transfer populations. Once more, this is a matter not so much for the main parties as for the local authorities living in the border areas to decide.'[55] The fuzzy thinking on this critical question was the fatal flaw in the Partition plan. Nobody had foreseen the risks of unprecedented population movements as a result of the plan and only feeble mechanisms had been put in place to reassure, protect or secure the position of the petrified communities living in the border regions of Bengal and Punjab. In the event, the resulting movement of people was so large that it changed the very nature of the newly independent states of Pakistan and India and altered the entire meaning of Partition.

Even as the plan was being agreed, the slow trickle of refugees had started and the decision to flee was weighed up. Those who could afford to travel left their keys with their neighbours or moved away from the Punjab to be with relatives. Anxious and confused students, businessmen and government employees penned tense and sometimes furious letters to the government or to their political heroes. The choices before them were limited. The very existence of the new state meant that those Hindus and Sikhs in Pakistan or Muslims in India immediately fell under the label 'minority'. It no longer mattered at all what their political inclinations were as, by the logic of the state, by a twist of fate decided at birth people were classified as members either of majorities or of minorities. Reports from the Central Provinces suggested that the ministry regarded 'every Muslim as a Pakistani' and that Muslim policemen were being encouraged to leave.[56] The Chief Minister of the province, as he reviewed the smart ranks of the Hindustani Seva Dal cadets a few days after the Partition plan was announced, suggested jokily that the Muslim minister sitting next to him on the platform would now have to find a new home in Pakistan. Rather less jocularly, he added that, 'even though religious and cultural freedom may be conceded to the Muslims living in Hindustan they will have no representation in the legislatures or in the services'.[57] The fundamentals of ethnic identity now looked as if they trumped everything else.

Masood Hussain, a twenty-three-year-old bachelor from the North Indian district of Moradabad, turned to Jinnah for help. Educated at Aligarh, with a Master's and a law degree, he was deeply worried about supporting his family. He had no capital, no business prospects and was worried about discrimination from local Congressmen as he had fought on the side of the League during the 1946 elections. As an unemployed student, his first concern was making a living and finding a modicum of economic security. 'Most Respected Quaid-i-Azam,' he wrote,

> I am ready to serve anywhere you order me – Sindh, Punjab, Sarhad, Baluchistan, Bengal or overseas . . . I assure you that I am passing very anxious days and nights. My father is dead and I have no property which can yield any income for the maintenance of my family. The capital left by my father, he having been a railway official, has gradually dwindled and has now come to Rs. 5,000 only. How long will it help, as our monthly expenditure is no less than Rs. 275 per month? I am in suspense and the future is uncertain. The last thing I could do was to approach you for help and sustenance.

Like many others, his attraction to Pakistan was framed in the language of economic and personal safety and security: 'It is my earnest desire that I should serve Pakistan and thus my family and myself.'[58]

The wealthy, far-sighted and well-connected made sure that their assets were safe. It is no surprise that the great industrial magnate G.D. Birla who had long been advocating Partition managed to extricate 80 per cent of his liquid assets from Punjab and Sind months before Partition. By May 1947 the capital shifting out of Punjabi banks to Delhi was being estimated at 250 *crores*, or 250 million pounds, and a banking magnate announced 'we are leaving the "Pakistan" an economic desert'.[59] Penderel Moon advised his 'unduly sanguine' Hindu friends in West Punjab to get out. 'One of them took the hint and expressed gratitude to me afterwards. The rest clung obstinately to their ancestral homes and in the end escaped with little more than their lives.'[60] Nobody leaves their home without a good reason, though, and the poor lacked the means to pack up and go, even if they wanted to. There was an urgent necessity to give rock-solid reassurances to these groups and to guarantee citizenship, property and security rights for all Hindus, Sikhs and Muslims, irrespective of where they lived. Catastrophically, this was not done in time and petrified communities threaded throughout India and Pakistan thought that they would suddenly be reduced to the status of 'minorities'. The corollary, they believed, was second-class citizenship, persecution and even death. In this light, waging a violent sectarian battle to preserve the land from intruders or outsiders became a perversely logical option.

Some leaders heard the 3 June plan as the starting gun for a *de facto* civil war; the demagogue Purushottam Das Tandon declared it would be the duty of the youth to take back the parts of the country that had been sliced away and appealed to the young, especially students, to train in arms even at the expense of their studies. 'It is the crying need of the hour. We are being subjected to onslaughts from every direction and enemies are waiting like hungry wolves to pounce upon us.' In Karachi, a packed crowd gathered to hear the provincial League president swear to 'fight to the last ditch for the honour and prestige of the Muslims of these two provinces', that the Muslims would 'never part with an inch of the Punjab' and that Pakistan might have to be claimed with 'the might of the Muslim sword'.[61]

Deluded and earnest attempts were made to bypass the plan and to reshape Pakistan along alternative lines. In the United Provinces, politicians in the west of the province set up committees to patch up a Pakistan corridor which would branch across from east to west, linking up the two wings of the new state. The secret Indo-Pakistan League campaigned doggedly for the 'original Pakistan' right into the earliest days of Independence, claiming that the British had ignored cultural and social considerations in their division of the country, that the separation of the two wings of Pakistan was illogical and that the remaining portions of the 'original Pakistan', such as Delhi, UP and Kashmir, should be released immediately.[62] These moves were entirely unrealistic by this date and reflect how detached many Leaguers had become from the politics of decolonisation and nation state formation being played out in New Delhi.

Numerous unambiguous warnings arrived daily in New Delhi and London of the turbulent state of affairs in the countryside, particularly the increasingly urgent and insistent warnings of the British Governor, Evan Jenkins, in Punjab. In London, politicians washed their hands of responsibility and showed vague, but uncommitted, concern. In a private conversation Attlee sombrely said that 'he was hopeful that there would be no bloodshed but feared that there would be'. The onus was on the South Asian leadership to take control and in the detached official colonial mind, Partition violence was perceived as *their* problem, a highly dubious perception considering the fact that the nascent governments had not yet begun to function and that, when they did, they would be understaffed, under-resourced and sometimes operating from under canvas. In a frank and astonishing exchange between Sir Paul Patrick of the India Office and American diplomats, the British official admitted that 'widespread violence and bloodshed' was likely from the first week of June and that 'legally there was no way of avoiding full British responsibility for public security in India until after the passage of the act and power transfer'.[63] It had taken six years to piece together the last major parliamentary act regarding India in 1935. Now, in less than six weeks, the final act of Parliament which unhooked India from its imperial master, 'a nice tidy little bill', in the words of the Secretary of State, was hurried through Westminster.[64] It is difficult to avoid the damning conclusion that, in the minds of British policy-makers, the duty to protect the lives of South Asians had already ended.

6

Untangling Two Nations

At the end of June, the Muslim League held a meeting at a large, private house in Lahore to decide the collective reaction to the boundary commissions. All the parties now scrambled to present their viewpoint to the commissions, to justify and explain why certain parts of territory should be destined to fall inside Pakistan. Penderel Moon attended the meeting and entered the house where a crowd of prominent Leaguers had gathered to deliberate over Pakistan's proposed boundaries, to decide what claims they should stake to the Punjab: 'On the floor and on a big table a number of maps of the Punjab were strewn about, variously coloured and chequered so as to show the distribution of the population by communities. We all fell to poring over these maps,' he later remembered. 'It became plain in a very few minutes that no-one had any definite idea of where we should claim that the dividing line should run – indeed, except for Gurmani [his colleague] and myself, no-one seemed to have given much thought to the matter or even to know the basic facts about the distribution of the population.'[1]

The open-ended, conveniently ambiguous Pakistan demand now came crashing into territorial realities of population ratios and land usage. Between 3 June and 15 August the imaginary, but deeply felt, attachment to Indian and Pakistani nationalism was to metamorphose into two, real sovereign nation states. Land, assets and armies were to be severed in seventy-three days. As Gandhi put it, intuiting the chasm between conflicting understandings of nationalism, 'Pakistan is not something imaginary. India is not something imaginary . . . No poison must be spread.'[2] Regrettably, however, the poison had already seeped deep into the arteries of the nationalist firebrands. Like a distorted fairground mirror, India and Pakistan became warped, frightening, oppositional images of one another.

The political decisions could no longer be made in a sealed bubble away from prying eyes. Penderel Moon was taken aback to see a young, junior official present at the League meeting in Lahore, one Mohammad Ali, with whom he had worked four years earlier in Amritsar. Mohammad Ali, a subordinate revenue official, was standing in a group of people near the window. Moon was surprised that someone so junior should have found his way into the inner circle of decision-making about depositions to the boundary commissions. He crossed the room and asked, 'What on earth are you doing here?' to which came the reply, 'My friend brought me along and we just walked in. Nobody stopped us.' Information was leaking profusely from the party strongholds, giving ample opportunity for rumours and misinformation to take hold. The centre of political gravity was shifting from New Delhi to the offices and front rooms of clerks, petty officials, policemen and administrators. Friends and relations passed news to one another as the political classes tried to extract information and to steer the boundary award in their own favour.[3] Simultaneously, decisions and statements were couched in so much uncertainty that ordinary Punjabis were left completely in the dark about whether their homes were soon going to be in India or Pakistan.

The border had to be decided against the clock. The Bengal Boundary Commission and the Punjab Boundary Commission, both under the chairmanship of Cyril Radcliffe, were formed on 30 June. Radcliffe was a respected judge, well known for his piercing intellect, but had none of the requisite technical skills for drawing a border, and had, infamously, never been to India before. The British government considered this an asset lending itself to impartiality rather than the self-evident drawback which it proved. Until he arrived in India, on 8 July, Radcliffe did not realise quite what he had bitten off: there were eventually 3,800 miles of border between the two countries. The terms of the commissions' briefs included not only the statistical proportions of Hindus, Muslims and Sikhs by district but also a woolly and muchdebated reference to 'other factors' – cultural, geographical and historical – which left the boundaries open to repeated challenges. In the long run this undermined the moral authority of the final settlement. In Punjab, over half of the districts were contested, making the provisional boundary line a sham. For Radcliffe it was, quite simply, a thankless task.

The census the commissions worked with was six years out of date and of dubious veracity in the first place; the trickle of refugees which had already started and the bunching of communities together for safety during the ongoing violence meant that the population ratio of the land which was being divided was shifting beneath both boundary commissions' feet on a daily basis. Pakistan itself had never been fully defined in a territorial way by the League, which had laid claim to the whole of Punjab, while the imagery of Indian nationalists staked a claim to the whole of the subcontinent. Now the precise landmass of Pakistan had to be carved out. 'The Assam government invited the commission to come to Shillong but they have refused on the score of shortness of time,' the disappointed Governor of the province remarked.[4] The commissions declined all the other polite invitations to come and visit affected areas. In the end, they retreated behind closed doors, working from maps using pen and paper, rather than walking the land and grasping for themselves the ways in which vast rivers, forests and administrative districts interlocked and could best be separated.

Faced with the impending reality of this arbitrary borderline, Indian groups and parties were bitterly torn among themselves about what to claim and what to relinquish and on what basis. The land question now seized centre stage. Rather than ameliorate and assuage, the 3 June plan was sparking unknown consequences. There was a 'very mixed' reception to the Partition plan in Lahore and Amritsar – and the imposition of the sudden division froze people together, making superficial association with one group or another more difficult to avoid. 'The belief that the Punjab will be partitioned has intensified the communal split and most officials are wondering who their new masters will be and how best they can secure their own future,' warned the Governor, foreseeing the complete fissure which would soon tear through the administrative offices and the police forces in the troubled province.[5] Again, the implosion of the old colonial regime meant that there was very little reliable organisational infrastructure to prop up the transitional state: 'so far as the services are concerned we are going through a very difficult time with some men yearning to leave India, others trying to please new masters, and others again upset and apprehensive. The old administrative machinery is rapidly falling to pieces.'[6]

He was right; the old machinery was disintegrating. Punjab was now held hostage by volatile militias. In fear of a political backlash, the government of Punjab allowed well-known ringleaders to go free and British officials and Indian politicians wavered over the banning of weapons, including guns and the unsheathed kirpans of the Sikhs. 'There was nothing abnormal en route . . .' Moon commented, on his way into Lahore, except that on roads leading through the district of Multan, 'individual Sikhs walking or cycling were all wearing very large kirpans'.[7] Bombs, often left over from the Second World War, became a new feature of the attacks in Punjab in June. On the morning of 10 June a Sikh on a bicycle hurled a bomb into a horse-drawn cart carrying passengers in Lahore. The street exploded into confusion, leaving two dead and ten injured. Ten days later, on Brandreth road, a party of labourers heading off early in the morning for their day's work, perhaps as bricklayers or rock-breakers, were attacked by a bomb thrown from a neighbouring rooftop. One of the men died. In the vegetable market in Lahore, the next day, two bombs timed to go off one after the other caused havoc; splitting apart the stalls of piled-up pyramids of vegetables, killing nine shoppers and traders and injuring at least thirty-eight more. The Sikh leaders openly threatened an uprising to the British officials and one spokesman, Giani Kartar Singh, wept as he told the Governor of the Punjab that a fight was inevitable if no heed was paid to Sikh solidarity.

Terrified by their loss of control and shocked by the chaos and the mess which they would inherit on Independence Day, national leaders pleaded for order. 'Amritsar is already a city of ruins, and Lahore is likely to be in a much worse state very soon,' Nehru told Mountbatten in the last week of June. 'You gave an assurance even before 3rd June and subsequently that any kind of disorder will be put down with vigour. I am afraid we are not honouring that assurance in some places at least, notably Lahore and Amritsar.' Jinnah, more bluntly, begged, 'I don't care whether you shoot Moslems or not, it has got to be stopped.'[8]

Claiming the land

At the same time, Pakistan was becoming a real, earthy reality. Rapidly, the greatest minds in law, statistics and administration turned to the maps in order to construct their case. 'I understand that a band of workers under Mr Abdur Rahim, I.C.S., has been working on the ethnological aspect of the problem. I venture to send a few figures in this connection,' wrote Professor Quraishi to Jinnah. He enclosed lists of numerical musings on *tehsils*, or small administrative areas 'contiguous to tentative districts of Pakistan where Muslims are in absolute majority'. These raw statistics make terrifying reading when we know, with hindsight, where this reduction of human beings to simple numbers was leading. Quraishi was just one of many who sent lists and he had scribbled in the margins whether the League had a case to make on the grounds of population. In *tehsil* Muktsar, he noted, 'Muslims in simple majority.' Moga was 'Predominantly Hindu', in Amritsar *tehsil*, 'Muslims are less than combined population of Hindus and Sikhs', but in Anjala there would be an 'Absolute majority of Muslims'. In Dasuya, 'Muslims are less than combined Hindus and Sikhs. But if Indian Christians are combined with Muslims, we get bare majority.' And so it went on.[9]

In this frenzied rush to calculate population ratios the reality of ancient and intricately woven homelands – and sensitivity to violent repercussions – was lost. Ominously, another League supporter in North India, A.R. Khan, was calling for limited movement of the population to strengthen the Muslim position, which he predicted would not be difficult in the rural areas 'where people have no stakes'.[10] The logic of this was to reduce individuals and communities to crass ratios and statistics which stripped bare the inner complexities of friendship, community and life itself. Gandhi distilled this beautifully into five words: 'today religion has become fossilised,' he told a gathering of saffron-clad *sadhus* and Hindu ascetics in early June.[11] Few talked about, or even contemplated, what this border would mean for the ordinary people who lived on either side of it. 'My anxiety now was to work day and night and get the case ready by Friday noon,' remembered the Muslim League's chief legal representative, Muhammad Zafrullah Khan, many years later. 'Even now, looking back, I cannot explain how it was possible for us to produce a case which we did by the Friday noon.' Immediately after submitting the documents to the Punjab Boundary Commission in Lahore, he went straight to a local mosque, where he led the Friday evening prayers and warned the anxious congregation to be 'vigilant' as he feared that the Muslims faced 'suppression'.[12]

There would be one chance for the parties to present a case to the boundary commissions at their public hearings held in the High Courts of Lahore and Calcutta in late July. The chattering classes could acquire permits and some went to watch the show, packing the press and public galleries. But it was not light entertainment. The Punjab Boundary Commission received fifty-one official memorandums from political parties and organisations, the Sikhs' memorandum alone was nearly 75 pages long and the star Bombay lawyer, M.C. Setalvad, who made the case for the Congress, with the Hindu Mahasabha's backing, spoke for over three hours. Ultimately, all this fevered activity only heightened expectations.

As Independence Day drew nearer, the response to the threat of an unknown borderline was, quite simply, frantic. The telephone at the Governor of Punjab's house was ringing incessantly around the clock with callers desperate to convey their position. Depositions and appeals came in the form of telegraphs and petitions, letters and phone calls, to the commissions themselves as well as, hopelessly, to those who were not allowed to intervene in their work in any case: Mountbatten, Attlee and even the King of England. There were so many memoranda and representations to the Bengal commission that the commissioners said it would be impossible for them to finish their hearings by the set date of 26 July (to which Radcliffe could only reply, 'I must beg you to complete by 26'). Journalists at the offices of the pro-League newspaper *Dawn* claimed that they had received hundreds of telegrams on the subject and warned uncompromisingly in front-page articles that local Muslim leagues were readying themselves for action against an unfavourable award. 'Muslims of Ambala,' the paper reported of one district which, objectively, had no chance of inclusion in Pakistan, 'demand demarcation of boundary lines on population basis. Any departure from this fundamental rule will be fought tooth and nail.' 'From start to finish,' in the words of the historian Joya Chatterji, 'the making of the borderline was shot through with politics.'[13]

'To Sikh solidarity the Mountbatten scheme will be what a knife is to a cheese piece,' warned a Lahore newspaper: 'it will cut through it easily and definitely.' The Sikhs, a community of only six million, in an all-India population of almost four hundred million, became desperate. The Sikh population was almost evenly spread across the Punjab. What were the Sikhs to do now, with 'no homeland in the whole world except in the land of the five rivers'?[14] They had lost their influence on the colonial state and felt the interests of their community were being sacrificed on the altar of a broader constitutional settlement. Many had called for Partition as a way of saving at least some of the Punjab from being swallowed up by Pakistan but now they appealed to the commission to consider the 'other factors' – the rich regional Sikh heritage, their extensive landholdings and architectural birthright. On this basis, it was not improbable that Lahore, home to six hundred gurdwaras, might fall to the Sikhs despite the population ratios which narrowly favoured Muslims in the city. There was a confused and divided response, with some appealing for a Sikh homeland, Sikhistan, and others pushing for reconciliation to broker a deal with the Muslim League. But for many, fighting to push back the boundary line was the only option if Radcliffe presented them with a raw deal.

Allegiances were swiftly sealed with Sikh princes whose own lands abutted these tracts and who had no intention of sinking their kingdoms in a wider sea of Pakistan if they could help it. As a collection of seventeen wealthy Sikh landlords spelt out in a searing appeal to the Viceroy, nothing short of a line along the Chenab River would satisfy:

We must now rise as one man and proclaim that we shall refuse to be put in a helpless position. We have fought and defended the country for over a century with our blood out of all proportion to our numbers. Our contribution in the economic field both in industry and agriculture and development of the canal colonies of the Punjab bears the deep impression of our sweat and toil. Our religion has given India a beautiful culture which if correctly understood would banish all communal strife and bitterness from our land. We have not done all this to earn slavery and domination.

Dawn bitterly retorted that it was unthinkable that 'the tiny little community of scattered Sikhs who have split themselves into two by their own scatter-brained policy may be awarded predominantly Muslim territories merely because there may be located in them a Sikh shrine here, or a Sikh shrine there'.[15] This was a gross and disingenuous reduction of the importance of Nankana Sahib, the fifteenth-century birthplace of Guru Nanak, the founder of Sikhism. As the Maharaja of Patiala told Mountbatten directly, 'The Sikh sentiment about this place is so strong that it would be most dangerous to minimise it, as under no circumstances they can be persuaded [*sic*] to allow this to go into foreign territory.'[16] Couched in royal niceties, this was a very thinly veiled threat. The Maharaja had already been roundly sacking his Muslim employees and openly supporting the idea of a revitalised Sikh state.

Princes and big parties could at least get a hearing with Mountbatten. Smaller groups such as 'untouchables', Christians and Anglo-Indians were simply pushed aside by the sweeping plan. Beyond the neat textbook polarisations of League and Congress were countless fragmented groups with their own worries and interests. Their voices could not be completely drowned out. Yet now these smaller groups looked as if they were up for grabs, only really able to make their voice heard through alliances with the larger parties. Chaudhri Sunder Singh was a member of the Legislative Assembly for Punjab, elected on a ticket as an 'untouchable'. He was so worried about the fate of his community two weeks after the 3 June plan was revealed that he forced staff in the Governor's office to send a letter to Mountbatten on his behalf. This met with a curt rebuff. Politicians of the Pakistan Achhut Federation, P.S. Ramdasia and Choudhry Sukh Lal, travelled to Delhi in order to try and confront the Viceroy in person and to push forward their viewpoint, 'in the hope that even at this eleventh hour [a] sense of justice may create an urge to minimise the wrong done to our unfortunate community at least in the province of Punjab'. Their community would prefer to be in Pakistan, they argued, rather than subsumed under the broader Hindu label. 'It is no longer a secret that the Hindus aim at re-establishing Vedic Raj – the so-called Ram-Raj – and the untouchables do not realise that they shall have to remain *chan-*

dals [untouchables] for ever under Hindu domination.'[17] There was neither the time, nor the will, however, to nuance sweeping understandings of 'Hindu', 'Muslim' and 'Sikh'. And nobody was clearly spelling out the guiding political principles behind the new India and the new Pakistan.

The basic building blocks of the new states, their economic policies and their attitude towards minorities, remained uncertain. Without this knowledge, those who feared that their land was on the verge of becoming Pakistan or Hindustan felt deeply troubled. People associated the idea of belonging to the hazy, unknown 'India' or 'Pakistan' with negative and upsetting connotations. Some feared infringement of their personal lives, the ruination of their religion, perhaps even the destruction of daily life as they knew it.

Portentous news began arriving in New Delhi: of the possibility of 'active resistance' to an unfavourable boundary and of people distributing posters in Punjabi villages summoning crowds to emergency meetings in mosques, temples and gurdwaras. On 8 July a massive *hartal*, as Sikh businesses, shops and markets closed all over Punjab, stretched into the cities of North India. Over half a million Sikhs wore black armbands to signal their depth of feeling. They collected together in gurdwaras to pray for the continued unity of their community. Abundant warnings stressed that violent protests were being organised in order to shape and influence directly the places where the borderline would snake through the land. Violence was the last tool of the desperate.

In this light, constitutional means were rapidly starting to seem an irrelevance. As a self-described 'common man' from Lahore expressed it to his Congress committee, 'Violence is bad but non-violence is hopeless.'[18] It was impossible to square the heightened sense of expectations which had been stirred by Independence with the bruising reality of a borderline penned hastily across a piece of paper. Uncertainty about the precise location of the new borderline collided with the intensely negative attributes ascribed to 'Pakistan' and 'India'. Among those who had been on the front line of nationalist campaigns, membership of 'India' or 'Pakistan' was reviled as potentially life-threatening and all-engulfing. If your home fell on the wrong side of the border when it was finally announced, many argued, you would not be living as a minority in a modern, democratic nation state. Instead you would suffer oppression, exploitation, the dishonouring of religion and perhaps even conversion or death.

Fears of British foul play were also festering. 'A nation that has regained a homeland that belongs to it never gives it up without a fight,' spat out editorials in *Dawn*, inciting its readers to action if the British reneged on their agreements. 'If that is what these last minute double-crossers want so that they may secure [a] renewed imperialist foothold under fresh excuses, they will get it.'[19] The plan was condemned as 'eyewash' and 'a sham' by others. Sikhs complained that their sons had died on the battlefields of Europe during two world wars and that this was how the British repaid them.

Collections were made for a Sikh war chest and Sikh *jathas* assembled, dressed in red and orange bandannas and distinctive turbans, armed, and stirred to action. Two private armies, the Akali Sena and Shahidi Jatha, went from village to village recruiting men. This was preparation for civil war by any other name. By July, Evan Jenkins, the Governor of Punjab, was sending unambiguous warnings, citing depth of anger about the division and proposed borderline as the major grievance. The boundary had become a live wire, or even 'a casus belli between the two dominions'.[20] The claims of the two sides were incompatible: the Sikhs could not forgo their principal gurdwaras, which lie in present-day Pakistan, just as Muslims claimed historical and cultural rights in Lahore, the home of the formidable Badshahi mosque, while it was feared that militants on both sides might destroy cities rather than relinquish them.

As Independence Day approached, life became nightmarish for people caught between the opposing sides. 'My head was about to burst. To me it seemed as if I was not in my senses,' the writer Fikr Taunsvi recorded in his daily diary after another difficult day in the war-torn city of Lahore, which had now been under siege for almost six months. 'I felt a hammering on my brain. My nerves were on edge, as if they would explode and destroy my body. The continuous sharp chain of the morning's turmoil enveloped me in its tight embrace.'[21] Fear was the predominant emotion in the middle months of 1947, particularly in those districts of Punjab where inclusion in Pakistan or India was, as yet, unknown. Here, policemen and magistrates had become completely unreliable and untrustworthy, slinking away from their posts or becoming openly partisan. Sleep was disturbed by unusual, threatening noises as riots broke out in distant parts of the city or militias made their rounds in the streets: there were the beating of drums and tom-toms, the striking of cooking vessels, bells and gongs, the wail of horns, trumpets, loudspeakers, whistles and sirens.[22]

Curfews and closed markets caused dire hardship. Taunsvi's local street was in turmoil: 'the washerman who lived on the ground floor . . . had become the father of a tiny baby at three in the morning and . . . was worried that the bazaars were shut. The sweet-seller who sold milk had locked his shop from inside and was hiding there. He had received no supply today because all milk-vendors are Muslim, and this being a Hindu locality, they couldn't step into it. Hospitals were not functioning, neither were doctors, nurses and medicines, and both the mother and the infant were crying. The children were asking, "Will the curfew never be lifted? Shall we never get milk?"' As he helplessly watched the washerman's newborn child become more sick, Taunsvi's feelings turned to anger against the politicians who had created the situation, 'I wish you had the strength to ask great brains like Jawaharlal Nehru, Jinnah and other statesmen and *maulvis* to wear the guise of this unlettered washerman for a moment. Then you may go and request the British to give you freedom. Then demand Pakistan and Hindustan.'[23] The brutality and daily privations of the time seemed far from the dreams of the long-awaited independence.

People experienced gradations of anxiety; some Punjabis felt paralysing and life-changing terror. In the worst-afflicted centres, in the hardest hit parts of Lahore and Amritsar, Rawalpindi and Sheikhupura, the most anxious took desperate measures – growing or cutting off their beards and learning the *Kalma* or Vedic phrases so that they could fake their religious identities if necessary. If possible, families sent their unmarried daughters away with guardians or relations, and decided upon hiding places in the roof spaces of barns or the small back rooms of temples or mosques. The optimists refused to take basic precautions but many minds turned to self-defence and the stockpiling of bags of sand and cooking fuel, and the collection of extra drinking water. Newly recruited watchmen patrolled villages and towns, and missiles and ammunition piled up. The family of Shanti Seghal, a young woman aged twenty at the time, made various attempts to find safety, moving from Gujranwala to Sheikhupura in 1946 because the family thought the city would probably end up in India. 'My father had a soda water shop; we put all the soda water bottles on the roof, lined them up, thinking that when they come we will attack them with bottles,' she later recalled, 'but they were no use because they came with machine guns.'[24]

Creating a believable border was impossible without the agreement of the people who would have to abide with it. The 3 June plan had exacerbated anxieties and accelerated the preparations for war. It was becoming more difficult to stay neutral and the formation of two new nations was forcing people to declare simple allegiances from much richer and more complicated pasts.

Making two armies

Fortifying the Punjab with a highly disciplined force of impartial, professional soldiers would have been one way of providing security and reassurance to people in the weeks between the announcement of the plan and its implementation. In the troubled district of Mathura, 'the sight of tanks careering round the countryside, often with the local police officer standing in the turret, had some temporary effect'.[25] In Bengal, there had been 'some ugly incidents' but, an American diplomat reported, 'the city is so bristling with armed troops and police that forays against public order have been discouraged and minimized'.[26] Troops did have a presence in city centres in Punjab, North India and Delhi – on Independence Day in Lahore Penderel Moon found the Lawrence Gardens 'full of troops' while 'the railway station was in the hands of the military and barricaded off by barbed wire'.[27] There was, in addition, a special boundary force constituted to deal with the prospect of a contested borderline.

But just as land was being divided, so were soldiers. Nearly half a million Indian soldiers commanded by a predominantly white British officer corps had to be cut and pasted into the new national formations. The division of the army along religious lines, which Auchinleck had reckoned would take 'between five and ten years', in March 1947, was hurried through in months, although it was only completed in full in March 1948.[28] In the midst of the most appalling killings which were ripping through North India and just at a time when a united, neutral army was needed to suppress militias – which were often composed of ex-soldiers themselves and hence not averse to engaging the authentic army in battle – the regiments of the Indian army were dismembered. Soldiers were combed out and mechanically divided according to their religious hue; blocs of Muslim soldiers were hastily packed off to Pakistan while non-Muslim soldiers were dispatched in the opposite direction.

Of the twenty-three infantry regiments in pre-Partition India, only seven consisted exclusively of Hindus, Muslims or Sikhs. Now, no Muslim who was resident in the Pakistan areas could choose to serve in India, and vice versa for non-Muslims living in India. Much effort had been expended by the British during the Second World War trying to keep the military immunised from the cross-currents of Indian nationalism. Before Independence, fervent nationalists were unlikely to sign up for careers in the imperial army. Now, though, more narrowly defined allegiances to the League and the Congress became irrelevant. The religion into which a soldier was born became the *sine qua non* of his new national identity. Now all Muslims were fundamentally equated by the state apparatus with Pakistan and all non-Muslims were assumed to have a natural allegiance to India, whether they had expressed support for the creation of the new states or not. Given this stark choice it was unusual for soldiers deliberately to choose to serve in a country where they would be part of a 'minority'. The chances of a quick promotion, family persuasion, marital prospects or judgements about personal safety rapidly took precedence.

Men of various castes and communities lived intimately alongside each other in the Indian army. Some companies remained immune from jingoistic outbursts, whereas others became more highly politicised. News of army indiscipline was suppressed and the army appeared to remain more 'reliable' and less polarised along ethnic lines than the severed and pugilistic local police forces. Nevertheless, the cart followed the horse as soldiers were encouraged to display patriotic feeling. Now, labelled Indian or Pakistani, many soldiers started to identify openly with one side or the other. 'Mussalman officers are jubilant and talking openly of being generals in the Pakistan army, and that Pakistan will eventually be greater than the previous Moghul Empire,' wrote one British colonel.[29] Many sepoys came from the Punjabi and North Indian heartlands where violence was raging and felt extremely anxious about the fate of their families. Nervous and irritable soldiers waited for information of their new postings in the maelstrom of misinformation and rumour.

As rail and road networks remained vulnerable to attack, the precise moment at which units of Muslim soldiers would be evacuated to Pakistan from India – and vice versa on the Pakistani side – was kept a closely guarded secret and usually announced at very short notice. A group of Pakistani cadets stationed in the northern hill station of Dehra Dun had just four hours' notice to pack for their new homeland, and their superiors bundled them out of their base in a heavily guarded convoy at 5.30 in the morning. The British medical officer Anthony Epstein, who was looking on, wrote home to his family about the sudden departure of the Muslim cadets. 'It was all very dramatic and tense, with a farewell parade in the dim lights of lorries and everyone cheering and very excited. This incident only heightens the sense of foreboding there is here as everywhere.'[30] Soldiers who had forged friendships over many years of shared daily routine were suddenly separated and there was genuine sadness about the division; glasses were raised in heartfelt toasts, addresses were exchanged and pledges made. Every company of the 3rd Rajputana Rifles hosted a leaving party for their Muslim co-soldiers before they took their leave for Pakistan. As a senior officer in 1947, Sahabzada Yaqub Khan, later a Pakistani Foreign Minister, remembered in discussion with the journalist Andrew Whitehead,

Many of the men I commanded, Punjabi Muslims, they had homes in what would become Pakistan, but in the villages there had been many cases of abduction of women, and some of the men were affected, their families and so on had been abducted . . . but I must say this also, their Sikh comrades made many efforts to go down to those villages and to try and secure release of abducted women, not always successfully; but you can imagine that events of that kind, which touched so deeply . . . were bound to prey on the minds of the people concerned; these events were a strong indication that the fabric would not be able to hold together.[31]

In the shadow of the continuing Punjabi violence, the fragmentation of mixed regiments was a constant concern despite the strong thread of comradeship running through the armed forces. Whole squadrons of Sikhs and Muslims waited cheek by jowl for movement to their permanent units in Jhansi and as rumours of their impending transportation came and went, alongside new stories of calamities in Punjab, there was a risk of the soldiers turning on each other. As they nervously waited for news of loved ones the strain could become too much. In Gujranwala there was a mutiny in one Pakistan battalion and the non-Muslim soldiers had to be urgently removed to safety, while in Ambala an inquiry found Pakistani troops guilty of firing at civilians from the carriage windows of their passing train, killing or wounding sixty people. A Sikh captain was charged after a shooting incident in an unspecified Punjabi suburb in which eighteen people died.[32] On board a ship sailing from Bombay to Karachi after Independence, General Tuker, who was no stranger to the extent of Partition's damage, was astonished to find just how many soldiers on board had had relatives killed in the violence or had not heard from their families for months.

Some soldiers, once they had been segregated for dispatch to their new homeland, passionately adopted the slogans of their new state and fired their rifles into the night sky as they passed through train stations *en route*, yelling 'Pakistan Zindabad' or 'Jai Hind'.[33] Food and water were handed through carriage windows to troops as they crossed into either India or Pakistan at the Wagah border crossing, and the air was filled with morale-boosting cheers and flags. In the later weeks of 1947, with increasing regularity, soldiers – on hearing of villages wiped out or sisters abducted – deserted to join militias to assist in the ethnic cleansing of Punjab.

As a result, the reliable manpower available to cover the vast tracts of land that were already up in flames, or likely to descend into the clutches of violence, was shockingly thin. At the same time, preparation for the departure of the British army was in full swing. Only a few hours' travel from the Indian capital itself, in the flat expanses of Gurgaon, guerrilla warfare against a rural population known as the Meos was decimating whole villages. The state was unprepared and there was a botched attempt to send troops. A 'British' policeman, William Chaning Pearce, who was actually Canadian-born and educated in Switzerland, was in his late thirties at the time and responsible for policing the neighbouring district of Mathura. 'Our resources for this task were pitifully meagre,' he recalled. Ingenious arming was taking place in the countryside. 'Although open violence ceased for the time being the extreme tension remained and both sides realised that the major storm was yet to come.' There was a lull in the Gurgaon massacres, during which time Chaning Pearce remembered the bustling activity that took place:

> The whole countryside therefore started at top speed to arm themselves for the supreme test. Practically every village started a gunpowder factory and village blacksmiths did a roaring trade converting any old piece of gas pipe into a so-called gun. Some surprisingly effective weapons started to appear. There were swords and spears by the thousand and even some home made sten guns and mortars. The latter, often made from the back-axle casing of a car, were usually mounted on strategic rooftops in villages to repel invaders.

There was only one jeep available in Chaning Pearce's district. For a while he and his men had the assistance of the Poona Horse, the Indian cavalry regiment, but soon, to their frustration, this was posted elsewhere. 'We could not spare more than twenty or so armed men in static pickets.'[34] In many places, policemen and soldiers were no match for the creative enterprise of amateur forces. Parties of volunteers could be seen marching along the major roads from the frontier and gathering along the Grand Trunk Road, reaching into Punjab, on their way to join the battle armed with swords, spears, *lathis* and muzzle-loading guns. One gang intercepted on their return from fighting in Gurgaon even had an elephant with an armoured *howdah*. The militias were also working hand in glove with the local leaders of princely states who acted as conduits for arms and transport.

During these fraught days, the state was trying to do two contradictory things at once: split the army in half, and prevent civil war. The chances of maintaining the peace looked increasingly slender.

Crisis in the capitals

'In Delhi I found everyone extremely tired.' Less than 50 miles away, a young American journalist Phillips Talbot recorded the frenetic activity in the capital in July 1947. 'A viceregal adviser who is the essence of politeness yawned in my face. Jinnah looked haggard and drawn. Nehru's always explosive temperament had according to people working with him got the best of him more frequently than usual. Some feared he was nearing a nervous breakdown. Everywhere weary worn men were struggling with problems that were too vast and too complex for them to comprehend fully in the available time.'[35] Partitioning the states in such a short time required immense physical and mental stamina. A photograph published in *Life* magazine in 1947 shows a frowning young official with his head in one hand, a pen in the other and a balance sheet spread open on the desk before him. All around him, piles of leather-bound books tower in great heaps. One pile of the books is labelled with a large white sign that says INDIA, while the tottering stack on the other side of the table is marked PAKISTAN. The official is dividing up a library between the two new nations. The division of library books was an especially contentious matter. Alternate volumes of the *Encyclopaedia Britannica* were meticulously allocated to each country.

New Delhi's offices had spun into overdrive. Partition had become a policy decision to be implemented and the loosely defined nationalistic aspirations of Indian and Pakistani people were now moulded into modern countries. Nationalist ambitions had to be squeezed into the prosaic boundaries of sovereign states. A literal interpretation of the words 'Partition' and 'Pakistan' now came to the fore, as the future shape of the subcontinent pivoted on delicate extrication of the resources needed to form a new Pakistani state from the old administrative husk of the Raj. Government staff separated all the physical and paper belongings of the former British Indian government. The task was left in the hands of civil servants and a Partition Council was established on 1 July, steered by two civil service officers, a Hindu, H.M. Patel and a Muslim (later a Prime Minister of Pakistan), Chaudhuri Mohammad Ali. This had the power to decide on the division of the spoils between India and Pakistan, and ten sub-committees dealt with splitting every arm of the government, from the most trivial to the most essential. Decisions that could not be made by the Partition Council were referred on to an arbitral tribunal. A general rule of thumb was agreed by which the division of physical, or movable, goods would be made along statistical lines, with 80 per cent of all goods going to India and 20 per cent to Pakistan. Every item of government property was counted and clerks drew up itemised lists. The goods to be counted and divided in the Indian Health Department included the following:

1. Durries 2. Table Lamps 3. Iron Safes 4. Cash Boxes 5. Cycles 6. Type-writers 7. Electric Heaters 8. Steel Trays 9. Stirrup Pumps 10. Time pieces 11. Clocks 12. Calculating machines 13. Locks 14. Magnifying glasses 15. Steel Racks 16. Steel Cupboard 17. Inkpots with stands 18. Curtains 19. Waste Paper Baskets 20. Paper Weights 21. Stationery 22. Officers' Tables 23. Other Tables 24. Chairs 25. Almirahs 26. Screens 27. Arm Chairs 28. Wooden Racks 29. Wooden Trays[36]

The pathos of such a doctrinaire division carried out against the backdrop of the carnage unfolding nearby is not difficult to imagine.

Political tension, despite the optimistic and self-congratulatory assessments in the Viceroy's camp, did not abate. 'There is no let-up in the negotiations with the parties,' Mountbatten wrote to the Governor of Bombay, 'and every day something fresh occurs which threatens to break down our slender basis of agreement.' The speed with which so many small but cumulatively impor-tant decisions had to be made placed a nervous strain on the administrative elite. 'An air of breathless haste seems to hang over the city,' observed an American diplomat on the other side of the country. 'Harassed government officials and politicians scamper around Calcutta as if pursued by the avenging angel.'[37]

In June 1947, every Muslim who worked for the government and resided in an Indian, rather than a Pakistani, area received a letter or was asked to make the choice of serving India or Pakistan. A propaganda war between the Indian and Pakistani governments started over the potential opportunities that would be on offer to young officers in the new states. Some hoped to gain promotion by plugging the gaps left by the departure of British officers. Frantic calculations about salaries, pensions, pay scales and promotions ensued. One cynic commented that 'All senior Muslim officers, with or without substance, are busy planning and manoeuvring for their own uplift in Government employment.'[38] Officers made tortuous decisions, based on a combination of political and personal reasons.

For Muslims in the more junior services, though, there was concern that promotion would become difficult because of suspicions about political loyalty if they stayed in India. It is an exaggeration to imagine that the members of the services who departed for Pakistan, as is sometimes suggested, were purely the elite. The majority of government employees who were given the chance of opting for Pakistan came from more humble jobs, on the rail-ways or in the postal service. The decision whether or not to leave for Pakistan was most difficult for these low-ranking, low-earning workers: 'An average man is in a great fix,' confided a Muslim lawyer from the Central Provinces to Jinnah, 'and every day railway and postal men are coming to me to consult.' Visitors came to the lawyer's door asking for advice on the question of migration. 'I feel I am unable to give them proper directions without first consulting you.'[39] The decision was momentous – more momentous than many of them realised. When some of them wavered, changed their minds or tried to return to their old jobs they would find it difficult or impossible to resume their old lives.

Manzoor Alam Quraishi, a Muslim staunchly in favour of a united India, had just celebrated his thirtieth birthday and had taken up the position of District Magistrate in Pauri in the idyllic foothills of the Himalayas. He had no intention of opting for Pakistan, although his brother, Badre Alam, was a keen League supporter, and was making his way to the new state. 'Even I got some threatening letters that I should migrate to Pakistan, otherwise I and my family would be wiped out by my own Hindu police guard,' he later wrote. Quraishi stood his ground, although he took the precaution of carrying a loaded pistol while touring the district, and he had a long and distinguished career in India.[40] For many others, though, even if they had never been keen on the League, Pakistan could seem like a safe haven.

As thousands of officials, railwaymen and clerks did make the choice to leave for Pakistan the logistics of the division became preposterous: 25,000 government employees relocated from one side to the other with 60,000 tonnes of baggage. From late July special trains set off across Punjab and Bengal carrying government workers to their new locations. Crates of belongings trailed behind civil servants who did not have clean clothes to wear to work when they finally arrived. Entire government departments operated from tents and barracks in the new Pakistani capital and those officials who had come from India remained intensely worried about the families they had left behind, many of whom could not accompany them immediately. 'We were not allowed to take files, typewriters, or anything,' recalled one administrative official, 'we used to work in tents, and I remember using thorns instead of paper clips. Only one goods train of our office equipment ever reached Pakistan.'[41] A national myth was being forged and the solidarity and camaraderie of the situation dissolved class differences and pulled new compatriots together, if only momentarily. As the nationalist newspaper *Dawn* patriotically reported, 'Cabinet ministers of Pakistan use packing cases as desks and crack jokes with painters who drip whitewash on them.'[42]

The reality was more gritty. The problems facing the Pakistani machinery and the confusions of the time were such that the new 'Pakistanis' – the word itself was still strange – requested that the first sittings of the Pakistani Constituent Assembly be held in Delhi. This request, which would have meant the two new constituent assemblies working in the same city at exactly the same time, was, not surprisingly, met with rapid refusal by the Indian ministers. So a new capital had to be built almost from scratch and quickly made ready for the tide of people coming from India.

The beleaguered new capital city of Karachi, a port city of around 600,000 people, was suddenly home to a new army of administrators and officials who were mostly Urdu speaking, from Delhi and the United Provinces, and quite at sea among the local Sindis, with their distinctive culture and language. The city became a building site. Big hoardings declared 'Central Pakistani administrative buildings: under construction'. Immediately, these newcomers or *Muhajirs* as they liked to be called, started to make Pakistan in their own image. They hoped to be welcomed with open arms and wanted to play a leading role in shaping the future direction of Pakistan. 'I continued to be idealistic and felt that a migration of such magnitude ought to have a meaning,' recalled the novelist Intizar Husain, looking back at those times.[43] It seemed only natural to the *Muhajirs* that Urdu, which was the old administrative language of British India and which had been the first language of many of the leading members of the Muslim League, should be the new state language. In deciding this, the *Muhajirs* began to trample on the rights and culture of the local Muslims in Sind – who might, of course, have had very different dreams of Pakistan and for whom Urdu was alien. This was storing up trouble for the future.

While this gradual division was being carried out in the summer months, clerks and officials had to continue working side by side, as they disentangled files and paperwork. In numerous offices, relations between officials deteriorated rather than improved. The sudden division of material goods – and human beings – brought out the worst pettiness and pedantry within the bureaucracy, as people reconstituted themselves as new national citizens, in opposition to one another. Clerks and junior officers played their part by accusing each other of hiding goods to prevent their reallocation and of substituting poorer quality furniture and stationery for better goods. This was the starting point for new imaginings of India and Pakistan and the perception of 'the other' within their most senior national institutions.

Even those who had attempted to stay aloof from the nationalist struggles were now pulled into the oppositional foundation of the two nation states.

Political interference added to the difficulties. Liaquat Ali Khan told Mountbatten that the situation had become so tense between Pakistani and Indian officials that he did not know how much longer they could continue working together.[44] The situation was even more fractious in the provincial Partition committees, which had the task of splitting the nuts and bolts of the Punjabi and Bengali Legislative Assemblies, and the Governor of Punjab complained of receiving 'poor political essays' from the civil servants responsible for the job, rather than 'objective reports'. Magistrates in Punjab, he added, were now 'completely unreliable'.[45] In the extraordinary conditions of the time many urban office-workers had their everyday life – and their own ideas – profoundly affected by the partitioning process.

Revealing the borderline

Still, few, if any, were contemplating a mass migration of any description. Some leaders mooted the idea of moving people long before 1947. 'Quite a number of people, especially educated people, might be expected to migrate,' a leading Muslim Leaguer, Choudhry Khaliquzzaman had breezily told the Cabinet Mission delegation in 1946.[46] And others had advised that co-religionists cluster together in 'pockets' for safety in the towns and cities afflicted by rioting. Some Sikh leaders had talked up the exchange of population as a solution to their own community's anxiety. Tara Singh told his Sikh followers in a press statement that they faced 'extinction' and that they should start shifting eastwards in Punjab.[47] This could all be written off too easily as bravado and posturing.

   The thought that the intermingled populations of towns such as Amritsar, Lahore, Calcutta or Dacca would be systematically weeded out and completely shorn of minorities was simply too far-fetched and preposterous for most people to contemplate. One Sayyid 'Abd al Latif of Uthmaniyah University had put forward a strategy involving the mass exchanges of population of tens of millions of people in the late 1940s as a possible solution to the constitutional gridlock. 'This was so utterly impracticable that even its author subsequently rescinded the suggestion and favoured a federal constitution,' commented Wilfred Cantwell Smith in 1946, similarly agreeing that any exchange of population was simply too unfeasible and too undesirable to bear thinking about. 'Some people hoped Pakistan would be formed but no one thought that they would have to migrate,' was how Intizar Husain remembered those days.[48] This myopia about the risk of mass upheavals was still very much present as the Partition plan was being put into operation in June and July.

Yet, by the summer of 1947, before Independence, the first trickle of refugees had already started. Soon it would turn into a torrent. 'There is some movement of bank balances to "Hindustan" and a certain fall in the value of real property in Hindu areas. There is also vague talk of emigration to Hindustan,' said a government report from Sind. Phillips Talbot, an American journalist, took things more seriously: 'trains and planes are loaded, according to local stories with gold bullion, jewelry and local currency. Bank accounts are being transferred in large numbers. Houses which sold six months ago for 60,000 $ are being offered for 20,000 $ if their owners are Hindu and anxious to get out of Pakistan.' He concluded that 'the amount can safely be estimated at tens of millions of dollars'.[49] In the early days of Partition, the well-informed put arrangements in place to transfer precious objects and savings. People often regarded this as a precaution rather than as permanent evacuation.

G.D. Khosla, a judge of the Lahore High Court, and later author of several well-known books about Partition, described how he received a letter from his wife who was staying with their children in the cooler hill station of Musoorie, in the summer of 1947; in it she insisted 'that I must withdraw all her jewellery from the bank locker in Lahore, take it to Delhi and deposit it there in a locker without fail'. He complied with his wife's demand and safely removed the jewellery to Delhi.[50] Others were not so fortunate as they hid or buried gold in their own locality with the intention of returning to recover it at some later stage, such as the 'rich Muslim woman from Amritsar' witnessed by Margaret Bourke-White, later in the year, who 'had thrown her jewels in the bottom of the well, when her home fell on the Indian side of the line. She had run across the border to Pakistan, and when I saw her there she was trying hysterically to hire a driver to go back and retrieve the jewels from the well.'[51]

These were danger signs which the politicians failed to pick up on. If families did move, it was still regarded as something transitory and reversible. Those who packed up a few bags and left their homes to find a place of greater safety with relatives or friends did so with the full expectation of returning when things returned to normal. Most politicians impressed on people the need to stay put. The super-rich could make their own insurance policies, by keeping a foot in both camps. The Nawab of Bhopal bought two houses in Karachi in July, planning an escape route if things became really awkward for his family in India. 'I may have to be in Karachi quite often and I must have a place in Pakistan where my womenfolk may take shelter should things begin to get really hot here.'[52] But underneath the surface of these grand gestures was a quieter, more dangerous, story of fearful people, weighing up their position and leaving their homes. The violence of the first six months of the year in Punjab had already seriously shaken communities. Over 100,000 people had already started to move internally within the Punjab, to be with relatives, to find safety in numbers, hopelessly trying to predict the borderline between India and Pakistan.

'The decision about the creation of Pakistan had just been announced and people were indulging in all kinds of surmises about the pattern of life that would emerge. But no one's imagination could go very far . . .' The novelist Bhisham Sahni captured the essence of public uncertainty as India stood on the brink of the unknown. 'The Sardarji [Sikh fellow] sitting in front of me repeatedly asked me whether I thought Mr Jinnah would continue to live in Bombay after the creation of Pakistan or whether he would resettle in Pakistan. Each time my answer would be the same, "Why should he leave Bombay? I think he'll continue to live in Bombay and continue visiting Pakistan."' Indeed, Jinnah continued to own a large white mansion house in Bombay and Liaquat Ali Khan had extensive farmlands in North India; such guesses were not so far-fetched. 'Similar guesses were being made about the towns of Lahore and Gurdaspur too, and no one knew which town would fall to the share of India and which to Pakistan.'[53]

It made good business sense at first to try and sit astride both new states. Initially, some businessmen with outlets and branches across South Asia reacted pragmatically to the situation. Lilaram and Sons, a silk merchant's and tailor's, placed an advertisement in the 15 August special Independence Day supplement of several national papers, illustrated with the black silhouette of the whole of undivided India. 'To all our patrons we offer our very best wishes on this auspicious occasion,' it boldly proclaimed. Similarly, the Punjab National Bank tried to continue straddling the border, wishing 'Greetings to all our countrymen of both Hindustan and Pakistan on this auspicious day.' Behind the scenes, though, industrialists and businessmen were trying to calculate where their businesses would be most secure and were withdrawing from Pakistani or Indian interests as conditions deteriorated. Mr B.T. Thakur, Managing Director of the United Commercial Bank told American diplomats that he wanted to keep some of his branches in Pakistan open but would close down those 'in areas where he fears police protection may be inadequate'.[54]

Meanwhile the two boundary commissions sweated over the highly secretive plans for the new national boundaries. These were ready on 12 August but were deliberately held back for five days, despite the requests of administrators coping with panicked border regions who implored the government for advance warning of where the boundary lines would fall ('even a few hours would be better than none,' pleaded Evan Jenkins to Mountbatten).[55] Nobody in India knew where the borders would lie on Independence Day itself; rumours, hints and suggestions flew around. Staff at the Viceroy's house leaked information. Newspapers published provisional maps with erroneous indications of where the boundary was likely to be drawn. Administrators complained about the manner in which the boundary was being sketched, and in Assam the Governor told the Viceroy '. . . the lack of an authoritative interpretation here is going to give us a lot of trouble'.[56] His feelings might have been echoed by every other governor in the country. Preserving good Indo-British relations, especially during the lavish ceremonial display of 15 August, was the unjustifiable excuse for holding back the award. The Radcliffe line was finally revealed to the public on 17 August – exactly the same day that the first regiment of British troops departed from Bombay.

Communicating the reality of the line and making it meaningful to the people affected was another matter altogether. The artist Satish Gujral, whose swirling, evocative paintings of mourning faces later depicted the horrors of 1947, remembered how he learned that his home city of Lahore would be in Pakistan: 'Curiously, the news of such magnitude was conveyed to us not by newspapers (which had ceased publication) but by posters pasted on the walls of our camp. These posters proclaimed: "Do not burn now. It is Pakistan's property."'[57] Others heard through the grapevine of rumour and news or through hurriedly distributed maps. Yet what did such maps and news about territory mean to those who had never known any place but their own home? Others found out because of the celebrations of football-like jubilant crowds on the 'winning' side, while others heard mixed and erroneous news. Nobody bothered to think about how to communicate the strange reality of this new world to peasants and villagers. 'One day I ran into a Muslim villager who had come to Lahore all the way from Sargodha looking for my grandfather, a well-known criminal lawyer,' Kuldip Nayar recalled. 'Poor chap he didn't realise that Partition had taken place and that the Hindus had left. It just shows how long it took for the implications of Partition to sink in.'[58] For many outside the grip of middle-class, nationalist mentalities, the line was irrelevant to their daily hardships. In the novel *Tamas*, one coolie describes to another how he had been carrying a heavy load on his head for a customer, when the man said to him, '"*Azadi* is coming. India will soon be free." I laughed and said, "Babuji what is that to me? I am carrying loads now and shall continue carrying them then."'[59]

For those who were caught up in the nationalist campaigns, though, the line meant everything. Radcliffe was aware of the contentiousness and unsatisfactory nature of the award and admitted as much in the final text itself, saying, 'I am conscious too that the award cannot go far towards satisfying sentiment and aspirations deeply held on either side.'[60] He waived the right to the generous salary he had initially accepted for the work. The final line, when it was revealed, came as a shock. 'With the announcement of boundary commission award our last hope of remaining in Amritsar disappeared,' a former tax inspector, Choudhary Mohammad Said, recorded. 'The morale of the Muslims was completely shattered causing great panic.'[61] This was something of an understatement as the result was uproar.

The line zigzagged precariously across agricultural land, cut off communities from their sacred pilgrimage sites, paid no heed to railway lines or the integrity of forests, divorced industrial plants from the agricultural hinterlands where raw materials, such as jute, were grown. Penderel Moon was urgently called to the scene of an irrigation plant on the Punjabi borderline shortly after Independence. He found a standoff and administrative chaos. There had already been a clash at the site between Indian troops and Pakistani police. It turned out that the line ran directly across the plant's headworks and protective embankments. 'It seemed extraordinary that there had been no-one to impress upon Lord Radcliffe the importance of including the principal protective works in the same territory as the headworks,' he later mused. 'This could very easily have been done, as the area involved was uninhabited and, for the most part, uncultivated. I fondly imagined that this absurd error would quickly be rectified. But it never was.'[62] There were many other jumbled parts of the line. The award bestowed a variety of eccentric features on the subcontinent's political geography. East and West Pakistan were separated by over a thousand miles, and travelling by sea between the country's two major ports of Karachi and Chittagong took approximately five days. The shaping of new borderlines left a complex and inflammatory legacy in the north-east, now only joined precariously to India by a 21-kilometre sliver of land. It was a very long, intricate border through Himalayas, dense jungle and river valleys. In sum, Radcliffe's line created a geographical settlement which would have been difficult to manage at the best of times, even if all parties were in agreement.

The inevitable result, particularly in the most contested districts in Punjab–Lahore, Amritsar, Gurdaspur, Hoshiarpur and Jullundur – and in parts of Bengal, was dire confusion about which places were in Pakistan and which places were not. In Malda district, the Pakistani flag brazenly flew from the administrative headquarters until 14 August, but then the area fell to India, inevitably leaving the local population in turmoil.[63] One woman, Maya, who had been a child in a Punjabi village that straddled the contested area, remembered stories flying about whether the place would ultimately go to India or

Pakistan. 'Each time one of these rumours became rife,' Urvashi Butalia, who recorded her story explains, 'people of the other community would abandon their homes and run, leaving everything behind. Maya and her friends watched this helter-skelter flight almost as if it was a game.'[64] Radcliffe's judgement – which was meant to be fixed and incontestable – instead appeared soft and malleable and had little real or imagined authority behind it. People could not see the line, nor did it seem that there were enough troops available to demarcate it even if it did exist. Even the national leaders, solemnly bound to the terms of the border, discussed some horse-trading about districts when the new maps were first revealed at a 'sombre and sullen gathering'.[65] Jinnah reflected the disappointment of the Pakistani people in an evening radio broadcast to the population when he described it as 'an unjust, incomprehensible and even perverse award,' although urging people to abide by it.[66] The repudiation of the line or ambivalence about it from the highest tiers of government exacerbated the potential for violence.

Bitterly disappointed groups who found themselves on the 'wrong' side of the boundary would now fight to purify and cleanse their home areas, to reverse the line or to rob it of meaning. The unforgiving calculus of Partition, which depended on head counts and the percentages of people living in districts, now came into full effect. From 15 August the violence would be utilised to achieve new ends: to drive out the other and stake a claim to land, while killers attempted to mark out the limits of the two new countries' 'rightful' borders with different sorts of macabre signposts: dead bodies floated up irrigation canals, or were left in visible spots, on display. 'The dead,' as Shail Mayaram has graphically expressed it in a powerful study of Partition violence, 'thereby became signals to the living of the construction of ethnic boundaries.'[67] The violence was designed to eliminate and drive out the opposing ethnic group while forging a new moral community. For all the superhuman effort which had been invested in untangling the two nations – their land, possessions and military stores – few had turned their minds to the new nations' most precious asset: their people. Emphatic clarification about *who* was a bona fide citizen of India or Pakistan was urgently needed. Yet, it was still unthinkable that elaborately embroidered communities would be permanently unpicked.

7

Blood on the Tracks

By August 1947 all the ingredients were in place for ethnic cleansing in Punjab: a feeble and polarised police force, the steady withdrawal of British troops and their substitution with the limited and undermanned Punjab Boundary Force, and a petrified, well-armed population. The violence which preceded Partition was grave, widespread and lethal. After 15 August 1947, it took on a new ferocity, intensity and callousness. Now militias trawled the countryside for poorly protected villages to raid and raze to the ground, gangs deliberately derailed trains, massacring their passengers one by one or setting the carriages ablaze with petrol. Women and children were carried away like looted chattels.

The British evacuation was in full swing by this stage. Far away in Bombay, British soldiers were parading through the monumental Gateway of India and boarding their troopships, kitbags slung over their shoulders, guns still in hand as crowds cheered from the shore. They were waved on by nationalist leaders and the imperial withdrawal meshed conveniently with the nationalistic stance of the Congress and League leaderships. 'Foreign armies are the most obvious symbol of foreign rule,' Nehru allegedly told the first contingent of British troops before they sailed away from the Indian coastline just two days after Independence Day in 1947. 'They are essentially armies of occupation and, as such, their presence must inevitably be resented.'[1] His viewpoint neatly overlapped with the interests of the British establishment which was eager to bring its war-weary and homesick soldiers back to Britain.

The terrorised public in the polarised atmosphere of Punjab might not have agreed. Instead of using these troops to quell the trouble, the British command confined them to barracks and evacuated the men as quickly as they possibly could. Mountbatten's instructions confidentially stated that British army units had no operational functions whatsoever, could not be used for internal security purposes and would not be used on the frontier or in the states. There was only one exception: they could be used in an emergency to save British lives.[2] The Punjabi Boundary Force – a toothless and dreadfully inadequate response to Partition's violence – was the alternative British initiative to protect life and limb in Punjab.[3] It was in existence for just thirty-two days. At its peak, the Punjab Boundary Force, in which Delhi's administrators had 'remarkable faith', covered only the twelve most 'disturbed' districts of Punjab and included, at most, 25,000 men. This meant that there were fewer than two men to a square mile. Sharing a train compartment from Delhi to Bahawalpur at the end of July with a young Sikh army major who was about to join the Boundary Force, Penderel Moon recalled that, 'He was himself about to join it, but was utterly sceptical of its capacity to maintain order.'[4] As a cartoon at the time expressed it, showing a goat sliced in two by a knife, 'You asked for it.' The message from London seemed to be that this was the price of freedom.

Violence must sit at the core of any history of Partition. It is the phenomenal extent of the killing during Partition which distinguishes it as an event. It affected women, children and the elderly as well as well-armed young men.[5] Grisly scenes of violence in Punjab have been better described in fiction, poetry and film. Children watched as their parents were dismembered or burned alive, women were brutally raped and had their breasts and genitals mutilated and the entire populations of villages were summarily executed. Eyewitnesses in Punjab reported the putrid stench of corpses and the crimson bloodstains on walls, station concourses and roads. After an atrocity in Hasilpur in Bahawalpur state, in August, when approximately 350 people were gunned down by rifle fire by a gang of Pathans, Penderel Moon groped for an analogy. 'Men, women and children, there they were all jumbled up together, their arms and legs akimbo in all sorts of attitudes and postures, some of them so life-like that one could hardly believe that they were really dead. I was forcibly reminded of pictures that I had seen as a child of Napoleonic battlefields . . .'[6]

Broken bodies lay along roadsides and on train platforms, while charred wood and rubble were all that remained of large quarters of Amritsar and Lahore. The two cities were *de facto* war zones: barbed wire had to be coiled along the length of station platforms in Lahore to keep people apart, looted objects lay abandoned in deserted streets, vultures perched on walls, broken and grotesquely splayed carriages and rickshaws lay at jarred angles, large suburban areas of bustling jewellers, bakeries and bookshops were now reduced to voluminous debris which took many years to be bulldozed away.

Human figures in photographs of the time look pitifully small against the mountains of rubble left behind.

All this has been written about in lurid technicolour and from jarring perspectives. Partition stories of Punjab in 1947 are marked by specific details and are layered in unique and entirely individual family memories. Yet these descriptions are also shot through with generic imagery and the haunting motifs that have entered the popular imagination of South Asia: the corpse-laden refugee train passing silently through the province, the penniless rows of refugees streaming across new international borders, which submerge individual tragedies in wider community histories. Generalisations do not do justice to the multiple atrocities. Poets and novelists offer more carefully calibrated, fragmentary insights into personal agonies and ruinous dilemmas of the time. The best have turned the emptiness of this moment into poetry, and grown new creative life into the hollow abyss of Partition's worst moments. The sound of silence in Punjab remains resounding, however. Partition is both ever-present in South Asia's public, political realm and continually evaded.

How to record these acts and disentangle rationality from madness, political intent from momentary insanity? In the sheer diversity and density of the violence, killers acted out of fear or in self-defence, were swept away on a buoyant tide of killing-induced euphoria, felt the intolerable pressure of their peers or found themselves conditioned by the conformity and regulations of institutions such as the police or by the inducements of their friends and colleagues in armed militias. One devout Khaksar, Mujahid Tajdin, who later stormed the gurdwara on Temple Road, Lahore, remembered being trained for the task for four days by a local police sub-inspector. The men in his gang were promised martyrdom or heroism, depending on whether they lived or died, and he remembered how they were told tawdry stories about the massacres of Muslims elsewhere in the country. They set up defence posts and stormed the walls of the gurdwara in the middle of the night, with cries of 'Pakistan Zindabad.' Someone took a petrol canister along. At least twenty to thirty Sikh men and women burned to death in the inferno that followed. Today the former Khaksar bakes *naan* bread on a street in Lahore and prays for forgiveness for his part in the murders.[7] Sometimes such actions are inexplicable, even by the perpetrators.

At the time, testosterone-fuelled ideals of martyrdom, bravery, honour and heroism sanctioned the killings. The spoils of looting attracted others who mopped up after the murderers, acquiring land, jewels and houses from the detritus of massacres. Even those untouched by ideological concerns were able to seek opportunities in the aftermath. Maya Rani, a young sweeper at the time, was not involved in the fighting but accrued valuable dowry goods in the wave of looting which followed, almost as if it was a game. 'From one shop we stole pure ghee and almonds; at other places we found cloth, we collected so many utensils that we filled up a room as large as this one.'[8] Harcharan Singh Nirman who was a child of just six at the time recalled people looting and carrying things from houses, in heaving gunny bags and on their heads. 'I also brought out a small chair . . . I could lift only this thing because it was very light . . . the impression in my mind was people are taking things, I should also take something.'[9] Explaining actions long after the event is sometimes impossible. Many memories become shrouded with the overcoat of regret and cold reason.

Others killed members of their own family and community, or committed suicide, preferring an 'honourable' death to the shame of rape or conversion of their loved ones, while it is impossible to know how many people eliminated romantic rivals or murdered long-standing adversaries with impunity while disguising their actions behind the façade of Partition's carnage.

This was war by any other name, and the principal aggressors were para-militaries composed of former soldiers and well-trained young men working hand in glove with the armed forces of the princely states. Young men stood on the front lines. Political interpretations of freedom, self-rule and power gave these men credibility and a sense of legitimacy. As Ram Dev, a young man working at a university in Lahore in the spring of 1947, who was arrested and detained for rioting, later recalled in an evasive, implicit acknowledgement of his own personal role, 'there was no tradition of fighting or killing in my family, but I wanted to keep Punjab together at all costs'. He claimed he acted to give a 'warning signal' to the 'other' side but also remembered 'a lot of milkmen and wooden sheds, and a lot of haystacks, there were thousands of tons of wood; someone threw kerosene, someone threw a bomb, it was set on fire and for twenty miles you could see the smoke; there were thousands of thousands of buffalo there, the entire milk supply of Lahore came from there; it was a milkmen's colony – all Muslims.'[10]

This was not haphazard, frantic killing but, at its worst, routine, timetabled and systematic ethnic cleansing. Large groups of men, with their own codes of honour, and often with a sense of warlike righteousness, set out day after day in August and September to eliminate the other. It is no coincidence that it is a war veteran who organises the defensive preparations of the village depicted in the novel *Tamas*: 'he had taken part in the Second World War on the Burmese front and he was now hell-bent on trying the tactics of the Burmese front on the Muslims of his village'.[11] In Punjab these gangs used military tactics, mortars, bombs, traps and automatic rifles. They covered large distances in formation and cut off supply routes and exit points for the fleeing refugees.

The result was terror. Krishna Baldev Vaid, a youth at the time, later a distinguished writer, lived through a prolonged, and life-threatening ordeal, and had to wait over a day and night for rescue with his family after they escaped from Dinga, a small town near Amritsar which fell under siege:

> we were numb . . . we were six of our family . . . and three more people . . . it's an awful feeling . . . we could hear the gunshots, we could guess from the shouting that people were being killed, that several houses were on fire . . . and we were numb with terror . . . my father was quiet, but my mother was constantly mumbling something, prayers . . . everyone was tense and short-tempered . . . this man he wanted to smoke . . . and he was very curious as to what was happening . . . and peeped out . . . partly out of idiocy, and everyone would snap at him.

After Krishna Baldev Vaid was rescued, one of his most graphic memories was of arriving at a makeshift camp in an office compound in the early light of dawn and the horrible sight of the survivors, bandaged in every way imaginable, and the traumatic process of counting the victims. It was here that he discovered who was alive, dead, raped or injured.[12]

The poet Louis MacNeice witnessed similar scenes. He was part of a British BBC features and news team sent to the subcontinent to record the imperial transition. The team drove out from Delhi on 26 August in a BBC van, heading for Peshawar. *En route* they passed overspilling *kafilas* making their treacherous journey across the Punjab. Somehow, the BBC team found their way to Sheikhupura, a satellite town of Lahore, which had been badly devastated by violence during the preceding weeks. The hospital held eighty seriously injured Sikhs and Hindus, covered with flies and attended by one doctor, with little or no equipment. A further 1,500 were packed into a nearby schoolhouse. The scene carved itself deeply into the minds of the helpless onlookers. 'A v. large number of these had been wounded with swords or spears & their white clothes were covered with rusty-brown blood. Some with their hands cut off etc. & again the hordes of flies. But hardly any moaning – just abstracted, even smiling in a horrible unreal way.'[13]

Breaking bodies

Of all the horrors of 1947, the experience of the women who were raped is the most difficult to write about. It is a history of broken bodies and broken lives. Rape was used as a weapon, as a sport and as a punishment. Armed gangs had started to use rape as a tool of violence in Bengal and Bihar in 1946 but this now took on a new ubiquity and savagery in Punjab. It sparked the deepest feelings of revenge, dishonour and shame. Many women were silent about what had happened to them: 'in most households the woman said no, no, I was hiding in the jungle or I was hiding in the pond, or I was hiding in a neighbour's house,' recalled Ashoka Gupta, a volunteer who worked with distraught women in the aftermath of attacks in Noakhali; 'they will not declare, or they will not confess, that they have been raped or molested . . . because it will be a confession of shame, and once confessed there will be quite a possibility that they will not be taken back in their own homes.'[14]

Rape was the unspoken fear at the back of many minds by the summer of 1947. News had been circulating of the atrocities committed against women – indeed, these were the most powerful and graphic rumours reaching the villages. Women feared for themselves and their own bodies. Their brothers, fathers and husbands feared for the shame and honour of their family and the wider community. The women themselves now became mere shell-like repositories of the new national identities when attacks on them – or threat of attacks – were used to prise families from their homes, to punish, mark out and terrify. The voluntary and enforced suicides of women and the murder of relatives by shooting, poisoning or drowning was not uncommon as it was, in some cases, regarded as preferable to the life worse than death which, it was believed, was certain to follow after rape. Other families faced with the choice of life or death traded their young daughters in return for the safe transit of the rest of the family. A Sikh woman, Taran, told her story to the writers Ritu Menon and Kamla Bhasin:

> One night suddenly we heard drums and our house was encircled. A mob gathered outside. I was 16, brimming with vitality. My two sisters were 17 and 14, and my mother was sick with worry. She trembled with fear. She took out all her gold, tied it up in handkerchiefs and distributed it among different family members for safekeeping. She made us wear several sets of clothes each, one on top of the other, shoes, socks everything and she asked

us to hide the gold. We did not know where each of us would end up – this gold was our security. She kept crying and kept giving us instructions.[15]

Taran escaped. But many others in Punjab were snatched from their homes and villages by marauding gangs or literally carried away from the slow and under-protected *kafilas* that made their way on foot towards the border: 'when we were travelling in a caravan we had some people who had guns, four or five guns among us . . . but women or children would trail behind, after all, travelling 150 miles some people would get tired, they never rejoined us so we believe somebody kidnapped them and took them away'. As another young woman at the time, Durga Rani, recalled, 'The Muslims used to announce that they would take away our daughters. They would force their way into homes and pick up young girls and women. Ten or twenty of them would enter, tie up the men folk and take the women. We saw many who had been raped and disfigured, their faces and breasts scarred, and then abandoned. They had tooth-marks all over them. Their families said, "How can we keep them now? Better that they are dead." Many of them were so young – 18, 15, 14 years old – what remained of them now? Their "character" was now spoilt.'[16] As vessels of the honour of the whole community, the shame and horror fell on everybody associated with the girls: these were not individual tragedies.

Women's bodies were marked and branded with the slogans of freedom, '*Pakistan Zindabad*' and '*Jai Hind*', inscribed on their faces and breasts. Those who survived were often humiliated and grossly scarred. They had become symbols of terror. Even worse, many of these victims were not really 'women' at all. Girls under the age of twelve made up at least one third of the women recovered in the state-sponsored recovery operation that followed. The rest of the women tended to be under the age of thirty-five and from villages. They were not then, most tellingly, members of the political classes who had fought for, or who had rejected, Partition. Instead they were victims of political debates that had, up until now, barely impinged on their lives. At the worst extreme women were traded on a flesh market, 'in the same way that baskets of oranges or grapes are sold or gifted', in the words of Kamlaben Patel, an Indian social worker who was stationed in Lahore as part of the recovery operation for five years after 1947 and saw the bleak and complex aftermath of these attacks and abductions.[17] Policemen and soldiers, as well as men of their own community, sometimes colluded.

After their ordeals, the women suffered the fears of unwanted pregnancies, tried to induce miscarriages or sought out illegal abortions. But above all, many women feared that their families or husbands would not be able to

1 Communist delegates marching during the Punjab Provincial Delegates Conference, 1945. The Second World War radicalised Indian politics on both the left and the right; 1945 saw an unprecedented number of strikes, marches and political conferences.

2 Royal Indian Navy mutineers in the streets of Bombay, February 1946. The mutiny of thousands of naval ratings started in Bombay as a protest against low pay and bad food. It sparked riots and sympathetic demonstrations by soldiers, factory workers and police-men from Karachi to Calcutta, placing unprecedented pressure on the British Raj.

3 Mohammed Ali Jinnah, Muslim League leader and first Governor-General of Pakistan, holding a press conference in Bombay, January 1946. By this time personal idolisation of Jinnah had reached new heights among League supporters. On the right-hand side sits Liaquat Ali Khan, who became the first Prime Minister of Pakistan.

4 People in Bombay lining up to vote in the general elections held during the winter months of 1945–6, which electrified India and proved critical in later negotiations. As well as creating popular provincial governments, the elections acted as a de facto referendum on the idea of Pakistan.

5 A co-educational zoology class at Aligarh Muslim University in May 1946. Established in the late nineteenth century and located a few hours from Delhi, the university was at the centre of the battle of ideas surrounding Pakistan's creation.

6 Lord Pethick-Lawrence, Secretary of State for India and member of the British Cabinet Mission delegation, looking over papers. The Cabinet Mission plan would have resulted in a federal Indian state but it collapsed in the summer of 1946.

7 A peace procession after the riots in Calcutta, 1946. The deaths and destruction in Calcutta in August 1946, in which both Hindus and Muslims suffered, proved a political and psychological turning point. Unfortunately the Calcutta killings also fuelled propaganda that was exploited in subsequent riots in Noakhali, Bihar and Punjab.

8 Villagers in boats fleeing under cover of darkness from their burning villages during riots in Noakhali, an eastern district of undivided Bengal, 1946–7. Around the river basins in the east of the country, Partition refugees moved in precarious boats or by foot.

9 Crowds look on during Gandhi's visit to Noakhali in present-day Bangladesh. Extreme ethnic violence started in the district in October 1946. Gandhi based himself in the region from November 1946 to March 1947 and preached social harmony, removing himself from the political negotiations continuing in Delhi.

10 Muslims and Hindus attempt to promote peace by jointly flying the flags of the Muslim League and the Indian National Congress, Calcutta, 1946. Peace activists, often associated with communists and other left-wing groups, worked hard to stem the riots: running ambulances; protecting and evacuating stranded minorities; denying rumours; and standing up to militants.

11 Nehru and Gandhi with refugees from West Pakistan at Haridwar in India, late June 1947. Thousands of people started to move out of Punjab even before Partition was confirmed. After the plan was announced on 3 June the numbers increased as people were displaced by riots or left fearing violence or discrimination.

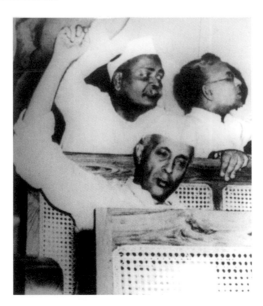

12 Nehru votes for Partition at a stormy Congress Working Committee meeting held on 14 June 1947. At this meeting Congress ratified the plan to divide the subcontinent which had been made public eleven days earlier. Directly behind Nehru is the Congressman Govind Ballabh Pant from the United Provinces.

13 The meeting with Mountbatten in his study at which the plan for Partition was agreed on the morning of 2 June 1947. Eight leaders are seated around the table: Nehru, Vallabhbhai Patel, Acharya Kripalani, Jinnah, Liaquat Ali Khan, Sardar Nishtar and Baldev Singh. This meeting was carefully stage-managed by Mountbatten, who later recorded that 'The atmosphere was at first most tense. I got the feeling that the less the leaders talked the less the chance of friction and perhaps the ultimate breakdown of the meeting.'

14 'A Happy Ending Indeed!': cartoon from *Hitavada*, 15 August 1947. Gandhi, Nehru and Jinnah head the funeral procession for British Imperialism in India.

15 British troops board their ships for departure at the Gateway of India, Bombay, 1947. The British military withdrawal began in August 1947 and continued until mid-1948; at the very time that the violence in Punjab was at its most intense, British troops were kept in their barracks and then evacuated from the subcontinent.

16 'Refugee Specials': trains stacked with families and their belongings make the perilous journey through Punjab. Over eight million people had moved across the region by November 1947. Hundreds of thousands went by train but others went on foot, in trucks and motor vehicles and even by aeroplane. For many, their destination was unknown and this became the first in a long chain of displacements and forced journeys.

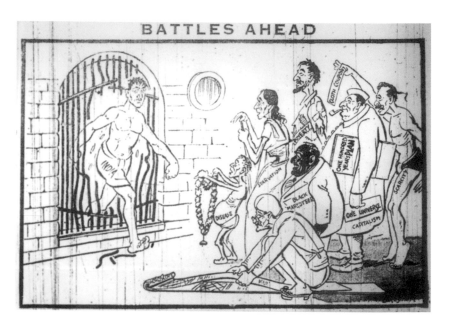

17 'Battles Ahead': cartoon from the *National Herald*, 15 August 1947. Shortages of cloth and essential household goods, deaths from starvation and a strong black market were just some of the problems facing newly independent Indians and Pakistanis.

18 Refugees at a shelter near the border between West Bengal and the newly created East Pakistan, 1947. Refugees slept wherever they could: on railway tracks; in schools and municipal buildings; in temples; in mosques; in gurdwaras; in tents; and in requisitioned property.

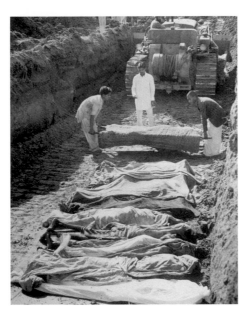

19 Men near the Indo-Pakistani border in Punjab placing bodies in a mass grave using a bulldozer, October 1947. The numbers killed in the violence of 1946–7 have never been fully known: figures suggested range from 250,000 to one million people.

20 Nehru addressing the crowds from the historic Red Fort in Old Delhi the day after Independence Day, 16 August 1947. Indian prime ministers continue to hoist the national flag from the same place every Independence Day. On the horizon is the Jama Masjid, Delhi's largest mosque.

21 Lady Mountbatten touring riot devastation at Multan, Punjab. Although many local relief agencies played a role in the recovery operation, much was left in the hands of the two new governments. In some places in Punjab it took eight years to clear the rubble.

22 News of Gandhi's assassination reaches Calcutta, 1948. Gandhi was shot in the chest by an extremist Hindu nationalist in Delhi on 30 January 1948. The news of his death helped to stabilise a highly divided society at a critical moment and undoubtedly gave ascendancy to Nehru and his ideal of a plural Indian state.

23 Nehru at a refugee township in Ludhiana, Punjab, 1949. Many refugee camps eventually became permanent settlements and townships. Refugees, especially the poorest ones, were often dependent on the largesse of the Indian and Pakistani states, both of which created their own Relief and Rehabilitation ministries to attempt to cope with the crisis.

24 Jinnah's sister Fatima Jinnah (middle of the back row) surrounded by women during their weekly Saturday meeting making clothes for refugees at Government House, Karachi, December 1947. Many middle-class women in India and Pakistan became closely involved in the recovery operation, as social workers and nurses and by running orphanages, schools and institutions for the displaced.

25 Refugee children at Kurukshetra camp with Nehru and Lady Mountbatten, February 1949. In total, at least 75,000 women were abducted, attacked or forced into marriage during Partition on both the Indian and Pakistani sides of the border. Countless children were orphaned, or lost or separated from their families, while others were abandoned in the aftermath.

accept them or welcome them again. These fears were not unfounded. The old taboos and rigid social customs of marriage and purity had been shattered. For those who had never been married there was the fear that they were ruined and now placed beyond the social pale. They believed that their families might be better able to rebuild their lives without them. Prostitution, life on the street or in a state-run home became the grim options if women were rejected by their families, and many preferred to convert or melt into the society of their abductor, becoming a new 'wife' or a family servant, rather than openly admitting the shame of rape. Ironically, the misogyny and patriarchal values that cut across North Indian society at the time meant that Indian and Pakistani men had much more in common in their attitudes and actions than they ever would have admitted. Women became, as Gandhi later described them, 'the chief sufferers' of 1947.

Rather than being raped and abandoned, tens of thousands of women were kept in the 'other' country, as permanent hostages, captives or forced wives; they became generically known simply as 'the abducted women'. Official government figures spoke of 83,000 women kept back, taken away from their families, on both sides of the border.[18] Why did men keep the women they had attacked? Some became servants, forced into unpaid labour, and converted and were assimilated into a new family; others replaced sisters and wives, who had themselves been taken away. Others became 'wives' and started a new life with their abductor or captor, with the full knowledge of others, who were complicit or who at least turned a blind eye to the new arrivals in the family. In all these different ways, the driving force was the impulse to consume, transform or eradicate the remnants of the other community.

Complicity and compassion

These waves of killing were not neatly bound by the provincial boundaries of Punjab but spilled into other places. In present-day Rajasthan, in the states of Alwar and Bharatpur, as the historian Ian Copland has unflinchingly described, ethnic cleansing killed tens of thousands while the mass killing in Jammu and Kashmir in 1947–8, which is usually forgotten or incorporated into the history of Kashmiri wars, shared far more characteristics with other Partition slaughters. The princely rulers of the states of Bharatpur and Alwar complied with targeted violence against the ethnic Muslim group, the Meos, who formed large minorities in their royal fiefdoms. Perhaps 30,000 Muslims were killed in these areas and 100,000 were forced to flee.[19] The princes used their state forces to kill the Meos or to run them out of the region.[20] There were stories of state police escorts killing Meos as they left the state, and the Maharaja of Bharatpur's younger brother was even reported to have boasted of how he had led an attack from his jeep and had used his sporting rifle on fleeing Meos.[21]

The methodical attempt to wipe out whole populations depended on a well-prepared, trained, uniformed and efficient body of former soldiers, policemen and students who took the shame, honour and protection of their communities into their own hands. Gangs armed with machine-guns in jeeps were able to inflict far more harm in one or two hours than villagers using *lathis* and pitchforks, were less alarmed by military patrols, on which they even launched unprovoked attacks, and could cover large distances. Communities gave succour and support to these militias in return for protection. To take just one example, B.L. Dutt, a government employee living in the suburbs of Lahore recalled providing a safe house for RSS meetings in the midst of the riots and hid killers in his home in the aftermath of an attack on part of the city: 'in my own house I had lodged two men . . . RSS men, who had attacked the Muslims and whatnot . . . they remained two or three days; . . . government servants' houses were not searched at all'.[22] The perpetrators were cushioned by sympathisers who fed or housed them in return for protection or even paid out blood money.

Neighbours sometimes looked the other way or gave tacit support from the sidelines. One of the nastiest and least discussed features of Partition was the active or passive social connivance in Punjab which radiated out beyond the province. During Partition social complicity was routine, even when those involved absolved themselves of blame and passed the responsibility for violence on to madmen, thugs and strangers. Although the timetables were supposed to be secret, it was common knowledge when trains specially arranged for refugees would run because the information was leaked by office staff, enabling the organisation of attacks along the route long before the trains had reached their destinations. On one occasion the confidential departure time of a train carrying refugees into Pakistan was even broadcast on All India Radio. Similarly, on goods trains the parcels of items belonging to refugees were selectively ransacked, suggesting that detailed information about the cargo had been passed on. Elsewhere slogans, marks on doors, census information and graffiti were employed in order to isolate and select victims. Staff on the railways were busily hoisting the new national flags on the railway stations and painting the engines with patriotic slogans. After another outrage when train passengers were robbed and slaughtered outside Macleodganj, 'the complicity of the railway staff in the outrage was quite manifest'.[23] Committed nationalists could become complicit killers.

Sometimes this complicity was motivated by fear or by the pack mentality that emerges at times of acute danger. During one attack on the Upper India Express train, when seventy or more people were killed just outside the pottery-making town of Khurja, the stationmaster refused to assist the investigating officer, denied that he would recognise any of the assailants, and said that he had been warned to stay in his office on pain of death. On a different occasion, when a man was stabbed and thrown out of a moving train, despite an immediate carriage-to-carriage search, 'Not a soul in the train admitted to have seen anything [sic], or heard anything.'[24]

Sometimes passengers directly defended the culprits. One train at Hapur was held up for nearly four hours while passengers protested about the arrest of some murder suspects and elsewhere desperately thirsty refugees found that the water taps on stations had been cut off.[25] The social status of those who looked the other way, or who tacitly sanctioned Partition violence, varied from prince to peasant, although the very poorest or the lowest castes rarely seem to have been the agitators. At one extreme, fabulously wealthy princes from states such as Bahawalpur, Patiala and Faridkot allowed the gangs to work freely on their lands, did precious little to disarm or suppress them and then suspiciously disappeared to summer capitals and on foreign vacations.[26] At the other end of the scale, rations dealers were accused of copying their lists and helping rioters to identify the occupants of houses, and some housewives and urban craftsmen boycotted markets, ruining local traders and shopkeepers and forcing them to leave for India or Pakistan. Sometimes the joy of independence or freedom itself would spill over into euphoric bloodlust: 'Hooligans looting in New Delhi yesterday . . . mob killed Muslims in shopping center while citizens hung out of windows and a sort of carnival spirit prevailed.'[27]

Expectations of justice plummeted. Magistrates and judges were not averse to siding with 'their' own community in the cases which were brought before them and acquittals were widespread on the rare occasions when Partition rioters were brought to book. Vallabhbhai Patel complained that the major problem in stemming an RSS revival after Gandhi's death in 1948 was the provincial High Courts' acquittal of large numbers of RSS men: 'In UP there have been several acquittals; in Bombay the acquittals have been of an almost wholesale nature and the Government has been asked to pay costs.'[28] Of course, distinguishing real from imagined partiality was difficult as people lost faith in the system itself. In some cases the lack of prosecution gave rioters a sense of immunity to punishment. Frustrated and overstretched administrators or policemen were forced to release people who, in any other circumstances, they would have charged. The complete turmoil of the state made even the most meagre efforts at justice difficult but it was often well known exactly who the ringleaders were. It was difficult enough to prosecute in the first place, though, when jails were bursting at the seams. Disarming people became the next-best thing when it was impossible to put them behind bars.

The illiterate depended on others for news. In Punjab some entrepreneurial unemployed made a few rupees by cycling to the nearest town to harvest the latest stories about events and then selling them on. Rumours were not necessarily the innocent by-product of violence but played a part in creating it in the first place. Exaggeration and hyperbole paid: with limited protection from police and troops it was essential to grab the attention of the authorities, to bring help to a potential riot scene. Telegrams and appeals for help were necessarily couched in the most extreme language. But there were more calculated uses of propaganda in addition to spontaneous gossip and snatches of newsprint. This had already started in 1946, when, for instance, a delegation of Pathans from the frontier visited the cities of Bombay and Ahmedabad, inquiring into reported atrocities and carrying with them photographs of damaged mosques and half-burnt copies of the Qur'an.[29]

Now, in August and September 1947, professionally produced pamphlets that had an air of governmental legitimacy circulated widely. *The Rape of Rawalpindi* was one: a forty-page palm-sized brochure full of gruesome black and white photographs, showing burnt skulls, orphaned refugee children and ruined temples accompanied by one-sided and inflammatory captions: 'All this is the result of the aggressive ideology of Pakistan. This is a foretaste of Pakistan.'[30] Partition was a modern event: the technology of the printing press was fully utilised to promote killing and pressmen and propagandists played their role in Partition violence behind typewriters as bureaucratic killers in word if not in deed. These propaganda networks stretched tautly across the subcontinent. Such propaganda was part of a strategic plan to polarise the communities and helped embolden those at the forefront of gangs. Some journalists and rumour-mongers in South Asia, then and now, are not detached commentators on the clashes between communities but are deeply involved in stoking the fires to which their partial stories give legitimacy, and sometimes spur on the rioters by creating tableaux against which they believe that they can act with impunity.

Against this bleak backdrop, many people carried out unusually brave, heroic and humanitarian acts. Some individuals saved the lives of neighbours, friends and strangers of different communities, even by risking their own lives. Others gave word of impending attacks to their neighbours, sheltered large numbers of people, smuggled food to the stranded and helped secretly move them from danger in the dead of night by lending transport or arranging disguises or armed protection. 'In the end I feel honour-bound to record that the lives of my children and those of about six hundred educated Hindus and Sikhs, male and female, of the Civil Lines, were saved by the efforts of some God-fearing Muslims who gave them shelter in their houses, even at the risk of their lives,' noted the Civil Surgeon of Sheikhupura, a survivor of the atrocities in the district which became a byword for terror in the weeks that followed. [31] Many of the acts were anonymous but abundant stories from all parts of India and Pakistan provide compelling evidence of a counter-flow to the polarisation of society in 1947. Even a future President of India, Zakir Hussain, owed his life to the intervention of a Sikh captain and Hindu railway employee who saved him from a gang at Ambala railway station. The Punjabi president of the Gujranwala City Congress Committee, Narinjan Das Bagga, was killed when he went to try and pacify an angry mob and rescue an injured Muslim.[32] An unknown policeman labelled as a 'South Asian Schindler' used a stick to fend off a marauding gang and saved two hundred Sikh lives.[33] Individuals built Hindu–Muslim unity leagues and peace brigades, and British observers, who had little reason to emphasise artificially the fraternity between Hindus, Muslims and Sikhs, frequently noted the extraordinary acts of heroism and generosity that occurred in the midst of Partition's worst atrocities. Groups ran ambulances and extricated the injured, ensuring that they got to hospital. Sometimes peace committees were well organised and sometimes individuals acted with spontaneous charity.

'No words can express the innermost feelings of gratitude and thankfulness which sprout from my grateful heart every moment when I cast a look upon my children and wife who have escaped from the very brink of the other world,' wrote one survivor to Dr Khushdeva Singh: 'you are doubtless an angel doing humanitarian work which befits a true doctor.'[34] Singh was the superintendent of a sanatorium and tuberculosis adviser to the government of Patiala in 1947. He also acted as a rationing officer for the area. Once the scale of the crisis became apparent he poured his energies into humanitarian work, collecting hundreds of rupees from local people to send to the Indian Red Cross society and urging peace. He worked with the wounded and the suffering at his clinic. Soon, he caught wind of the fact that truck drivers were leaking news of the planned evacuation of a large group of local Muslims. Avenging refugees had blocked their route out of the town and planned an ambush. Kushdeva Singh hatched a plan to evacuate the refugees secretly and to send them in an alternative direction. The doctor received 317 letters of gratitude from Muslims whose lives he had saved or from their family members.

Friends and neighbours relied upon each other. 'I still have more non-Muslim friends than Muslim and I have reasons to be proud of them,' wrote one Muslim author, Mahmud Brelvi to the Congress.[35] Others felt guilt for not doing more to save their neighbours or lamented the destruction of life as they had known it. Joginder, a small shop owner, who was a child in 1947 recalled, 'as soon as the Muslims left the others started coming . . . they took away everything, loaded them on bullock carts, and even took away the cattle . . . we felt very sad, we were completely heart broken, we'd been with them for generations, the elder people in our community were extremely sad, we still talk about them . . . we used to cry after they left . . .'[36]

Acts of mercy and charity were very common. Violence was not all encompassing. The complexities of these emotions cannot be easily stereo-typed. Nationalism was entirely compatible with love for an individual neighbour, member of staff or colleague. In other ways, the passage of time makes it incredibly challenging to disentangle slivers of memory and frag-mented stories. 'On the one hand individuals like Amiruddin could save the lives of members of other communities at considerable personal risk,' the historian Ian Talbot writes of the city's mayor, who conveyed Hindu and Sikh friends to safety under showers of bullets but also later glorified the 'marvellous' way that the Muslims in Amritsar 'put up a fight' in 1947. 'Simultaneously they could gloat at the removal of their "enemies" symbolic and physical presence.'[37]

The compulsions of violence forced many to look the other way, or made them too fearful to intervene. In mixed *mohallas* and villages, acute anxiety about the safety of neighbours could sit flush with nationalistic feeling and fear for one's own family. At its worst, this became a Judas-like denial or incrimination. Shanti Seghal was a young woman of twenty in 1947 and lost two sisters, their children and a sister-in-law. She was caught up in an attack outside Shiekhupura in which troops lined people up against trees and mowed them down with guns. She tried to convince the attackers that her family were Muslims but believed it was a neighbour who revealed their true identity as Hindus.[38]

Partition was accompanied by an acidic paper trail of pamphlets, letters and newsprint that created a sphere of paranoid and partial knowledge. Abundant rumours and their magnifying, generalising tendencies made it impossible to distinguish truth from fiction, reality from apprehension. Rumours and panic spread to areas such as Sind, which remained mercifully free from violence until January 1948 as well as to those where it was becoming endemic. The shortage of sound information, among political elites as well as villagers, was a two-way process and official actions – from sending out troops to ordering mass evacuations – were based on hearsay and rehashed stories just as much as localised violence depended on distorted stories from a distant Delhi. Leaders were overwhelmed by painful stories and inundated with tales of horror. Leaders and ministers, especially in Punjab, became conduits for news between members of their rank-and-file. Mumtaz Daultana, a senior Pakistani minister, was to be found sitting near a petrol pump in August 1947 in the Punjabi countryside, on the outskirts of Okara, 'surrounded by a group of men'. Often, the political imperative was to believe the worst about the other, a tendency still apparent in the contemporary national press of both countries: that it was the other side that was *really* the chief aggressor and the other side that was *really* responsible for the horrors of 1947.[39]

News was shaped so that it became entirely partial and was chiselled in such a way that people often only heard about the crimes against their own community: in the North West Frontier Province, the Muslim Pathan knew all about the terrible atrocities committed against fellow Muslims in Bihar but little of events in Bengal, where Hindus had been the victims. The public news sphere was sophisticated enough for news to travel rapidly, and between different parts of the country, connecting people together in imaginary religious communities across time and space.

Translation from English to vernaculars also offered scope for creative inventiveness. Crude tales of violence proved the most problematic obstacle to peace. Sometimes news was inverted, so that news of riots was turned entirely upside down and the real victims were painted as the culprits. After the violence in Garhmukhteshwar, 'the propaganda was so blatantly false that in the beginning it only caused amusement'.[40] Rumours of various kinds included details of major atrocities that sometimes had not actually taken place, in particular of grotesque acts against women, which intersected and overlapped with rumours about the actual course of political events – whether or not Pakistan was or was not being made, and where it was going to come into existence, what it would be like when it did.

Outside Punjab people started to worry about what was happening there, 'Events in the Punjab and NWFP are occasioning concern,' wrote the Governor of Bombay. 'It is difficult to follow what is happening here as information is confusing.'[41] Subsidiary rumours fed like tributaries into the wider stream: about where relief could be found, who was responsible for the trouble, preparations for attacks and stories of impending disasters. Slogans warned soldiers of the danger of rumour in watchwords reminiscent of the Blitz spirit: 'Careless talk costs lives. Keep a 24 hour guard on your tongue. Do not listen to Rumour', 'Rumour-mongers are public enemies', and 'Do not spread bazaar talk and gossip'. The potency of rumour should not be under-estimated, and more recent calamities in South Asia have continued to spark lethal rumours across the country long after events have receded from the media's purview: after the tsunami disaster in South India in 2004, news of another giant wave sparked mass evacuations along several parts of the Indian coastline, and in 2005, in Bombay, eighteen people were killed and over forty injured when a stampede broke out after word spread that a tsunami was approaching. During Partition the circulation of false information – whether intentional or accidental – frightened people in a parallel way and caused stampeding and panicked evacuations. To try and counter false propaganda the Indian government air-dropped over 20,000 newspapers to refugees in the distressed districts of Jullundur, Amritsar, Lahore and Ferozepore. Even a year later, rumour of impending riots was still a powerful weapon and a 'whispering campaign' among refugees in Delhi put all the law and order authorities on red alert in May 1948.[42]

India and Pakistan emerged shattered, but intact, as two separate nation states at the end of the summer of 1947. Nobody had imagined that the Partition plan or Pakistan's creation would lead to this scenario of death and destruction. Nobody had thought that freedom would come in this guise. Newly anointed Indian and Pakistani leaders now had to juggle the ceaseless flow of distressed and penniless refugees, to set up a feasible and functioning state, and to integrate princes and provincial interests in the shadow of Partition. Although no one could be naïve enough to suggest that only one side was responsible for the terrors of 1947, it is little wonder that nationalism was given a new edge. The two states necessarily saw each other through the prism of the violence that had taken place and eyed each other warily across the expanses of the ruptured Punjab.

8

Leprous Daybreak

By Independence Day, the national leaders of both countries were badly
shaken by their personal experiences of witnessing the violence at first hand
or by hearing the stories of the survivors and distressed refugees flooding into
the national capitals. Daily, anguished crowds queued at the residences of
political leaders, asking for recompense, help with finding lost ones or for
vengeance. Maniben Patel, the Indian Deputy Prime Minister's daughter and
secretary, records in her diary for late August and September how these early
morning callers became part of the Deputy Prime Minister's regular routine.
On 1 September 1947, typically, 'Large crowd from Punjab waiting in early
morning in the compound. Whole day passed in seeing visitors.'[1]

A national crisis

New Delhi was in chaos, with constant murdering and rioting in August and
September, throngs of refugees arriving, local people living under the daily
threat of death, armed gangs roaming the streets and thousands waiting in the
camps at Purana Qila and Humayan's Tomb to be taken to Pakistan. The ornamental fountains at the picturesque sixteenth-century monument Humayan's
Tomb became so fouled with human dirt that they had to be filled in with
sand. The Quaker aid worker and author Richard Symonds witnessed
Kafkaesque scenes in the Delhi camps:

I joined Horace [Alexander] in the largest camp, the Purana Qila, which
was sheltering 60,000 refugees in tents, in corners of battlements and in the
open, together with their camels and tongas and ponies, battered old taxis
and luxury limousines. There were orderly rows of tents which organized
bodies of college students had put up. You might meet anyone from a

nawab to a professor. Rich men offered you thousands of rupees if you could hire them an aeroplane to Karachi. It seemed possible to buy anything from a taxi to the hawkers' boxes of matches, which were now the only ones available in Delhi. From time to time Europeans hurried through looking for their bearers who had fled from their houses.[2]

Ordinary life had been turned upside down.

Knitted together in a collective feeling of crisis, the Congress – now the party of government – turned to the citizens of Delhi. Military reinforcements were meagre. 'Only a small number of Gurkhas and Madras paratroopers could be made available quickly. Madhya Pradesh contributed a contingent of armed police.' So instead of using more conventional troops and police, 'every possible source of trained and disciplined manpower was tapped'. The government gathered together under its wing all manner of groups from Boy Scouts to members of the Jamiat-ul-Ulema. Congress corps and Home Guards were armed by the Central Emergency Committee with shotguns. The government seized hold of private vehicles owned by the public and asked people to donate spare parts for vehicles, while 'trained mechanics were literally rounded up from their homes'.[3] This was the first *national* crisis for the free India and the free Pakistan.

Administrators and politicians hovered on the brink of nervous exhaustion; Dr Zakir Hussain, a future President of India, reporting on the state of the refugee camps in the city to his colleagues, suggested 'that these places could not properly be called camps, but rather areas in which humanity was dumped'.[4] In the imperial capital in mid-August food and milk were scarce, rubbish rotted uncollected in the streets and in the heat of summer all car windows were firmly sealed, or vehicles were mounted with guns. Many politicians personally suffered, nor were they personally immune from the terror sweeping the country; the daughter of Ghulam Mohammad, later Governor-General of Pakistan, was abducted and the brother of Rafi Ahmad Kidwai, a leading Congress politician, was stabbed to death on his way to work in a government office one morning. Dr Zakir Hussain himself was narrowly saved from death when he was attacked at Ambala train station. Leading political figures waited frantically for news of loved ones or tried their best to use their political clout in order to obtain information, to secure the safety of a specific train or to get access to a telephone line.

Guilt, shock and profound sadness had to be reconciled with the wider ideal of freedom for which the country had been striving. Indian leaders grieved for the bloody mess that they saw around them. Nehru was shattered and depressed, looking 'inexpressibly sad' at the first Emergency Committee meeting.[5] The Prime Minister reportedly jumped out of his car when driving through the streets of Delhi one day when he saw a Hindu pushing a handcart full of goods looted from a Muslim neighbourhood, grabbing the man by the throat when he refused to take them back.[6] The military general Ayub Khan, who was serving with the Boundary Force at the time of Partition, later wrote that 'this was the unhappiest period of my life'.[7] Even the optimistic and pragmatic industrialist G.D. Birla reflected sombrely that 'Unless we can cope with the situation India is doomed.'[8] There was a feeling that the new states might be on the brink of falling, irretrievably, into an abyss. 'Most prominent and persistent was our absolute uncertainty whether we should succeed in restoring and maintaining order,' remembered Penderel Moon who was trying to piece back together the princely state of Bahawalpur after murderers and looters had ransacked the city. 'This gnawing anxiety amounted sometimes to the fear that not only Bahawalpur, but the whole of northern India and with it Pakistan, might sink into utter and irretrievable chaos . . .'[9] Other administrators and officials shared this concern.

Politicians felt the full force of the refugees' grief – and anger. When Nehru went to meet refugees clustered in the pilgrimage town of Haridwar, he tried to be conciliatory and to talk to them of human losses on both sides of the border. A moving if hagiographic account by the Urdu journalist Shorish Kashmiri captures the tension at the camp:

Some young people, whose parents had been butchered and whose sisters and daughters had been left in Pakistan surrounded Panditji [Nehru]. . . One young man lost his temper and gave Panditji a resounding slap; a slap on the face of the Prime Minister of India. But Panditji said nothing to him. He just placed his hand on the young man's shoulder. The young man shouted: 'Give my mother back to me! Bring my sisters to me!' Panditji's eyes filled with tears. He said, 'Your anger is justified, but, be it Pakistan or India, the calamity that has overtaken us all is the same. We have both to pass through it.[10]

Nevertheless, elite leaders, often the product of imperial schools and colleges, were as likely as the British that they had replaced to cite the madness of the masses, and apply the vocabulary of craziness, insanity and of a fever gripping the people, blaming 'crooks, cranks and . . . mad people' to try to explain the inexplicable devastation that had taken place.[11] The language of class could be a convenient way for the leadership to wash their hands of their own explicit or inadvertent culpability. The poor and the uneducated must, of course, it was naturally assumed, have been mostly culpable. The information that militant, and often middle-class, organised cadres, sometimes fully answerable to Congress and League politicians, were at the forefront of events was known but glanced over. Nehru called for the rounding up of leaders causing trouble and demanded to know who was issuing orders, but the general tendency by the dramatis personae of politics was to patronise those caught up in violence and to dissociate their own actions and decisions from riots.

This intense anxiety and fear clutched hold of a broad sweep of North India. Even in places where violence hadn't occurred, communities became nervous and tense. Suhasini Das, an East Bengali Gandhian and social worker, who was in her early thirties at the time, and an indefatigable peace worker, covered miles of territory in the district of Sylhet, which joined Pakistan, persuading her fellow Hindus to stay in their homes, trying to assuage their fear and confusion. Her diary, written at the end of long days and evenings crossing the East Pakistani countryside attempting to spread reassurance and calm, conveys the tensions of the moment and the ubiquity of angst. In Sylhet, from July to September, she found people 'tense', 'worried', suffering 'mental agony', consumed with 'panic' and 'troubled'. 'Although no major mishap had befallen people here, they were still tense and anxious,' she wrote in her diary, and a few weeks later, in Sunamganj, 'People plied us with anxious queries as we went from house to house.'[12] Work in government offices ground to a halt and all the talk was now of Partition and Pakistan. The daily grind of petty incidents and random stabbings kept affected populations suspended in a state of anxiety.

Far from the major sites of devastation, people were caught up in Partition's ramifications. Some had migrated far away to find work or to marry but remained worried about news from home. 'The day before I left Ranchi [the summer capital of Bihar] for good, Inayat Khan, one of my staff-car drivers came to me to say goodbye as he was going off to Pakistan,' recalled General Tuker. 'His home was in Jullundur in the Indian Union. It had been destroyed with all his property. His father had died some years before. His grandfather tried to get his mother and sister away to Pakistan but the old man was waylaid by Sikhs and disappeared. His mother escaped and wrote to say that his fifteen-year-old sister had been taken as a concubine by a Sikh. To leave the Indian Army with this as the last sight of my own soldiers and friends was deeply painful.'[13] In Mathura in western UP corpses floated to the surface of irrigation canals for at least four months after the first wave of massacres in nearby Gurgaon as ghostly reminders of Partition and part of its invisible but important psychological rupture.

Families negotiated a semblance of ordinary life around the edges of violence, curfews and travel restrictions. The Urdu writer Masud Hasan Shahab Dehlvi, who was living in Delhi at the time, was married in the weeks preceding Partition and had to procure curfew passes for his wedding guests, some of whom faced difficulties returning home after the celebrations. 'These joyous moments were completely overshadowed by the atmosphere of violence and suffering,' he later remembered.[14] Gathering with relatives was preferable to being alone. Signalmen on the railways deserted their posts, afraid of spending lonely nights in their huts dotted along the tracks. In one hospital, in the northern city of Bareilly, a British army doctor found a loaded revolver under the pillow of a patient. 'He claimed he must keep it in case anyone came in during the night.'[15] In the later months of 1947 people walking unaccompanied in the afflicted parts of the country could be knifed from behind, even in broad daylight. Living through 1947 was an ordeal for many Indians and Pakistanis, even for those who escaped physically unscathed.

Partition was, then, a national crisis for India and Pakistan, notwithstanding unanswered questions about national belonging. Partition penetrated, and disrupted, normal life beyond Punjab and Bengal as people began their new lives as Indians and Pakistanis. Militias and gangs, especially the Muslim League National Guard and the RSS, were still operating with impunity on train lines in September and October 1947. Random stabbings, bombs and hate-crimes continued to pierce the social fabric far beyond Punjab. 'The frequency, callousness and darings of these killings on trains and at stations has made staff very panicky,' reported an East India Railway official on the line that stretched from Delhi across to Bihar, 'and on occasions it was with difficulty that we could keep them at their posts and keep trains going.' People travelling on passenger trains ran the risk of murder at night or could be thrown unsuspecting from the train. On this line alone, the daily reports make grim reading: on 8 September, an unidentified dead body was found in a luggage van at Ghaziabad. On 9 September a Muslim passenger who alighted from the train to drink water was dragged away and stabbed, but found alive. On 10 September, an 'upper class' passenger reported his two servants missing. The servants' compartment was full of blood and the two corpses were found later that day further along the tracks.[16]

Limited services were achieved by pushing trains through the landscape at almost any cost. Railwaymen often worked for little or no pay, while in East Pakistan they were housed in railway wagons, huts and tents up and down the

East Bengal line. Here, there were no passenger services at all and the 'refugee specials' were the only functioning services – trains carrying refugees covered some 200,000 miles in 1947 on the North Western line alone. Train services were still abnormal at the end of 1947. Ticketless travel had become rampant across the subcontinent (Gandhi complained that 'people evidently thought that under independence travelling by trains or buses was free for all' – another echo of the pervasive nature of social dislocation, opportunism and confusion of 1947) and to add to the disorder, after Independence, several of Pakistan's services were brought to a complete standstill because of shortages of Indian-supplied coal.[17]

'The Delhi in which I arrived on 11 September appeared physically and nervously shattered,' Richard Symonds later remembered. 'Stabbing and looting had spread from the narrow streets of Old Delhi to the broad boulevards of Lutyens' New Delhi. Those shops which had not been plundered in the commercial centre of Connaught Circus were boarded up. There was a rigid curfew after 6 p.m. There was no bread for ten days in the Imperial Hotel where we lived off tinned food.'[18] Nehru later questioned if the public ever realised how close India had come to complete internal implosion. 'If the disturbances had not been halted in western UP,' he wrote to his chief ministers while reflecting on the gravity of events, 'they would eventually have spread eastwards right up to Bihar and west Bengal and the whole of northern India would have been in chaos.'[19] The situation was grave enough in September 1947 to lead some to consider 'a compulsory evacuation' of Delhi and the removal of the national capital to another location.[20] Dealing with Partition's aftermath bled the state's income and inhibited essential economic and governmental reforms. 'Since we assumed office my Government and myself have been spending the best part of our time and energy in dealing with this grave crisis which continues to assume greater proportions as one disaster follows another,' admitted Jinnah.[21]

Post offices and airfreight offices degenerated into chaos, the floors were stacked with unclaimed parcels, letters and hessian-wrapped packages with 'sacks of unsorted messages lying in the telegraph office'. In the Indian capital, all public holidays for bureaucrats, including Sundays, were cancelled. Profiteering was rife. Tonga and rickshawallahs charged inflated prices for those desperate to travel and precious seats on outgoing trains could be secured for the right bribe, while coolies ratcheted up the cost of carrying heavy packages. A photograph taken at Ambala station in Punjab shows a man with a rickety bamboo ladder charging two *annas* per trip for people to clamber up from the platform to the roof of a departing goods wagon.[22]

People trying to contact relatives jammed telephone exchanges and the Partition crisis disrupted the lines for several weeks but when an unidentified woman, named only as 'Kamila', tried to get through to find out news of her husband's whereabouts even the telephone operators were consumed with nationalistic loathing, neglecting their jobs and shouting down the telephone lines '*Jawaharlal Nehru Murdabad*' or '*Jinnah Murdabad*' [death to Nehru or death to Jinnah] so that it was impossible to hear anything on the line. 'They'd be fighting among themselves and we'd be left saying, "Hello? Hello?" We just couldn't talk. We booked so many urgent calls, but nothing. So we couldn't consult each other.'[23]

Both administrations had to untie other logistical knots. Food was still desperately scarce. In one district of Punjab, in 'dismal camps', the ration was a *chittack* (two ounces) of flour a day, enough to make one chapatti, and nothing else. Far beyond Punjab, in the north-east, the food crisis was exacerbated by Partition and in the Chittagong Hill tracts thousands wearing rags were begging for food while 'reports of deaths from starvation were constantly dribbling in from the villages'.[24] Rumours were still rife and could bring towns to a standstill. A British officer living in the imperial summer capital, Simla, reported. 'The other day a rumour was spread that the water supply had been poisoned. Every person on the road was talking about it. After several hours' anxiety, we managed to contact, by phone, the Health Officer who informed us that the water had been tested and that it was quite all right.'[25] The transition of power in South Asia was overcast by a cloud of fear.

The wider South Asian public could not avoid the drama of Partition: news about the suffering of the refugees was everywhere. Anybody listening to All India Radio would have been struck by the poignant litany of names read out on air as people tried to ascertain the whereabouts and safety of their relatives. This started off as a five-minute bulletin but by the first week of November up to 1,400 messages were being broadcast daily using three hours of airtime.[26] Similarly, newspapers ran adverts placed by people attempting to locate their missing relatives. 'Mr Abdul Waheed, Traffic Inspector, Ferozepore city, wants to know the whereabouts of his son, Abdul Fahmid, who lost contact with him at Kasur station. Mr Waheed is now staying at a hotel in Lahore near the Taj company on Macleod Road.'[27] By reading these advertisements, listening to the radio and producing and circulating the news, the wider public became caught up in Partition's cold war and, inevitably, in the shaping of ideas about the neighbouring country.

Whose freedom?

'At the stroke of the midnight hour, when the world sleeps, India will awake to life and freedom.' Jawaharlal Nehru's haunting words filled the night air of the midnight session of the Constituent Assembly in New Delhi's Council House on 15 August 1947. The remarkable speech was broadcast throughout the country and reproduced in special newspaper editions. Huge jostling crowds thronged Lutyens's commanding sandstone buildings in New Delhi to take part in the tryst with destiny. They had done so in Karachi just twenty-four hours previously, where, in parallel, Jinnah had addressed the Pakistani Constituent Assembly meeting and spoken to the people over the airwaves of a 'supreme moment' and of 'the fulfilment of the destiny of the Muslim nation'. In Karachi, the celebrations were 'carried off with very scanty means and not in as perfect a manner as at Delhi', recalled one member of the audience, '. . . but that never struck one as incongruous . . . it was improvised, Pakistan itself was being improvised'.[28] Euphoria, an unprecedented collective feeling, marks many of the recollections of those who stood in the vast crowds, dazzled by the fireworks and illuminated buildings, not only in New Delhi, but in the major cities throughout South Asia. 'We have to celebrate 15 August in such a way that people's psychology is metamorphosed into that befitting the citizens of an independent nation,'[29] instructed a Congress secretary, and every effort was made to make it a memorable occasion. There was a profound sense of catharsis; a feeling of order up-ended and old constraints removed.

Popular expectations meshed with political generosity. The moment promised new power, new potentialities and a sense of release. Provincial and district governments flung open the jailhouse doors and prisoners were released early at the moment of Independence. In Bombay on Independence Day every prisoner who had been behind bars for ten years or more was allowed to walk free, alongside those who had served two-thirds of their sentences. Death sentences were commuted to prison terms. Some of the recently arrested prisoners charged with violence in the Hindu–Muslim riots of the preceding weeks were also allowed to walk free or promised early release. More than 3,000 prisoners in Bombay City gained their freedom on the evening before Independence Day and, astonishingly, some 13,000 prisoners were released on 15 August in the Central Provinces.[30] In Pakistan, prisoners might have preferred to stay within their cells; mobs reportedly lynched those who could not prove they were Muslims outside the prison doors.

There was a darker side to freedom, though. The particular irony of Independence, and its interlocking with Partition, was the way in which it forced a new moment of national identification. Where there had been myriad localised groups, patriotic allegiance to either India or Pakistan was now mandatory. No Muslim was immune from the charge of disloyalty and many had to bend over backwards to try and prove themselves. 'Half of my life I had to suffer such humiliation as a Congressman at the hands of the British Government in India,' protested the Muslim Congressman from Bihar, Syed Mahmud, after his house and car were searched by police. 'Now it seems for the remaining period of my life I have to suffer all these indignities and insults at the hand of the Congress Government. Am I wrong in this conclusion?'[31]

Employees in intelligence branches intercepted letters to Pakistan and prosecuted anti-national behaviour – the familiar actions of governments that start to suspect the fidelity of their own citizens during a time of terror. Some Muslims, especially those with families living across the border in Pakistan, wavered, and did not express their allegiance to either India or Pakistan as they continued to reside in a grey netherworld in which these new borders remained porous. Others used subterfuge in order to explore the possibilities of making a new life elsewhere. One police sub-inspector in the northern industrial city of Kanpur, Mohammad Rizvi, caught corresponding with relations in Pakistan under a fictitious name while attempting to secure a permanent settlement permit in Pakistan, was arrested on discovery of the correspondence and dismissed. Considerations about whether to depart for Pakistan, often driven by mundane economic motives, were always interpreted by the government in the paradigm of loyalty or disloyalty to the nation state.[32] This was a complex emotional and political process for all those people living in the former Raj but particularly difficult for millions of people who felt themselves to be in the 'wrong' country, were financially or physically ruined by Partition or had other, deeply felt, sub-nationalist identities. Was it right to celebrate in the middle of violence? Who was an Indian or Pakistani citizen now? Should you celebrate the creation of one state, both states or none? How could people's 'psychology' be 'metamorphosed' so that they became loyal citizens?

There was ambivalence about whether Independence should be a day of jubilation at all, given the contingencies and trauma of the ongoing violence. V.D. Savarkar, the Hindu nationalist supremo, and others in the Hindu Mahasabha and RSS who staunchly opposed Partition boycotted the celebrations. Gandhi was also conspicuously absent, praying and fasting in Calcutta and promoting peace: 'This much I certainly believe – that [the] coming August 15 should be no day for rejoicing whilst the minorities contemplate the day with a heavy heart.' He urged a day of fasting, praying and spinning instead. 'It must be a day for prayer and deep heart-searching.'[33] In his refusal to endorse the festivities, Gandhi was sensitive to the perversity of holding firework displays, dances and feasting as massacres continued elsewhere, but this also placed another question mark over the legitimacy of Pakistan and the new Partition settlement.

In public places the line between religious rituals, holy institutions and the national cause was blurred. Both India and Pakistan included a significant religious component in their official state rituals of celebration. Listeners to Pakistan Radio at one minute past midnight on 14 August heard the announcement of Pakistan's birth followed by readings from the Qur'an. In New Delhi, at a private residence, Nehru and his ministerial colleagues sat cross-legged around a holy fire as Hindu priests from Tanjore chanted hymns and sprinkled holy water on them. N.A. Sherwani, a Congress minister and a Muslim, unfurled the striped gold, green and white national flag over the Bharat Mata, or Mother India, temple in the sacred city of Varanasi.[34] Elsewhere, diverse and impulsive ceremonies centred on historic sites associated with the heroes who had fought the British in the uprising of 1857, or the Quit India movement of 1942. Others organised ecumenical, multi-faith ceremonies with readings and prayers from all religions.

In the Punjabi cities where massacres were still taking place, there were far fewer signs of celebration. When Penderel Moon arrived in the imperial centre of Lahore on 15 August he recalled a deathly stillness. 'The Mall empty, every shop shut and as silent as the grave. I made for the railway station to find out about trains to Simla. As I passed down Empress Road a fire station was coping with a burning house, and to the left, from the city proper, numerous dense columns of smoke were rising from the air.'[35] At the 'festivities', later that day, only one Hindu and no Sikhs attended the Governor's inauguration for which only one-fifth of the invitations could be delivered. For many who had not yet escaped the risk of violence, the memories of Independence Day were overshadowed by fear and this fuelled the resentment of refugees who felt abandoned by their compatriots. 'The evening was drawing to a close. I turned the radio to Delhi,' recalled a refugee from Lahore.

> The babble of tongues, the excitement of the vast assembled crowd near the Red Fort could be clearly heard. The announcer was giving a running commentary on the whole show; the Independence of India was being inaugurated ... Just then a bullet was fired in the Sanda Road Chowk, hardly fifty yards from my *kothi* [bungalow]. . . Of course the Delhiwalas must have had a gala night. Stuffing themselves with fruit, sweets and drinks, soft or strong, they must have gone to sleep dreaming of pleasant

dreams . . . Of course, a few of them had seen but many of them had only heard that there was 'some trouble' in the Punjab. But what was Punjab's trouble as compared to the Azadi of the other parts of the country?'[36]

Meanwhile, in private homes some people fused the secular and the profane, improvising ceremonies, distributing coloured sweets or hoisting flags. Families and individuals found their own way to negotiate rocky questions of national loyalty and allegiance to one state or the other. 'On Independence day, when the announcement came on the radio,' remembered the Punjabi journalist Amjad Husain, who was in Lahore in 1947, 'father took the Holy Qur'an in hand and made all family members take an oath of loyalty to Pakistan. I still remember that every family member took an oath.'[37] In much the same way, elsewhere, people were busy designing and improvising their own ceremonies to mark the occasion. A Sikh, Saroj Pachauri, a child at the time, recalled painting Pakistani flags and watching her father participate on the dais in the Punjabi town of Rawalpindi during the Independence Day cele-brations, only weeks before the whole family fled to safety in India.[38] Many people celebrated Independence Day in the 'wrong' country, as they later moved as refugees from India to Pakistan or vice versa. Some even celebrated it twice, once in each state. For some, participating itself was a kind of insur-ance against violence and 'proof' of loyalty to the new nation, and for the terrified, newly converted Muslims, seen along the roadside near a hamlet in Bahawalpur, it must have been a strange kind of 'freedom'. They were jigging desperately around 'a miserable bit of green cloth' which was 'a stick with a little green flag tied to the end' and protesting 'this is our flag. We now have Pakistan and Muslim Raj.'[39] In fact, the group had been forcibly made to convert to Islam and had gathered under the flag for safety, to try and prove their Pakistaniness.

As the 3 June plan had been so rushed and inadequately thought out, there had been little meditation on who was a rightful Indian and who was a rightful Pakistani. At the heart of these uncertainties and dilemmas was the undefined question of citizenship. Did this just depend on religious identity? As each new government tried to earmark its own citizens, a diplomatic quarrel erupted about *who* should be celebrating Independence and which country they should be endorsing. The Congressman Acharya Kripalani suffered his own family's displacement from Sind. He was personally badly shaken by Partition's events. Now he issued a directive to provincial Congressmen living in areas that were soon to become Pakistan: 'The hearts of all Congressmen and Congress sympathisers in Sind, East Bengal, West

Punjab and the North-West Frontier Province are lacerated at the division of the country,' he wrote; 'they are, therefore, in no mood to rejoice with the rest of India. Under these circumstances there is no need of celebrating August 15, in these areas which have been separated from India.'[40] A bad-tempered row broke out immediately with Pakistani politicians who saw things in a different light; weren't these Hindus and Sikhs now Pakistani citizens and, if so, why should they not take pride in Pakistan's green and white crescent moon flag?

Flags had become powerful, sometimes lethal, symbols. The Pakistani flag had unmissable Islamic connotations. This provoked anger and confusion among Hindus and Sikhs in Pakistan as they contemplated staying in the country. The Pakistani Prime Minister tried to fudge the issue, rebuffing a complainant with the claim that it is 'not a religious flag' and arguing that the 'Moon and stars are as common to my Honourable friend and they are as much his property as mine'. Such disingenuous claims hardly washed with a community already shattered by violence and frightened about the protection of its religious freedoms.[41] Similarly in India, Krishna Sobti recollected the fuzzy sense of belonging among different people, depending on their status, religion and outlook: 'Our entire family was gathered around the radio. Our servants, many of whom were Muslims, were also present. When Nehru spoke our reaction was very different from theirs. After tea, sweets were passed round (green and orange ones known as *ashrafian*). None of the Muslim servants touched them. But when the national anthem was sung and we stood up, they did too. They realized that they too, had paid a price for freedom.'[42] We do not know what was going through the minds of these particular servants. But as loyalty to the Congress *party* and allegiance to an Indian *state* got rolled up together, this could cause confusion and panic.

Emphasis on loyalty to Congress symbols, such as *khadi*, the Gandhi cap, and the spinning wheel, alienated many people who had been political opponents of the Congress but now felt pressure to submit to the emblems of the *party* as well as to those of the *nation state* in order to gain acceptance as loyal and law-abiding citizens. The Congress Chief Minister of the United Provinces made all the police in his province wear a Congress armband on Independence Day in August 1947. As the departing British Governor noted, 'Pant would have his pound of flesh out of the police in the UP.'[43] The Congress flag and the national flag – which were very similar in any case – were used interchangeably on Independence Day. People who had been involved in the intense electoral campaign in 1946 in opposition to the Congress or policemen and officials who had worked in the service of the colonial state strongly associated these symbols with an old adversary. In the past, they had rallied against these flags and ripped them down. These changes could be hard to bear, and the insistence upon these old symbols could be regarded as a show of Congress triumphalism.[44]

Now formally labelled as 'minorities' in the official mindset, groups of Hindus and Sikhs in Pakistan, and Muslims in India, felt thoroughly compromised. 'You are free; you are free to go to your temples, you are free to go to your mosques or to any other place of worship in this state of Pakistan,' Jinnah told Hindus and Sikhs in Pakistan in an acclaimed speech at the time of Independence, even as arson attacks on these religious buildings and the murder of their worshippers continued unabated.[45] Jinnah's commitment to a plural state was both principled and economically pragmatic, given Pakistan's position on an economic precipice. As the Chief Minister of the North West Frontier Province put it bluntly six months later, 'We had more than one reason for wishing the Hindus and Sikhs to stay on. They controlled all the banking, trade and industry in this Province and their sudden departure has hit us very hard.'[46] Some Pakistani leaders realised that the state had much to gain from stemming the flow of migration.

It was also possible for non-Muslims to be, at least in the early days of the state, enthusiastic Pakistanis. J.N. Mandal, an 'untouchable' from Bengal, was elected chairman of the Pakistani Constituent Assembly. The other members cheered as he signed the roll book in Karachi on Independence Day and he called on other Pakistani 'minorities' to be 'responsible, loyal and faithful to the state'. Soon afterwards he was promoted to a coveted ministerial position. Mandal's experience was hardly typical, though. Everywhere minorities were feeling deeply insecure about their physical safety and their citizenship rights. It was these fears that drove people from their homes and started one of the greatest mass migrations in history.

As well as marking the end of a nationalist struggle against colonialism, then, 15 August underscored the moment at which a new project began. People felt compelled to decide upon unalloyed national attachments, demarcate clearly their patriotism and express unwavering belief in the power of one nation state or another. This was all vastly different from the *mélange* of communities and national beliefs that had been in coexistence at the end of the Second World War in India.

Unforeseen exodus

It had been unthinkable that twelve million people would move, absolutely impossible to conceive, even if anyone had believed it to be desirable. The mass migrations were the sting in the scorpion's tail, the unknown face of the Partition plan. The tides of people flowing out of Pakistan and India were so fantastical, so vast and so thorough, that they unbalanced the entire substructure on which Pakistan had been built. As Danial Latifi recalled years later, the plan had backfired: 'I was in favour of self-determination . . . and to the extent that the Muslim League stood for self-determination I was with the Muslim League, but self-determination did not involve transfer of large groups of people.'[47] The movement of millions across the new international border meant that the plan did not work as originally envisaged and this massive upheaval changed the entire composition of India and Pakistan.

Once the Radcliffe line became clear, the numbers of refugees crossing Punjab and moving out of the state intensified frighteningly quickly. In 42 days from 18 September to 29 October, 849,000 refugees entered India in formally organised foot convoys alone. Between August and November an additional 2.3 million crossed the borders by train. Thirty-two thousand, mostly the rich, the privileged or essential administrative staff, arrived by air in both directions. In East Punjab in one month alone over a million gallons of petrol were consumed carrying people across the border and 1,200 vehicles moved back and forth carrying the stranded and vulnerable. In addition, there was a much slower, more protracted movement by sea and rail from all corners of the subcontinent, from Sind to Bombay, from Dhaka to Calcutta, from Lucknow to Lahore. Numbers involved in this were impossible to count. In November alone, 133,000 people arrived into Bombay's docks by steamer from Sind. By November 1947 perhaps eight million refugees had crossed the borders in both directions.[48] These figures are almost beyond belief. One in ten people in Pakistan was a refugee. Each country had to resettle, feed and house a group as large as the total population of Australia.

Overspilling trains have provided the most enduring images of Partition. In the opening scenes of Khushwant Singh's influential novel, *Train to Pakistan*, a train inhumanly crammed with refugees passes through Punjabi countryside near the Indo-Pakistan border. 'Like all the trains it was full. From the roof, legs dangled down the sides on to the doors and windows. The doors and windows were jammed with heads and arms. There were people on buffers between the bogies.'[49] Partition refugees did move in other ways, on foot, mostly in great columns or *kafilas*, but also by car and boat. Yet it is the trains piled high with people and hastily assembled goods that have provided the totemic image of Partition.

This was not simply an 'exchange' of population or a straightforward swap. In the months following Independence, Pakistan lost its bankers, merchants, shopkeepers, entrepreneurs and clerks – the wheels came off the machinery of the state. Jinnah became increasingly panicked, saying that knifing Sikhs and Hindus was equivalent to 'stabbing Pakistan'.[50] In India, similarly, the sudden disappearance of Muslim railwaymen, weavers and craftsmen, agriculturalists and administrators, brought gridlock to production and trade and crippled the state's ability to function. Large numbers of the incoming refugees arrived with quite different occupational histories and could not or were not qualified to plug the gaps left by those who departed. In the autumn months of 1947 the refugee movement was a tragedy for the refugees themselves and also a tragedy for the two new states.

In September 1947 Jinnah ordered a park packed with people in Lahore to 'make it a matter of our prestige and honour to safeguard the lives of the minority communities and to create a sense of security among them'. Nehru had long been stressing India as the land for all Indians. As he wrote to his chief ministers, 'we have a Muslim minority who are so large in numbers that they cannot, even if they want to, go anywhere else' and he urged that they must be given the same rights as other citizens and treated in a civilised manner, if the nature of the body politic itself was to be preserved.[51] Political safeguards for minorities proved paper tigers, however, in the face of the Punjabi tragedy and they offered too little and too late to those who had lost faith in the state's ability to protect them; the speed of events on the ground outstripped deliberations about the rights of citizenship in the constitutional arenas of India and Pakistan. Across Punjab, coexistent communities fragmented as the entire non-Muslim population was exchanged for the Punjabi Muslim population of India. Elsewhere, across the whole of Pakistan, and in Bengal, Rajasthan, Bombay and North India, people started to leave their homes at a dizzying speed and a mass and unanticipated movement of people began to occur.

There was a big difference in the way that people left. For the majority, especially in Punjab and the other heartlands of ethnic cleansing such as Gurgaon, it was part and parcel of the terror of violence, as they literally ran for their lives or were hurriedly formed into *kafilas* and made to march without as much as a few hours' notice. They did not know where they were heading or what their final destination would be. Rajinder Singh, who finally found his way to Delhi from Punjab, described to Urvashi Butalia how his family left in the middle of the night: 'Whatever people could pick up, big things and small, they put clothes on top of those they were wearing, and threw a *khes* or sheet over their shoulders. They picked up whatever they could and then they joined the *kafila*. Who could take along heavy things? And the *kafila* began to move.'[52]

Others adopted disguises or masqueraded as Hindus or Muslims to try and protect themselves. For others, with more forewarning, or further from the epicentres of violence, there were more tortuous and prolonged decisions about whether to stay or go, which sometimes divided families, as Damyanti Sahgal, living in a village 30 miles from Lahore, recalled. She tried to persuade her father to leave, but 'Father didn't agree . . . the workers in his factory were mixed: Jats, Hindus, but on the whole it was a Muslim village so most of the workers were Musalmaans . . . at the time they were respectful and humble. They seemed safe . . . When I tried to persuade my father he said, well if you feel scared you go. I said but bhauji, he said no bibi, if you feel scared you go.'[53] She left and made her way to Lahore, leaving her father behind. Further away from violence, the choices were different again. People could opt for one state or the other for ideological reasons, for business purposes or because they feared discrimination or job losses.

At first the new governments tried to stop these movements of people. The Partition plan envisaged that groups of religious minorities would remain in both states. If anything, these pockets of minorities formed part of the intended plan as it was believed that they would be 'hostages' or guarantors against any discrimination or harassment of minorities across the border. Both states showed rhetorical commitment to plurality and both countries started hammering out in their Constituent Assemblies the legal and administrative frameworks that would be put in place to secure these minority rights. The plan had not made allowances for any potential mass population exchanges and the ensuing two-way movement of people caught both national leaderships unawares, pulling the rug out from under their feet and invalidating the safeguards that had been notionally built into the plan.

At the end of August both governments reversed their initial strategy and admitted that, if the groundswell of refugees was beyond their control, they should be aiding rather than inhibiting it. On 7 September it was announced that the evacuation – at least across Punjab – was the 'first priority' and that Punjabi refugees would be given military and political support by both governments.[54]

What had begun as a spontaneous exodus was rapidly merged into an organised evacuation operation. In the first week of September a Military Evacuation Organisation was formed and by late October 1,200 military and civilian vehicles were being used to transport refugees across Punjab.[55] Twelve RAF Dakotas airlifted stranded officials. Gandhi disagreed with the policy at first and stood firmly in favour of replanting uprooted populations and continuously made the case for returning and resettling the refugees in their original homes. Others, with an eye on the fratricide and daily mortality figures and the grave dangers of unorganised and unsupported refugee columns, wanted the exchange to be as organised and rapid as possible.

More controversially still, this policy could be exploited to 'clean out' an area and purify it of minorities. Local administrators now had the chance – either accidentally or explicitly – to help with the ethnic cleansing agenda. Administrators and police forcibly shifted whole communities as the priority became dispersal rather than violence: 'there were certain people in plain clothes who were asking people to leave that place and go to Pakistan . . . but people were resisting this, people said: we won't go to Pakistan . . . then another military truck came, and on the top of it was some leader. He brought out a pistol and said you must leave, as soon as he said that immediately a caravan was formed, and everybody cooperated,' recalled one Punjabi eyewitness, Harcharan Singh Nirman.[56] In swathes of central and western India, Muslim communities were drummed out of India, just as Hindus and Sikhs were hounded out of many parts of Pakistan. Although some pleaded desperately for evacuation, others resisted the suggestion that they should migrate and felt angered by the confused message of the governments.

Elsewhere people wanted to leave but were being dissuaded by politicians and local magistrates, and in October, in the Punjabi district of Jhelum, a Gandhian envoy, Pandit Sundralal, called for the suspension of the evacuation in the local press. 'The Jhelum Hindus seemed perturbed by all this,' noted the aid worker Richard Symonds, who was co-ordinating local relief activities. 'They wanted to leave, not to be pawns in a political game.'[57] Politicians were accused of meddling in the internal affairs of the other state when they intervened and once again the political and the social were closely entwined; Acharya Kripalani raised objections to the obstacles preventing people's evacuation from Sind when he visited his former home in September.[58] Penderel Moon remembered asking the blue-turbaned leader of a group of Jat Sikhs, who had halted by the roadside with their bullock carts for the night, why they had left their villages. 'He replied, "*Hukum Hai*" (It is an order.) I asked him, "Whose order?" But to this he would give no clear reply, but just went on repeating, "It is an order. We have received an order. We have to go to Hindustan."' A little later in the month, Moon was shocked to hear that government officials were pushing Muslims out of East Punjab – 'If the Sub-Divisional Officer was acting under orders, where was this all going to end? We might have the whole Muslim population of India thrust upon us' – only to have the double shock of finding out that this transfer of people in Punjab, had, overnight, become official policy.[59] Such confusion only exacerbated the voluminous problems faced by ordinary people.

Whether the state encouraged them to leave or not, the greatest numbers of people on the long march across the border had no access to transport. Circumstances compelled them to travel by foot. Foot columns sometimes 30–40,000 strong, created human caravans 45 miles long in places. It was 150 miles for those Punjabis coming to India from Lyallpur or Montgomery districts, and Muslim Meos from the Gurgaon region of India took three weeks to reach Pakistan. 'According to our latest reports they are now without food and their cattle are rapidly dying for lack of fodder, or are being slaughtered by them for eating; their bullock carts (wherever they had any) are being used as fuel-wood and other difficulties are aggravated by the onset of winter which with their physical debility will make them an easy prey to diseases like pneumonia and influenza.'[60] The journey itself proved a cruel physical punishment for many.

Luggage was very often confiscated or looted along the way or simply abandoned as people became too weak to carry it; sores developed on bare feet; women gave birth to babies *en route*; and people died of starvation, exhaustion, cholera and grief. It must have seemed as if all the fates were conspiring against the refugees; to make matters worse the infernal temperatures on the Punjabi plains in June were followed by dust storms. A thick pall of dust caked the refugees and flies were omnipresent. 'We went on with the convoys week after week', later wrote the American photographer Margaret Bourke-White, 'until our hair became stiff and grey with dust, our clothes felt like emery boards, my cameras became clogged with grit . . .'[61] These were followed by unusually heavy storms and torrential rains in Punjab at the end of September. The countryside was suddenly awash with mud. These rains burst the banks of the Beas River, destroying railway bridges and roads, washing away camps and belongings, soaking and drowning some of the refugees who became caught in the currents. Fear of the descent into a bitter winter followed, and there were concerns that families would freeze or succumb to disease if living out in the open, badly dressed in thin cotton clothes or rags.

Both states snidely criticised the facilities provided for 'their' refugees and the treatment they received in transit camps and *en route*. Hanging over all this was the question of national belonging. This difficult question was grossly complicated by the influx of refugees. Who should have priority access to housing and accommodation? Should refugees or the remaining minority populations be given the same rights and protection as other citizens in India and Pakistan? This issue urgently needed to be clarified by the central leaderships. Some did speak out for liberal, plural, secular, multi-ethnic states but they were not the loudest voices. At the crucial moment, numerous leading politicians and their parties hesitated and dodged the question of citizenship – or actively promoted the idea of India for Hindus-Sikhs and Pakistan for Muslims. This bullishness of the top branches of the political networks intersected with, and was influenced by, the gravity of violence. Confusion about who was a legitimate citizen of each state was endemic. Disagreement sliced vertically through society from cabinet-level indecision, especially in conflict between Nehru and his Deputy Prime Minister, Vallabhbhai Patel, to uncertainty about who was a compatriot among ordinary people in the smallest villages and towns.

Crossing over

What of the experiences of the refugees themselves? Many refugees did feel, superficially at least, patriotic on reaching the new states simply because of their relief on reaching a place of safety. Crossing the border was a momentous act. Breaching the border became a spur, and something to aim towards for those who had lost all motivation, and is remembered in a remarkably similar way in refugee accounts. One convoy pitched camp 'with much more cheer than usual' on an evening when they knew that the border of Pakistan was only 50 kilometres away.[62] On crossing into India at the Wagah border post another convoy was momentarily united in relief as people called out, '*Bharat Mata Ki Jai*' (Long Live Mother India). In 1947, Kuldip Nayar, who later became a distinguished Indian journalist and parliamentarian, crossed at the Wagah border post on foot, on his long and painful journey from Sialkot to India, and remembered that there was nothing there on the windswept Punjabi plain, just a solitary Indian flag flying on a wooden pole and some overturned drums, partly painted white, partly black. 'And I just crossed. Nobody checked to see if I had any documents, nothing.'[63]

Ironically, those who had been living with ambiguous and multivalent ideas of 'Pakistan' 'India' and 'Freedom' were being remade into loyal citizens. Passengers arriving by boat at the port of Karachi cried '*Allah-O-Akbar*' when they first sighted the unfamiliar Pakistani coastline. 'The engine driver started blowing the whistle,' Khushwant Singh writes in his fictional but evocative novel of the time, as a train steams through the Punjabi farmland, 'and continued blowing till he had passed Mano Majra station. It was an expression of relief that they were out of Pakistan and into India.'[64] Nasreen Azhar, a

Pakistani feminist, was a child when she crossed the border into Pakistan on her journey from the imperial hill station of Simla, and similarly remembered 'we felt very safe because we arrived in Multan and it was the day after Bakr Id . . . and people were sacrificing goats openly . . . people were being Muslim openly, so that was a very wonderful feeling.'[65] Crossing into the new country was marked with its own symbolic significance.

Certainly, some of the new arrivals, as elsewhere in the subcontinent, were met with hospitality. Arrangements were made along the tracks and at stations to greet Pakistani clerical staff passing through their new home – at Bahawalpur, 'to cheer them on their way and offer them refreshments'.[66] The Mayor of Lahore later claimed that the inhabitants of the city baked *naan* bread for the displaced and gave 'a right royal reception to the newcomers. Cauldrons of rice could be seen cooking all over the place for distribution among the refugees.' Radio appeals were broadcast for donations for the hungry and shopkeepers, housewives and bakers delivered food parcels to the refugee camps.[67] In Delhi, the local population baked 280 *maunds* of chapattis when news spread of two stranded and starving foot convoys, one of 30,000 people and one of 60,000, moving southwards from Punjab, and the Indian Air Force airlifted the food parcels to the refugees the following morning.[68] Newspapers in Punjab demanded charity from the prosperous and, in the language of the London Blitz, asked, 'Have you done your bit?' In all these ways, the refugees were being encouraged to see themselves as welcome citizens of either India or Pakistan, to submerge their other identities and to embrace their new nationality unreservedly.

It is doubly ironic then, that, taken as a whole, the refugees themselves completely rejected any simplistic affinity with their new national governments. They were experiencing unimaginable hardships and daily difficulties; their experiences were entirely at odds with the lip-service and promises of the politicians; and there were manifold political problems caused by the difficulties of assimilating new refugees at the crux of Independence. In reality, a definite tension was already emerging between the new national characteristics that were being imposed from on high, and the sub-identities of region, caste, class and community. Fleeting moments of *imagined* unity and camaraderie were almost immediately undercut by the *real* experience of the refugees and migrants.

The ordeal of the refugees on the trains did not end when they reached the inhumanly packed platforms of their new homelands in Delhi, Calcutta, Lahore or Amritsar, and their experiences clashed with the language of national solidarity. Greeted by scenes of misery, they had to pick their way through the crowds camped on the railway station concourse, cramped with their ragged belongings, lying or sitting in every available space. Pimps and brothel owners, gang leaders and paedophiles were not easily distinguishable from legitimate refugee camp workers who came to collect the new arrivals, and women and children were bewildered by offers of adoption, marriage or positions as domestic servants. 'All these brothel people used to stand at the platform trying to grab them, and we had to make sure that they are not taken away,' remembered Khorshed Mehta, a voluntary worker who looked after distraught women arriving at New Delhi's main railway terminus in 1947.[69] Able-bodied young men and united families were at a distinct advantage, as they could elbow their way to the front of queues, find information and watch each other's luggage while the frail, single women and the orphaned young were the most vulnerable. The weakest ended up in camps.

Refugee camps were ubiquitous and the crisis rippled out across the rest of the subcontinent. It could not possibly be contained in two corners of the former British India. The Indian government constructed more than half its camps outside Punjab, including thirty-two in the Bombay Presidency and even three in the most southern state, Madras. The largest and most notorious camp in India, Kurukshetra, was a proto-city, built over nine square miles in East Punjab and housing over a quarter of a million refugees. Hospitals and kitchens were established, cholera inoculations and cooked food were distributed. And yet, despite the war footing of the operation and the organised dispersal of quilts and tents, lentils, rice and flour, the camp buckled under the weight of the sheer numbers of people still moving across the border. Kurukshetra grew ten times in size in just six weeks from mid-October to the end of November 1947. Sometimes as many as 25,000 people would arrive, unanticipated, in the middle of the night – and even receiving them and guiding them to a suitable space was a difficult task because of the shortage of electric lighting. The Indian government resettled some as far away as the remote Andaman and Nicobar archipelago.

By the end of 1947 in South Asia there were perhaps three million refugees in refugee camps; over a million in the Pakistani camps of West Punjab alone.[70] The camps ranged from small temporarily improvised shelters near the refugees' own homes where people collected together for safety – in schools, temples, gurdwaras, mosques and municipal buildings – to vast state-run establishments which, in some cases, have not been dismantled to the present day. Some camps continued to exist in new incarnations in the 1950s. In Punjab many camps were wound up and dispersed within several years of Partition or deliberately transformed into more substantial housing colonies.

In the western provinces, canvas was gradually replaced by bricks and mortar and refugee colonies emerged from the ashes of the camps. But in West Bengal, the phraseology of 'camps' does not do justice to the enormity of social dislocation and the scale of change instigated by the arrival of Bengalis from the east.

The refugees were frequently exposed to bullying, extortion and profiteering by each other and by opportunists in their new homelands. Although organised refugee camps may have provided shelter and protection from sectarian warfare, other dangers lurked within them. The sanitary conditions beggared belief and cholera broke out in numerous Punjabi districts, with particularly bad epidemics in Sheikhupura, Ferozepore and Lahore districts, while dysentery and smallpox also killed hundreds. Intimidating figures established themselves as camp leaders and preyed on the vulnerable by extorting money or running protection rackets. In Jullundur, people calling themselves 'Barrack Commandants' were organising the seizure of food from others. 'I was pained to find that a certain section of evacuees grab the share of other less resourceful evacuees and sell it at exorbitant prices,' reported one eyewitness.[71] Unsurprisingly, people tended to try and re-establish their own caste and community networks and bunched together – ideally with members of their old villages or, if this was not possible, at least with people of their own caste. There was safety in numbers. Families strung up ragged sheets and bits of cloth to separate themselves from those around them. Preserving old hierarchies and ideas of ritual purity was a struggle and it was impossible to avoid sharing space with other, less desirable, castes. Sanitation was poor, old customs went unobserved and taboos were broken.

In particular, Partition made the long-maintained seclusion of daughters unsustainable, and young people – especially those who stayed in the camps for months or years – struck up liaisons and affairs. Social workers arranged abortions for women, some of whom had been assaulted during the Partition violence or molested in the camps, but some of whom had illicit affairs and consensual relationships facilitated by the extreme and unusual conditions of the time. Despite all this, refugees started the long journey to recovery and adjusted to their new lives – that would never be the same again.

* * *

Begum Anis Kidwai was forty-five years old in 1947 and had, until that year, lived the genteel life of a woman born into a privileged and political North Indian family. The family staunchly backed the Congress, and her brother-in-law was a leading Congress politician. They moved in a broad social circle, were friendly with the Nehrus, and the extended family lived in a rambling house around a courtyard in the heart of the city of Lucknow. Kidwai opposed the Muslim League and she had worked for the Congress in the 1946 elections. In the autumn months of 1947 her life changed for ever as the violence of Partition started to surround her. Stuck in Lucknow, in September she started to worry intensely about her husband, Shafi, who was working in another part of the country, in the hills of Mussoorie, several hours away. As a civil servant he was charged with running the local municipal board, a run-of-the-mill post in the civil service which would normally have involved dealing with problems of sanitation and food supply. But conditions in Mussoorie were deteriorating and his letters, which were still arriving in the post, were beginning to show the signs of strain in the town. He was due back in Lucknow towards the end of September but postponed his return. He had started working with the Punjabi refugees who poured into the hill station, needing relief and shelter.

Before long, attacks on the local Muslim population in Mussoorie started. 'While I am writing to you,' Shafi wrote to his wife, a few days later, 'I hear the din of the populace down below, the sounds of firing and the shrieks and wails of the victims. Houses and shops are on fire, shops are being looted and the police is watching the spectacle. This is happening in broad daylight.' Soon he was informing her that the telegraph lines had been cut. 'Both the telephone and telegraph are useless.' In Lucknow, meanwhile, Anis Kidwai fretted about her husband's security, and agonised about whether to try and catch a train to go and join him.

As he was a Muslim, albeit one who had worked against the League, it was an unspoken fear that Shafi was in great danger now as he was living and working in a town where the Muslims were a small community, and there was a risk that he might be targeted. 'You should not worry about me,' he instructed his wife sanguinely. 'Despite the rain, I am attending the office except for one day a week.' But within a few days, anxiety had entered his letters again. 'I used to listen to the news on the radio. But for three days, the radio has also stopped. I do not know why I cannot telephone Pantji [the Chief Minister] nor talk to my brother on the phone.' There were stories of hate-mail and threats; he acquired police protection. Anis was in a paroxysm of anxiety by this time, and tried to encourage him to leave and return to the family. In one of his last letters to her, he wrote, 'Anis, do not weaken me. Let the riots be over then I will tell the truth to everybody. Otherwise, whatever be my fate, only pray to God that I may remain firm of step.' On 18 October, between nine and ten in the morning he was stabbed to death on his way to work at the municipal office.[72] Anis Kidwai's life now took a new turn, as with great moral courage she plunged herself into social work; she moved to Delhi and began, at the behest of Gandhi, to work in the refugee camps, where she dedicated herself to the service of destitute women. Anis Kidwai's story is unique, more especially because she kept a lyrical and convincing account of her difficult days in 1947. It does provide a sense of how couples, families and individuals, far from the Punjabi centres of the worst devastation, became entangled in Partition's miseries. It also suggests how social norms had collapsed and how far the primacy of religious labelling had spread.

The 3 June plan had evidently gone catastrophically wrong. As people made the tortuous transition from subjects of the British Raj to citizens of two free states, countless communities got swept up in the chaos and panic. The violence, and its aftermath, glued people together, temporarily at least, in a new spirit of nationalism. But this was crisscrossed with deeper confusions and anger about the place of class, caste, language and religion in public life. There was no simple blueprint for becoming an Indian or a Pakistani. One thing people could agree on, though, was that the 'other' state was rapidly looking like an adversary, or even an enemy. Nationalist politics had collapsed into two national tragedies.

9

Bitter Legacies

On the evening of 3 January 1948 Delhi's Superintendent of Police was making security arrangements for Gandhi's imminent arrival when he was summoned by another superintendent and they both rushed to Phatak Habash Khan, a Muslim district of the city. He was astonished by the intensity of the scene that greeted him. Refugees had illegally taken possession of houses that had previously been owned by Muslims and were refusing to vacate them. Most striking of all was the sight of hundreds of women standing at the front of the crowd who steadfastly refused to budge. 'Police had to face great difficulty in getting the houses vacated,' the police chief wrote, 'as they were the target of sallies from women'. The police turned to tear gas to disperse the crowd. Despite this, the following morning the men and women had reassembled. Once again the refugees picketed the main gate to the colony and continued to try and force their way into the houses for five hours or so. 'The number of women was about one hundred, and thousands of men refugees were backing them . . . Police applied all sorts of tactics to disperse the crowd but in vain.' Eventually they once again resorted to tear gas and the anxious superintendent appealed to the government, saying that the men and women were determined to occupy the houses and that there would be no peace in the city until a solution was found to the situation.[1]

The angry resolve of refugee women to take possession of homes for themselves and their families provides a rare glimpse not only of the frustration of refugees – male and female – and their determination to remake their lives but also of the political risks of the situation. As their demands went unmet and ambivalent feelings about their new national status arose, in some cases refugees turned away from central government towards other political groups who championed their cause.

Picking up the pieces

In the three years after Independence, India and Pakistan both faced relentless and protracted difficulties because of the refugee crisis. The South Asian political leadership did not yet have power firmly in its grip. Nether state had, as yet, a fully functioning military, clearly consolidated territory or smoothly functioning parliament. In this grey transition zone between regimes, the movement by so many people began to threaten the very existence of Pakistan and menaced the development aspirations of the Indian state, as government agencies struggled to cope with the incessant, desperate demands that they provide shelter, sustenance and protection for the displaced.

To make matters worse, in Calcutta, and Bengal more generally, the crisis was only just beginning. Bengalis from East Pakistan started to arrive in small groups as they pulled into train stations in Calcutta or made their way across in precarious, packed boats: this movement was slower and, superficially, less dramatically violent. Nonetheless it marked the emergence of a refugee culture that has never ceased to be a feature of the city's life. Twelve thousand people shifted to West Bengal every day in 1948 from East Pakistan, and the camps themselves could only accommodate a fraction of the numbers so that hundreds of thousands poured on to the streets, railway platforms and into squatters' colonies instead.

On the two sides of the subcontinent – in the east and the west – the complications of the refugee movements were distinctive and there was no catch-all solution to 'refugee rehabilitation', a new and unrefined government responsibility, which had to be managed locally and through a process of trial and error. The problem was daunting. The two nation states consolidated themselves in the shadow of Partition. 'This matter of refugees continues to be practically the only topic of discussion here. Newspapers are full with statements and counter-statements,' the exasperated Governor of West Bengal told the Indian government in 1948.[2] In the early 1950s, numerous political controversies turned on the vexed question of 'refugee rehabilitation' and news about refugees peppered the newspapers well into the post-Independence era. Partition was not a discrete event, rapidly dispensed with in 1947, but had, and has, ongoing repercussions in South Asia.

To add to their difficulties, the two new governments had to solve the crisis almost entirely alone, with the international community barely involved. The International Committee of the Red Cross stood on the brink of insolvency and had actually closed its delegation in India in February 1947. Europe turned inward as it attempted to heal its war wounds and to solve its own post-war refugee crisis. In December 1947 the Red Cross sent a fact-finding mission to India and Pakistan, which pessimistically reported back that the Partition crisis was 'so enormous' that it was beyond the scope of the international Red Cross's capability.[3]

Christian missionaries and small foreign organisations already operating in the subcontinent, such as the Quakers and the National Christian Council of India, ran relief operations alongside local volunteers from at least fifteen different organisations, from the Scouts and Guides to the YMCA and St John's Ambulance. This was only a drop in the ocean. There were no tried and tested responses to a mammoth disaster like this. Partition happened too early in the century to benefit from any of the post-war global institutions such as the United Nations High Commission for Refugees, which was established in 1950. The international tensions emerging between India and Pakistan meant they preferred to act independently; both states shied away from the United Nations Refugee Convention which was passed in 1951 and, to date, neither has ratified it. Through choice and circumstance, both states had to deal with their crisis alone.

Nor were regional governments much help. Overstretched provincial ministries across India and Pakistan dug in their heels and tried to resist taking responsibility for refugees. Across South Asia the provincial governments panicked at the prospect of absorbing trainloads of refugees, especially at a time of endemic food shortages and fragile social peace. They had to be cajoled, bribed and ordered to take responsibility for quotas of displaced. The UP state government steadfastly resisted the arrival of refugees in 1947 and attempted to seal the state borders. In Gujarat, the government announced that it would not be giving any aid to itinerant Gujarati traders coming 'home' from areas that now lay in Pakistan, although many of them had been away from Gujarat for generations. After Independence, non-Muslim Sindis continued to land in Bombay harbour after crossing the Arabian Sea by boat, but when the Bombay government lobbied against this, Nehru dejectedly concluded that 'there is no help for it' and instructed the ministry to prepare to receive more boatloads of displaced people.[4] On the other side of the country the Chief Minister of Assam, less than a year after Partition, was reporting such tensions in local towns – where Bengali refugees were camped out – that he was already playing his most serious trump card against the centre: provincial separatism.[5]

These conflicts reached fever pitch in Sind where dislocation to the local economy caused by Partition and conflicts between old local Sindi stalwarts and patriotic Pakistani refugees became controversial from the earliest days of

Independence. Pro-refugee papers such as *Dawn* waged a campaign of resistance to what was regarded as the Sind government's parochial or 'anti-national' stance while, jealous of their city's autonomy and culture, Sindis resisted Karachi's transformation into a national capital under centralised control. This tension has existed to the present day.[6]

Regardless, the Indian and Pakistani governments overcame the resistance put up by their regional ministries to receiving refugees. They imposed their own formulation of the crisis as a 'national problem', boosting political centralisation and enhancing their own executive powers in the process. In their desperate desire to wind up the camps, ministers turned a blind eye to refugee preferences and regional jingoism, and whole groups of refugee peasants were arbitrarily selected for dispersal to regions where they could not speak the local language and had no familiarity with crop patterns, cultural practices or weather conditions.

At first, relief efforts were completely improvised; operating from their old party headquarters Congress Party workers, Muslim League volunteers and others handed out blankets and food, built temporary shelters, and administered medicines and emergency relief to people in camps and on the streets. By the end of 1947, refugees were dying of cold on the roadside in Lahore, where the mercury dropped to almost freezing point in mid-December; a journalist of the *Pakistan Times* reported the scenes:

> After midnight on Wednesday I accompanied the Bait-ul-Mal workers on their 'mercy round' in the city in a truck loaded with *razais* [quilted blankets] and other woollen stuff. We rattled through the wide, empty streets and halted near the Braganza Hotel, outside the railway station, where one can generally find hundreds of homeless people huddled up together for the night. We debussed, carrying bundles of *razais*, and fanned out into different directions for their distribution.
>
> As we approached the place we heard subdued groans that escaped hundreds of lips as the slashing, icy cold wind cut into their limbs. They were lying huddled together with their legs drawn up to their bellies to have some warmth. As we approached them we saw that a fairly large number had only one cotton *khais* [shawl] to cover them and the rest had a thin *razai* or a blanket to warm them up. Many mothers were leaning over their children to protect them against the biting cold. Many others blew at the dying embers of a *chilam* [hashish pipe] and toasted their hands at the glow. Men, women and children were coughing and sneezing and suckling babes were crying with cold. That night we visited many places and distrib-

uted about 250 *razais* and some 100 blankets, a number which is hopelessly inadequate to meet the present requirements.[7]

As the sheer magnitude of the crisis sank in, in the autumn of 1947 India and Pakistan launched vast and unprecedented relief operations. Both states set up full-blown ministries in September to deal exclusively with the refugee crisis. They had to respond to the whole spectrum of human needs. Refugees badly needed basic essentials as well as everything with which to start a new life, from clothing, food rations and manufacturing materials to loans, accommodation and bank accounts. Some needed proof of identity or qualifications. Both governments had already lost millions of rupees because of unharvested, rotten crops, the closure of banks and shops and disruption to national and international trade. The Indian central government estimated that it spent 940,078 million rupees between 1947 and 1951 on the relief effort. This staggering amount was surely equalled in Pakistan, where the Walton refugee camps in Lahore alone cost 30,000 rupees per day to keep running. A special refugee tax, which stayed in place until the 1950s, was surcharged to existing taxes; Pakistani train travellers even paid a refugee supplement that was added to the standard cost of their railway ticket. In short, there was a major and prolonged wrench to the economy. Centralised planning was seen as one way of reasserting control over the crisis.

The refugees inundated the government with their demands: the illiterate employed letter-writers or a caste or community association to write for them, and signed with poignant indigo thumbprints; these became paper records of personal suffering as people described precisely what had happened to them, listed the possessions and land they had lost, as well as, not infrequently, providing the names and addresses of the attackers when they were known to the victims. One refugee from the NWFP who had worked for the Congress Party but now found himself in North India, penniless and unrecognised by the local politicians, wrote, 'I am of 56 [years] and forcibly exiled from my home I am wandering disappointed. Will you kindly advise me what to do and where to [go] in this critical moment of my life.' [8] Others were in desperate need of medication or wanted to find their children or other family members. State banks loaned former businessmen and entrepreneurs money to found factories so they could tentatively resume business. Special quotas were set aside to ensure that refugees had priority access to government jobs and university places.

These state-sponsored efforts compared well with the apathetic approach of the British colonial state in the face of disaster, as seen during the Bengal famine of 1943, and meshed with the general swing towards state-centred policies favoured by many in both countries at the time. It was the age of the expert bureaucrat and economic specialist, as India and Pakistan stood on the cusp of a new age. In this light, men such as the Indian Planning Commission supremo, P.C. Mahalanobis, argued that Partition could even be regarded as an opportunity if refugees who were part of the old, unmodernised, agricultural order could become industrial workers, working on large public works projects and in the giant factories of the future envisioned in the five-year plans. 'The expansion of the national economy initiated under the two Five Year Plans by itself,' one government pamphlet commented reassuringly, 'provides numerous opportunities for rehabilitation of displaced persons possessing initiative and enterprise.'[9] Partition had to be integrated, in government eyes, into the bigger story of nation-building.

Beginning a new life

Extensive government intervention touched the lives of large numbers of refugees who benefited from state-backed plans, schemes and novel initiatives. In both countries, the state paid for the construction of schools, dispensaries, houses and workshops. The government created job centres, employed refugees in public works, cleared land in forested areas to make space for displaced accommodation, built training centres to teach women skills such as soap-making and embroidery, re-trained men as mechanics, carpenters, spinners, paper-makers, shoemakers and printers. Orphans and widows were housed in welfare homes and young girls with no families to provide for them even had their marriages arranged by the state, which literally assumed a parental role: 'A Marriage Bureau has been organized to put displaced men and women in touch with each other,' reported another of the many government-produced pamphlets outlining the state's diverse attempts to help the refugees. 'As soon as news about its establishment was published, applications from eligible men began to pour in.' In some cases the state stepped into parental shoes, providing small gifts, clothes and money as dowry.[10]

Nevertheless, the actual experiences of the refugees stood at odds with grand public rhetoric about refugee rehabilitation. The best schemes favoured the 'hard-working', the middle class and the literate.[11] These were the people who were allocated the best new accommodation or received the biggest loans. Middle-class refugees did not act as one undifferentiated, victimised mass but looked after their own kith and kin and organised quickly along these lines. The Frontier and Punjab Riot Sufferer Committee requested housing colonies near business centres for 'the deserving and the middle class men from the NWFP', while the Pakistan Sufferers Cooperative Housing Society was open only to Hindu and Sikh government servants and businessmen, and membership was restricted to refugees of 'good character and sound mind'.[12]

Certainly, Partition was indiscriminate in its cruelty at times; all kinds of people could find themselves in wretched conditions. But there is no doubt that, rather then starting completely from scratch, those who already had education, contacts and status were, on the whole, eventually able to ease themselves into a new, and sometimes more profitable, lifestyle by lobbying for jobs, gaining access to the most desirable vacated properties and extracting government loans, while the poor were the ones who suffered forced resettlement, or who languished forgotten for decades in displaced person homes, camps and squatters' colonies. Professional networks, deference to one's status and accent or simply the ability to understand and act upon news on the information grapevine gave elites a head start in recovering from Partition. In the scramble for access to compensation, as Ravinder Kaur has shown, the richer refugees already had inbuilt advantages, as they could read the lengthy paperwork, and knew how to 'break the codes that the state had invented' while those who had managed to transfer at least a few of their savings could use this to smooth their path. Partition did not completely shatter the social pecking order.[13]

The refugees lobbied for improved food and accommodation and used the tools of Gandhian *satyagraha*, or non violent resistance, to their own advantage long after 1947. Sit-ins, strikes and peaceful protest methods, acquired and honed during the nationalist struggle, were now turned against the new post-colonial governments. In Durgapur near Jaipur, part of the refugee camp was burned by fire in 1949 and seven hundred refugees started to protest at their conditions. A group attempted to travel to the provincial government ministry to stage a protest but when these plans were thwarted, after initially refusing to alight from the train, they sat down on the railway tracks, causing delays up and down the line. Government impatience could be lethal, however: in this instance, the Ministry for Refugee Rehabilitation itself sanctioned police firing on the group.[14]

Other refugee groups besieged the homes of national leaders and rejected the housing that was offered to them. Sukh Ram, a refugee from the NWFP living in the nascent city of Faridabad, led a hunger strike against the proposal to house his community in mud huts. 'The displaced persons thought mud huts was a mad idea . . . they argued, "Look, after all, the mud-huts are for our convenience . . . we do not want them. Do not waste precious rupees. Please stop."'15 Handouts and gifts, sanctimoniously celebrated in the official literature of the Indian and Pakistani governments, were not always received with unalloyed delight and a rare window on to the feelings of a group of poor Punjabi women, who were being taught new crafts at a women's 'industrial home', suggests that they could see the potential flaws in rehabilitation schemes. 'These hardy woman [*sic*] of West Punjab are ready to take up any sort of job from needles to spade without any grudge,' wrote the principal of the institution, 'but there are occasions for them to feel down hearted when they forecast their future covered with gloom and blackness. They sometimes come and ask me "Do tell us how are we to settle up by learning Weaving or Sports Goods Making? Where are we to get so much equipment from so as to start this trade? Is it not wastage of Government money and woman power to teach us a craft which we can not take up in future?"'16 The despondency and common sense of these faceless women is palpable in this report.

Refugees who had lived in towns before Partition wanted to stay in city centres – even if this meant living in slum-like conditions – because it was here that they could hope to make a reasonable living, and ambitious but naïve government schemes to house refugees on bleak suburban outskirts or in the rural wilderness of cleared jungle areas resulted in expensive losses to the treasury. When twenty-one families were ordered to move to Kashipur in Uttar Pradesh in 1951, they elected two nominees of the families to go and inspect the land first. 'These refugees are not inclined to accept the offer of land in village Kesri-Ganeshpur,' the District Magistrate tactfully informed the Ministry of Relief and Rehabilitation, after the refugees had visited the spot. 'It shall be much appreciated if they are given some other land in Kashipur area where there is no threat of wild animals so that they may be asked to shift from Gandhinagar.'17

Others protested when the state reneged on promises, or started asking for rent. A group of refugees in a housing scheme at Netaji Nagar in Agra were ordered to start paying rent on huts which they had been allocated. The refugees reacted with fury, calling it a 'hoax played on refugees' and 'nothing short of high handedness'. The president of their colony wrote to the government, describing the huts in which the refugees were living:

> . . . bamboo walls with hardly half an inch coat of mud and with roof of galvanised sheets . . . Mostly this mud coat has also vanished away and one can see inside the room from bamboo walls . . . In summer this tin roof becomes very hot to such an extent that none can live in the said alleged

house and due to this heat, many suffer from eyes trouble and many other diseases and income earned by the occupants is wholly spent on medicines. In winter hard and fast winds enter these rooms from pores and there is extreme cold. Not only this, but there is no privacy for night sleeping ... There is neither kitchen nor bath room.[18]

Wantonly sacrificed to the demands of making two new nations in 1947, the refugees often felt disgusted and abandoned by a callous state, which had promised them the moon and given them, in the words of the Urdu poet Faiz Ahmed Faiz, a 'leprous daybreak' instead.

Paying the price

Nonetheless, as refugees arrived in India and Pakistan they were encouraged to see themselves in a new light – to set aside their hardships momentarily and to appreciate that they were now, after all, independent citizens of free countries. Refugees were repeatedly told that they were now 'Indian' or 'Pakistani' and that they should rejoice in spite of their shattered lives. Pakistan was promoted as a safe homeland from violence and Jinnah was depicted as the refugees' saviour. The victims of Partition violence were called *shahids* and bathed in the language of martyrdom. Partition quickly became repackaged as a war of liberation. The West Punjab government lost no time in engraving a stone plaque and dedicating it, 'To every Mussalman man woman and child who fought suffered and won the first battle for Pakistan through the Punjab Muslim League 1947.'[19]

When Jinnah visited camps in Lahore in November 1947, refugees lined the route and shouted League slogans enthusiastically. An old man approached Jinnah and, at least according to newspaper reports, 'thanked him for establishing Pakistan where they could live safely and prosper'.[20] Officials used every opportunity they could to boost national morale in the camps. On Jinnah's birthday in December 1947, after the Friday prayers, the refugees were entertained with a programme of poetry recitals, volunteers handed out sweets, games were organised for the children and the camp was lit up with bright lights. When the Lahore camps were disbanded the following year, and some of these same refugees were forcibly resettled in other Pakistani provinces, often against their wishes, the trains taking them to their new destinations pulled out of Lahore station to the sound of brass bands playing the national anthem, while hired hands waved Pakistani flags along the platforms.

These efforts could not paper over the sheer desperation of the refugees, however. A visitor to the Walton camps in Lahore found that 'a major portion' of the refugees were 'complaining about the mismanagement in respect of food, supplies, sanitation and medical aid'.[21] There were, as in India, fears of anti-government insurrection, bread riots and fighting between local people and refugees who had moved into their space. Jinnah made a surprise visit to the camps in Karachi in a stage-managed attempt to boost national feeling in September 1947. Even the patriotic journalist of the *Pakistan Times* could not disguise the contradictions of the situation: 'The refugees were greatly cheered by the visit but there were two poignant moments when a former wealthy merchant now destitute broke down in relating the hardships he and his family had undergone, and a villager whose family had been wiped out, sobbed uncontrollably.'[22]

In India, the propaganda may have been more nuanced but the Congress was similarly anxious about the loyalty of the refugees and the wider public to the Congress government. In northern India, the Hindu Right, particularly the RSS and the Hindu Mahasabha, which had played such a provocative role in the months leading up to Partition, and had been hand in glove with violent rioters all along, now swung firmly behind the refugee cause. Working with refugees was a direct way in which members of the Mahasabha and the RSS could challenge the power of the government, and these groups swiftly stepped in to fulfil social service functions that the state was woefully unable to provide. The Mahasabha established an All-India Hindu Refugees Committee immediately after Partition. In Delhi the RSS operated four large refugee camps and RSS members later recalled the time with nostalgia: 'they had a sense of actively participating in a great event in which their services were both demanded and appreciated,'[23] while they could simultaneously spread their political ideology. In Bengal, on the other side of the country, and in stark ideological contrast, the CPI and leftist groups gradually took the lead in organising the refugees, triggering mass protests and land occupations in the 1950s. This provided the building blocks for the communists' electoral success in the region into the late twentieth century. In Pakistan, similarly, the Jam 'at-i Islami was running a major refugee camp in Islamiyah Park in Lahore, and their leader, Maulana Mawdudi, who was himself living under canvas in the park at the time, having arrived from Delhi in July by truck, made a powerful public call for volunteers 'gifted with fellow-feeling, diligence, sincerity of purpose and honesty of work'.[24] The Jam 'at-i Islami quickly responded to the crisis, by burying unclaimed dead bodies, collecting funds and operating camps, doling out food and medicine and cleaning refuse, and is estimated to have helped over one-and-a-half million *Muhajirs* over the subsequent weeks and months. A small but vociferous core of grateful refugees became rank-and-file supporters and these efforts paid political dividends in future decades.

Domestically, the overwhelming concern for both the League and Congress leaders after 1947 was the internal threat posed by the refugee crisis to their political leadership. There was a serious risk that their own parties might be ripped apart by differences of opinion over refugee rehabilitation. In Pakistan, the League's treatment of refugees was soon causing headaches for the leading national party, which feared for its electoral future in the face of such a human catastrophe. The Governor of West Punjab was before long reporting on refugee demonstrations against the government in which the treacherous slogan '*Pakistan Murdabad*', Death to Pakistan, was shouted, and he told Jinnah that 'I am told that Shaukat [Shaukat Hyat Khan, Minister for Revenue] is afraid to show his face in the Muslim refugee camp here.'[25] In the context of increasingly vocal refugee restlessness, showing sensitivity to the refugees was a vote-winner, as well as a moral responsibility. The Refugee Minister of West Punjab, Mian Iftikhar-ud-Din, demanded land redistribution as a solution to land shortages for the displaced. When his plan was roundly rejected by the landowning political elite in his own province, he resigned, exposing deep fissures between the organisational and cabinet-level wings of the provincial League. Another dominant Punjabi politician, the Khan of Mamdot, the largest landowner in undivided Punjab, was shorn of constituents after Partition as he had lost his extensive farmlands that lay on the Indian side. Pragmatically, he tried to rebuild his power base and cultivated refugees as his new followers while the euphemistically named Allotment Revising Committee was his personal creation; it lacked official sanction but was used to siphon off abandoned properties and cars in Lahore for his followers and former tenants.[26]

Dealing with the refugee crisis opened up all sorts of avenues for corruption and profiteering, while also exposing deep cracks in the party-political ideological outlook – cracks which had been pasted over while the demand to create Pakistan was foremost in the leadership's mind. It is little surprise in the face of such extensive difficulties that one year after Independence Jinnah announced that 'a grave emergency has arisen and exists in Pakistan' and declared a state of emergency that gave the centre heightened powers over the provinces, enabling bureaucrats and administrators to rein in the politicians. In Pakistan, then, the Partition refugee crisis undermined the development of democratic politics and shook the unsteady foundations of the state.

In India, the crisis was just as acute, especially as there was, of course, still a large Muslim population living throughout the country. Controversy about how best to respond to the refugee crisis rocked the inner workings of the Congress Party. Nehru and Gandhi persistently reiterated the need to protect Muslims, to retain them in the country and to prevent their mass ejection from India. As Nehru told a group of Muslim labourers in Delhi, 'As long as I am at the helm of affairs India will not become a Hindu state.'[27] Barbed wire was fixed up in Muslim Sufi shrines and mosques, at Dargah Hazrat Nizamuddin Aulia and Dargah Hazrat Qutbuddin Chisti among others, and guards shooed away looters. Gandhi imperilled his life by fasting for peace and reconciliation in 1948. During Gandhi's fast, the government swung behind the peace effort, even franking envelopes sent by post with slogans urging social reconciliation. 'Communal Harmony will save Gandhiji', the messages declared and, 'It is only through communal unity that Gandhiji can survive'. The crux of the matter was keeping the minorities' faith in the state's ability to protect them.

Yet support for the refugee cause was strident within sections of Congress and was a touchpaper for broader ideas about the ideological tilt of the Indian state. It was a struggle between Nehru's secular ideal and a brand of Hindu-infused nationalism. The refugee cause, along with the stoppage of cow slaughter and the reconversion of mosques to Hindu temples, became a subject of mass protest. Many walls in Delhi and Uttar Pradesh were covered with graffiti demanding immediate abolition of cow slaughter, and these protests interlocked with deep anger about the creation of Pakistan, and the Congress's acquiescence to Partition. After Partition, any Muslim could be charged with being a 'Pakistani' and suspicions fell in a McCarthyite manner on fifth columnists, spies and those who displayed dubious commitment to the national interest. Speeches called for proof of loyalty. Large workshops of Muslim smiths or craftsmen were disbanded as their Hindu suppliers stopped advancing indispensable credit or materials, worried, they claimed, that the Muslim artisans would abscond to Pakistan without paying. By January 1948 the atmosphere had deteriorated alarmingly, and India's future as a secular state, and as a place with equal rights for all, looked uncertain.

Both the Indian and Pakistani governments worried about the damage caused to their international image by the crisis, especially as the relationship between the two new nations deteriorated. This was part of the crude process of making the two nation states. Effective rehabilitation was a moral duty but also a point of pride and nationalistic validation. Nehru, for instance, was anxious about international press coverage of the refugee camps in Delhi, and

Dr Mookerjee, a leading Mahasabha politician, suggested that foreign press correspondents should be banned from photographing the camps.[28] 'You might have seen Chandni Chowk is hardly passable because all the pavements and part of the roads are blocked by refugee stores,' Nehru complained, of one of Delhi's main thoroughfares a year after Partition.[29] The overspill of refugees on to the streets of the national capitals marred the leader's long-envisaged dreams of freedom, and soiled the international image of the new nation states in the eyes of the rest of the world. But it was the coverage of abducted and traumatised women about which both governments were hypersensitive. As so often happens, debate over the status of women became the focal point of much deeper anxieties.

During an Iranian dignitary's tour of Pakistan, a group of recovered abducted women arrived in a truck from a camp in East Punjab and were welcomed by villagers who wept and created a major scene. 'The whole show was so staged as to create an impression of Pakistan having recovered these women at great risk and cost,' complained the Indian Deputy High Commissioner who was stationed in Lahore, claiming that the entire situation had been faked: 'Villagers had been hired to act as fathers and relatives of the recovered women and immediately on arrival of the women very touching scenes of reunion were staged before the *Alama* [an Iranian scholar], which brought tears to his eyes.' It was feared that 'the *Alama* is carrying back with him deep impressions of Pakistani Muslims having suffered untold horrors at the hands of Hindus and Sikhs'.[30] In this international war of words and deeds, the Indian government lashed back, and Iran was notified about the stunt, while Patel suggested that pamphlets were compiled of the most 'glaring, barefaced and shameful pieces of propaganda by Pakistan' to be circulated to the foreign press under titles such as 'How Pakistan lies' or 'How Pakistan vilifies'.[31] Other tactics were for both sides to play down news of local Hindu–Muslim–Sikh violence, to limit news of fresh bouts of refugee departures (and to attribute these to economic causes alone), to criticise the provision made in exit camps for departing refugees and to emphasise state complicity in any poor treatment of the other country's minorities.

This was particularly the case with the restoration of abducted women initiated by both governments and nationalistic point-scoring trumped any consideration of refugee sensibility. The needs and rights of the refugees were overridden by nationalistic self-righteousness. Some women had reconciled themselves to a new life with their abductor. They were able, little by little, to piece together some form of normality, to find happiness in the arrival of

children or to adjust and bury their memories of life before 1947. The fortunate ones may even have found love. Women whose lives to date had already
been severely controlled by social values found that any small freedoms and
hard-won contentment that they had forged over the years – through family
life, routine and security – could be rebuilt. For some poor women, who had
never known control over their own lives and had always gone hungry, a life
in a more prosperous home or away from a violent or abusive husband could
bring some consolation. But now, to add to their miseries, the state intervened
and forcibly collected them by truck to repatriate them.

India and Pakistan now looked to each other as an inverted mirror image.
In India, the visible presence of mutilated and suffering refugees was viewed
as a manifestation of Partition's callousness, which was conflated with
Pakistan's creation, while in Pakistan, the incoming refugees and those who
died in Partition violence were represented as sacrificial martyrs to the
Pakistani national cause. So refugees were important citizens in the eyes of the
brand new post-colonial states which needed, after Independence, to account
for and justify the refugees' presence, assimilate and assuage them. Their
suffering and experiences were woven into the fabric of national history that
was constructed around the events that had occurred. 'We crossed a river of
blood to achieve independence . . .' wrote one future President of Pakistan.
'People were uprooted and driven like millions of dry leaves by a turbulent
gust of fanaticism and blind passion.'[32] Indian prose could be equally florid
and a government-produced pamphlet told how 'The people were afflicted
with sufferings and agony more terrible than has ever fallen to the lot of
human beings . . . This has been a legacy of insensate outburst of communal
frenzy, generated by the pernicious Two-Nation theory and its attendant cult
of hate.'[33]

Murder of the Mahatma

Circumstances suddenly changed in India because of one climactic event.
Gandhi was shot in the chest on 30 January 1948. He died shortly afterwards.
The murder was carried out by a Hindu nationalist who, although clearly a
fanatic, was also an articulate and well-connected member of the Hindu
extremist parties. The shock of the assassination (perhaps, as Ashis Nandy
has argued, almost a product of a 'death-wish' by Gandhi, who knew better
than anyone how his own death might help to pull together Indian society)
immediately helped to stabilise and enforce national feeling and undoubtedly
gave ascendancy to secular policy.[34] The assassin had opposed Gandhi's

powerful fasts for peace, his conciliatory policy towards Muslims and peace overtures to Pakistan.

Gandhi's assassination was carried out in the national capital itself and the ensuing funeral processions spread out like radial arteries from New Delhi, drawing people together in their shared grief and solidifying national feeling. Dazed and shocked crowds began to assemble outside the gates of Birla House to catch a glimpse of the Mahatma's body laid out on a simple bier surrounded by flowers as the news of the tragedy spread. The following day, the funeral cortège loaded with sandalwood logs, flowers and incense moved slowly through the dense crowds in Delhi, slowly winding its way through the streets to the *ghat* on the banks of the River Yamuna where the cremation took place. Thirteen days of official state mourning followed the cremation. In February, two weeks later, a special night train carried Gandhi's ashes for immersion in the Ganges at Allahabad. Along the train tracks from Delhi to Allahabad, mourners looked on with grim and curious faces and crowds collected as the copper urn was carried on a flower-bedecked trailer to the riverside. At the sacred meeting place of the Ganges and the Yamuna Rivers, swathes of people waded into the water as Gandhi's youngest son scattered his ashes.

The assassination proved a cathartic experience which enabled and embodied the beginning of the new nation. Beyond North India, the country was echoing and mirroring the ceremonies, united in observance of Gandhi's passing. Shops shut, public services were suspended and places of amusement closed. People collected by rivers and seafronts such as Bombay's Chowpatty beach, where vast crowds gathered to perform rituals of mourning and to hold religious services. In Karachi, too, many shopkeepers closed their shops as a mark of respect and Pakistani newspapers spoke warmly of Gandhi and sadly of his death. It was a moment for re-evaluation across the subcontinent.

Gandhi's death and its attendant rituals forged a new sense of unity and community in North India where these had been sorely lacking in previous months and Nehru spoke on the theme of unity in a radio broadcast to mark the end of the fortnight of mourning, raising a whole string of divisive issues on which the country now needed to unite. He appealed to the press to avoid criticism of the Congress Party, for his Congress colleagues to patch up their own factional differences, spoke out against provincialism and even made public his personal efforts at unity, by extending olive branches to his estranged colleagues Vallabhbhai Patel and Jayaprakash Narayan. Nehru, always alive to the importance of history and adept at writing Congress's history even as it was made, was quick to ensure that the tragedy of Gandhi's death was redeemed and put to a practical purpose by remodelling the nation along united lines. 'Even in his death there was a magnificence and complete artistry,' the premier himself wrote of Gandhi's assassination.[35] The institutionalisation of Gandhi's memory was a persistent feature of post-Independence politics and it was telling that the All India Congress Committee met for the first time in Independent India exactly eleven months to the day after Gandhi's death, in Gandhinagar, a newly built township for refugees displaced by Partition.[36]

Yet it would be misleading to see Gandhi's death, as is sometimes suggested, as the full stop to India's internal Partition crisis. Gandhi's death strengthened Nehru's ascendancy and, temporarily, facilitated an effective backlash against the extremists. The Government of India did at least attempt to imprison the culprits, compensate some of the affected and acted to quash the most brutal assaults. Nevertheless, despite these initiatives, numerous communities continued to live in fear in the years following Partition, discriminated against or economically boycotted. Nehru was surrounded by cabinet colleagues who had equivocal feelings about Indian Muslims' rights. Rajendra Prasad, the first President of India, opposed state intervention in reform of Hindu personal laws, wanted cow slaughter banned and in October 1949, while Nehru was abroad, the All India Congress Working Committee passed a vote allowing RSS members to become primary members of the Congress Party, although this decision was rapidly revoked. Partition boosted the strength of the Hindu Right and relegated Indian Muslims to a difficult and precarious position in the early years of Independence.

From Partition to war

A culture of high defence spending and militarisation in South Asia dates from 1947, and the roots of the ongoing Kashmiri conflict are deeply entwined with the moment of Partition. In October 1947, the pressurised Maharaja's hesitant accession to India overlapped with a rebellion in Poonch, in the south-western corner of the princely state. This was led by Hazaras, Punjabis and some militias under the command of former INA officers. Simultaneously, Indian troops airlifted into the Kashmir valley faced a tribal incursion of men from the frontier who fought with some covert support from the Pakistani army. The psychological ruptures of Partition undermined a peaceful solution to the Kashmiri conflict, and the war escalated in intensity until an official UN-sponsored ceasefire was announced on New Year's Day, 1949.

The vulnerability of both new nations was nakedly exposed by the dislocations of Partition: the refugee crisis, economic uncertainties and contestations over borders, twinned with the violent events in Kashmir, explain the intense paranoia that set in instantaneously regarding the relative strengths and motives of the other country. The Pakistani leadership – owing to the inherent limitations caused by their country's position as the seceding state and its smaller size – felt exposed to the risk of collapse or invasion. Indian intelligence written in purple prose warned that the Pakistani government was training ordinary people with arms and encouraging the 'war-minded', while in Pakistan, the official talk was of enemies attempting to paralyse the new nation. The Prime Minister spoke freely in broadcasts of 'the enemies of Pakistan' who 'indulged in their black hatred to the full'.[37]

Both national governments remained acutely aware of their shortcomings: their poor balance sheets, the loss of senior officers, the shortfalls in available bureaucratic talent and the urgent imperative of securing hundreds of miles of newly acquired borderland. Lack of supplies hampered Indian forces in Kashmir while troops airlifted from low-lying areas were exosed to the altitude and icy conditions. Pakistan turned to militias and vigilantes while its weak army was still being consolidated in the midst of the first war over Kashmir. Army ranks had been seriously depleted by the departure of British senior officers; before Partition 13,500 of 22,000 officers in the army were British. A few hundred, at the request of the undermanned Pakistani army, stayed on to train Pakistani soldiers but the majority swapped their uniforms for civilian positions in Britain or hunted down roles in other parts of the British empire. To the newly independent governments the solution to this strategic vulnerability, particularly the apparent weakness of the new armies, appeared to lie in spending money. The origins of habitually stratospheric defence spending can be found in these early days of Independence and such spending was a product of defensive weakness rather than hubristic swagger.

Only Gandhi had anticipated this. In July 1947, he said 'he visualised a definite increase in military expenditure' which would be 'all for fighting among ourselves'.[38] It was a prophetic statement. Within a year Indian and Pakistani soldiers would be fighting the first war over Kashmir and soon scientists in both countries would be racing to develop nuclear missiles, with their noses pointing towards the foreign border. But all this was in the future. Needless to say, little of it was in the original Partition plan.

Acute anxieties have beleaguered Pakistan's military establishment ever since. The ability to defend the new nation was in serious doubt, and there was a constant fear that it would be swallowed up by its larger neighbour. The army lacked arms, equipment, training centres and basic supplies and as Liaquat Ali Khan told the Joint Defence Council, 'an Army without equipment was as much use as tin soldiers'.[39] The army, the League leadership presumed, was essential for uniting the nation and cementing the component parts into one viable whole, whether by suppressing Sikh incursions on the Punjabi border, dealing with the reception of refugees or managing the violent domestic insurrections breaking out in the North West Frontier Province. Pakistani leaders blamed the weakness of the state and its problems on a deliberate Indian conspiracy to undermine the state's viability from the moment of its inception – a seam which ran deeply through the national psyche – and the dominant trope of 1947 was one of defiance and the will to exist in the face of hostility. 'Pakistan has come to stay' became a catchy political slogan during the early years of Independence.

The evocation of an external enemy waiting on the borders to subsume Pakistan was a useful bond between Pakistani people, some of whom had little conviction in the state's viability. A group of upper-class Muslims in Lahore felt so concerned that Pakistan could be attacked that they kept their cars filled with petrol and luggage, ready to flee from an Indian invasion at a moment's notice.[40] Luggage-carrying coolies at Karachi's airport talked of 'war with the Hindus'.[41] This was also a product of the overwhelming, almost revolutionary, calamities into which the state had been born and which it had faced from its inception. The Pakistani leadership tried to overcome these anxieties with overcompensation. Uncertainty about Pakistan's borders and the question marks over its creation before August 1947 were now replaced by a blatant form of pride in the nation state.

In India there was considerable defensive posturing and attempts to boost military capability – through the use of both conventional and less conventional methods. Both governments granted some official sanction to the armed militias that had helped to bring about Partition in the first place and absorbed them into the nation-making projects. Provincial governments assembled special armed constabularies, essentially upgraded policemen armed with weapons, and endowed them with new responsibilities and powers. The formation of such defence groups was explicitly tied to the protection of 'our people' from Partition violence, which at its worst was becoming indistinguishable from war.

They also had a local law and order purpose; ongoing student strikes, workers' protests and agricultural upheaval troubled numerous provincial governments across the subcontinent in these months, but preparations for war used up the scanty resources of both India and Pakistan. Governments bolstered home guards and strengthened their security apparatus. Policemen belonging to the minority religious communities were forced out of work in several states, and in India the Home Minister euphemistically called for the correction of 'communal maladjustments' in the police.

Meanwhile Punjab had a new status as a fragile border state and along both sides there was deep uneasiness. 'The West Punjab Government is freely arming its people,' the Indian Home Minister wrote to the defence ministry, 'and we must encourage the East Punjab Government to do likewise.'[42] In Pakistan, the frantic and overstretched government aimed to establish a Pakistan National Guard of 75,000 men only weeks after Independence. A remarkable photograph taken in 1948 in the highly contested Indian district of Ferozepore, lying flush alongside the Punjabi border, shows young women in crisp white *salwar kameez*, intently marching in formation with rifles at their sides. Members of the National Volunteer Corps of Ferozepore, these women are being trained in military tactics in case of trouble on the border. How far did this anxiety and paranoia exist in the minds of the leadership and how much did it reflect grassroots realities? This is difficult to say as both governments escalated their *real* militarisation in response to the *perceived* aggression of the other. What is certain, though, is that new groups of individuals, often former Indian National Army members, policemen or students, increasingly took part in a web of nationalistic activity which promoted India or Pakistan as 'the other' and created new jobs founded on these new ideologies in armed institutions such as the East Bengali Ansars, the Indian Provincial Armed Constabularies and the Pakistan National Guard.

By the time that the Pakistani and Indian governments concluded their first ceasefire in Kashmir at the start of 1949, the leaders could look back at eighteen months which approximated a revolution. Two new states, different in shape and social composition to anything they had ever anticipated, had come into existence, born in the cauldron of a traumatic transition. Old battles between Congress and League supporters looked outdated and parochial in this new environment. At the same time, a sense of the other state and of its innate violence had begun to grow. This would fuel a conflict which has lasted for the lifetime of all the Partition's survivors.

10

Divided Families

The north-western corner of the Indian subcontinent suffered the bloodiest violence and the most severe dislocation in 1947–8 but after just a few years visitors were surprised by the speed of change and the ways in which these events had faded from view. The energies and expenditure of the governments, the imperative quickly to begin farming again in the Punjabi breadbasket states that supplied vital food to the rest of India and Pakistan, and the rapid, total exchange of Punjab's population meant that, publicly at least, a line was drawn under events by the time of the first Indian general elections in 1950. Chiselled Victorian luminaries on plinths were removed and the names of streets and parks changed overnight. The landscape became increasingly alien to old inhabitants as shop names were removed and freshly painted signs hoisted up in their place. Marketplaces and segments of the old walled parts of cities were reinvented. As the new order began, and the old order fizzled out, cultural, linguistic and economic changes followed in the slipstream of Partition. Refugees made up almost half of the population of Lahore, almost a third of the population of Delhi.

Communities of refugee squatters could still be seen, camped on the outskirts of towns, and rubble still marked the sites of riots. New cities rose from the ashes, though, such as Le Corbusier's angular, uncompromisingly modernist Chandigarh, the new capital of East Punjab. The resourceful Punjabi refugee became a national stereotype and an actor on the nation-building stage. Inevitably, many of the residents who had stayed in the same place during Partition and witnessed these transformations felt nostalgic for the old cities where there had been less traffic, business had been done face to face, prices were at least remembered as cheaper, and it was possible to cross cities such as Delhi in minutes rather than hours; and they mourned the emergence of the 'vast sprawling multicoloured soulless monster of today which we continue to call by the same name'.[1] The public memory of Partition in the north-west of South Asia was gradually put to rest. Grave and invisible legacies lived on in less tangible ways, in emotional scarring and sporadic political friction, but observers were happy enough to buy into the story of regenerative enterprise told by both national governments.

Beneath the glossy factories and the meteoric rise and endless expansion of new cities, though, Partition left deep and ragged fault lines. These ran through individual lives, families and whole regions, pitching Indians and Pakistanis into new conflicts and paving the way for the troubled bilateral relationship which blights South Asia to the present day.

In the 1940s and 1950s people were not well equipped with the language of psychiatry and psychoanalysis; it was too much to hope for any systematic understanding of the collective trauma which a generation had experienced. Partition had a widespread psychological impact which may never be fully recognised or traced. This afflicted not only refugees but also eyewitnesses, perpetrators of violence, aid workers, politicians and policemen; arguably hundreds of thousands of people living in the northern and eastern parts of South Asia. The immediate trauma of the refugees was well testified in their frozen and fixed faces, uncontrollable tears and shocked inertia. More invasive mental health problems may have plagued some people for the rest of their lives. People who had managed to get away or who had been strong enough to secure themselves a place in a train compartment, or who had remained hidden while other members of their community were killed, felt guilt. Others experienced culturally specific shame and humiliation related to violations of religious or community rights that inverted the normal social order. 'One woman wept hysterically,' recounted Margaret Bourke-White, 'as she told me how her home was polluted by Muslim *goondas* who placed raw meat on the window sills.' For others, fear of starvation had left a deep mark – 'they started stealing food,' remembered Krishna Thapar who worked at an ashram in Punjab with rescued women: 'we would find chapatis under their pillows, under their quilts, and their beds . . . Some of them had become psychological cases.'[2] Some people went, quite literally, mad.

For women the trauma of rape, molestation and abduction was so grave, and made even worse in many cases because of the cultural taboos surrounding it, that it is unclear how recovery was possible at all. Relief workers were under enormous strain. 'None of us had the ability to understand the psychology of these women nor did we try,' admitted the social worker Anis Kidwai. 'The few sentences that are spouted at such occasions proved totally ineffective, and often we ended up saying very unpleasant things to them.'[3] Social workers often tried to steer the conversation away from memories of trauma, encouraged their charges to look to the future, and had a limited grasp of their psychological needs. They can only be judged against the standards and practices of the time. For those who saw scenes of devastation or lost loved ones, life was punctured by panic attacks and ugly nightmares for many years.

Some twenty years later, Begum Ikramullah wrote, 'I somehow have never been able to get over the shocked impact the Calcutta riots had on me' and Manzoor Quraishi's otherwise prosaic account of life in the Indian Civil Service is suddenly interrupted by the memory of a brother who lost his life on a train to Pakistan: 'I loved my younger brother and could not get over the brutal and tragic end of a brilliant career at the young age of 24 years. For months I could not sleep properly and insomnia that I got from this horrible and traumatic experience has haunted me now and then throughout my life thereafter. My mother whose youngest child [had died] was completely heartbroken and cursed "Pakistan" till she died in 1978 . . .'[4] Urvashi Butalia has pointed to the ongoing trauma of those who had been children in 1947, 'his wife told us that he still had nightmares, that he woke in the night feeling an intense heat rising up around him, the flames which surrounded him as he lay by his father's body in 1947', while in one instance a perpetrator of violence is also haunted by the events of the time: 'Another Sikh living in Bhogal in Delhi who had actually been part of a killing spree as a child, would often wake in the night screaming. His wife said he could not forget the screams of the Muslims he had helped to kill.'[5] These could have been exceptional cases but it seems more likely that Partition continued to echo, unrecorded, in anonymous stories of breakdowns, alcoholism and suicide.

A prolonged Partition

There were other invisible trails left by Partition. By late 1948, politicians were relieved that violence had subsided, and Nehru in particular was delighted that the annexation of the troublesome state of Hyderabad passed without trouble elsewhere in India. He saw this as a sign that the corner had been turned and was elated that 'not a single communal incident occurred in the whole length and breadth of this great country'.[6] Sadly though, questions of citizenship and belonging still hung in the balance and there were numerous people and communities who had grey, uncertain allegiances to India or Pakistan and had slipped between the cracks formed by these neat parameters of nationhood.

In Bengal, in contrast to the north-west, the physical reality of the refugee crisis was only just beginning to take shape in the 1950s. By 1951, there were at least three million refugees squeezed into every nook and cranny of Calcutta. They slept on pavements and in Nissen huts, made their homes on railway platforms and along riverbanks. The consequences could not be easily ignored and the unceasing flow of refugees brought India and Pakistan to the brink of war in early 1950. As Nehru wrote to the British Prime Minister, Attlee, in 1950 the treatment of minorities in both countries was 'far more important for the maintenance of peace than the settlement of the Kashmir dispute'.[7] A proclamation of emergency was kept ready to be used at a moment's notice in West Bengal and the Governor suggested declaring a state of martial law. The prolonged, tortuous Partition of Bengal would prove a whole chapter in the Partition story. It was a political and social drama which stretched well into the twentieth century. The war of 1971, and the secession of Bangladesh from Pakistan, exacerbated the human crisis in the region and, by 1973, West Bengal was coping with a refugee population of around six million.

After 1947 East Pakistan's ability to survive hung in the balance and the province's continued viability as a part of Pakistan was already in doubt. The desperately poor, waterlogged province, economically dependent on the unreliable jute crop and physically distanced from the Pakistani capital one thousand miles away, had to struggle with two dominant issues from the moment of its independence: on its borders it faced a refugee crisis of epic proportions and a brewing conflict with India, while East Bengalis also began a long battle with their compatriots in Karachi, who began trying to stamp their cultural and political imprint on the province. Jinnah declared Urdu the Pakistani national language in 1948, deaf to the passion of Bengali linguistic patriotism and the complaints of the majority of Pakistanis who could not speak the language. After Independence, East Pakistan suffered from inflation and shortages of basic goods as it was cut off from Calcutta, but the Chittagong port, which was critical for East Pakistan's industrial development and imports, was developed too slowly. All this was underlined by bigotry shown towards the rural Bengali peasantry and a barely concealed implication that the province was a poor cousin to the 'real' Pakistan: Jinnah took seven months to make his first brief visit to Dacca and although Liaquat Ali Khan announced that he would aim at two visits a year, he never managed to reach his own target. The fissures which would eventually result in civil war, the bloody cracking apart of the country and the creation of Bangladesh in 1970–1 were already visible in 1947.

Meanwhile, massive communities of Hindus who remained in East Bengal found little to commend in their poorly administered new country, and clung tenaciously to their older political affiliations. Many had ties to Calcutta and remained unreconciled to Partition, which was seen as an arbitrary imposition from outside. 'Their temple bells can be heard in the evening and in their shops in the bazaar are exhibited portraits of Nehru, Patel and other Indian leaders,' noted one foreign visitor to Dacca.[8] Hindus had overwhelmingly been the *zamindars*, or landlords, in undivided Bengal, while Muslims had been the tenants, and Hindus remained the wealthy gatekeepers of Bengali *bhadralok* culture; even in 1950 they still dominated the Dacca bar and held one third of the university's places.[9] Simultaneously, the promises of Pakistani nationalism had fired the imagination of Muslim tenants who hoped to improve their lot at the expense of their erstwhile masters. In this light, well-meaning Pakistani guarantees of a plural state decreed from the capital, and the promise of a 30 per cent reservation for the minority, looked hollow and capricious from the perspective of the East Bengali Hindu who, although represented in the provincial Legislative Assembly, had no figurehead in the cabinet and little reason to believe that his children or grandchildren would benefit from the same access to educational opportunities and legal rights as himself.

Fears of outright persecution were strengthened by real assaults and murders of East Bengalis in the grievous riots in Khulna, Chittagong, Barishal and Sylhet in 1950 and the ruthless requisitioning of Hindu property by a partisan and unaccountable state administration. Disentangling the truth from fiction about the persecution of East Bengali minorities is still immensely problematic, but as news of rapes, murders and massacres gained currency, fears of war between the two countries over Kashmir and the worried intercessions from family members and political groups on the Indian side of the border all added to the maelstrom. Rich and poor Bengali Hindus became fused in a new collective consciousness of their vulnerable minority status. The full ambiguities of Pakistan's territorial creation came to light as many Bengalis on both sides of the border lamented its creation and echoed Vallabhbhai Patel's declaration that Partition was a tragedy.

Ultimately, although some minorities held out in East Pakistan and tried to preserve their community rights, there was an alternative option for those who decided that they could not remain in East Bengal: migration to India. Many did not think this would be permanent, while some remained in East Pakistan for as long as possible and tried to claim their political rights, waiting for the storm to pass. Migration decimated ever more communities, leaving small isolated families targets for criminals and creating a vicious circle. By early 1950 some of the Congress regarded war as possibly the only solution that would stop the tide of refugees, push back Pakistan's borders and create a safe zone for non-Muslims in East Bengal which could be subsumed within Indian territory. Daily border clashes and riots in East Bengal started to threaten the security of Muslims in North India, in Calcutta and West Bengal and in March 1950 riots in East Bengal had 'repercussions' hundreds of miles way. The reflex action of many Indian Muslim communities was to pack up their belongings and to consider the possibility of migration to Pakistan. 'The common folks are concerned – peasants, artisans, metal workers, domestic servants and the like,' Nehru lamented. 'Their *panchayats* decide and whole groups pack up and want to go.'[10]

Independence had not delivered on its promises. J.N. Mandal, the leader of the local *dalits* who had vigorously backed the Pakistan demand and had been sworn in as a minister in the Pakistan Constituent Assembly, was racked with regret and dashed expectations. In 1950 he resigned from his post and migrated to India. It was the result of a long personal tussle with his own emotions and responsibilities. 'It is with a heavy heart and a sense of utter frustration at the failure of my life-long mission to uplift the backward Hindu masses of East Bengal,' he wrote sadly in his resignation letter, 'that I feel compelled to tender resignation of my membership of your Cabinet.' The daily persecution and harassment of peasants whom Mandal was elected to represent had become too much as 'untouchables' found themselves discriminated against, attacked and persecuted in East Pakistan, lumped together in popular thinking with 'Hindus' and exploited by unaccountable administrators who, Mandal was convinced, were determined to squeeze out all the minorities from the land.

The riots in East Bengal 1950 proved the final straw for Mandal like many others. 'The news of the killing of hundreds of innocent Hindus in trains, on railway lines between Dacca and Narayanganj, and Dacca and Chittagong gave me the rudest shock,' he wrote. 'I was really overwhelmed with grief.' Shortly afterwards, Mandal made his way to India. The final part of the sorry tale came afterwards in a twist which reflects both the ironies and the complications of defining citizenship in the partitioned subcontinent. Mandal's departure was rewritten as treachery and anti-nationalism. The Pakistani Prime Minister, standing on an airfield in Karachi, when asked about his minister's departure declared that he hoped Mandal would come back to Pakistan. 'A number of nationals betray their country and run away,' Liaquat Ali Khan declared imperiously to the assembled journalists, 'but by doing that they do not cease to be the nationals of that country.'[11]

Once again the murky lack of clarification about citizenship entangled the two states. The bitterness engendered by Partition was still palpable and in 1950 the prime ministers bickered in personal letters to each other about responsibility for the violence in 1947.[12] 'The disturbances which led to mass migrations covered three hundred thousand square miles in Pakistan,' argued an Indian government pamphlet, 'while the area affected in India was only eighty-seven thousand square miles.'[13] The real cost of Partition was lost in this scramble to attribute blame.

Both governments became blind to the real human misery of the refugees as the 'refugee question' became another focal point for Indo-Pakistani conflict. In provocative rhetoric the governments fixated on their own righteousness, undermined the journalism and reportage emanating from the other nation's press and denied their own culpability for what had happened in 1947. 'Wielding administrative power and having at their command the police and the military as engines of oppression, these [Pakistani] officials committed the worst savagery in human history. The riots in West Punjab had their natural repercussions in East Punjab, of which exaggerated reports were published in the Pakistan press and broadcast by the Pakistan radio,'[14] claimed the Indian government publications division while Pakistani propaganda perpetuated similarly partial interpretations in pamphlets such as *The Sikh Plan in Action*. The question of culpability for the crisis of 1947 remained a powerful silence in the background of later diplomatic discussions over Kashmir, and it still exerts a deep-seated force in the official mindset of both nations.

War over conditions in Bengal was narrowly averted in 1950. The Indian and Pakistani prime ministers sealed the peace – at least temporarily – by signing a far-sighted pact in April 1950. The Nehru–Liaquat Ali pact addressed desperately urgent questions of fair press reportage, protection for migrants in transit, affirmation of minority rights, the property rights of migrants and restoration of women who had been held captive against their will. It came just in the nick of time.

In Delhi in May 1950 newspaper editors gathered from India and Pakistan at a joint conference. The Nehru–Liaquat Ali pact encouraged journalists to tone down their alarmist coverage of what was happening in the two countries. Journalists spent hours talking, trying to get to the bottom of what was happening across the border and learning about life in a place which had now become mysterious and inaccessible. A Pakistani journalist admitted that he was relieved to find that the reports he had seen in Pakistan of gangs massacring Muslims had been exaggerated.[15] At the conference, journalists wept to see each other for the first time in three years. On hearing this, Nehru reflected that the two states had to find a way to get their people to meet as often as possible. Sadly, the pact was a temporary sticking plaster and this aspiration towards open borders remained a vain hope.

Visas and passports

Ahmad Hussain worked as a mechanic in a tin-printing plant in Lahore. He had a wife and young children to support and he performed well at his job, rising to the position of chief mechanic. During Partition, in 1947, the factory where he had been employed for over a decade was looted and his employer, the mill-owner Amar Nath Bindra, fled to India. We do not know what Ahmad Hussain made of this, or whether he was able to find alternative employment, as his life goes unrecorded in the archives until one day a year later when his former employer contacted him.

The indefatigable Amar Nath Bindra had managed to find his feet in the city of Mathura in North India. He had borrowed some money from the central government, and along with the help of 'some good-hearted capitalist' had managed to re-establish his factory, set up the necessary equipment and machinery and had even secured a supply of precious electricity. But now he faced a problem: he could not find suitably skilled workers needed to operate the newly installed plant. His mind turned to the men he had left behind in Pakistan. If they could come and help him, even for a limited time, he could get the factory running and use them to train some new staff. 'I had to request the Government to allow me to have my old five Muslim artisans from Lahore who worked in my factory there for about ten years,' he wrote to the Refugee Department: 'during that time they served me so honestly, sincerely and faithfully that I cannot still dream that they belong to other Nationality or Dominion and I hold implicit faith in them. [sic]'[16]

Remarkably, this appeal worked and Ahmad Hussain was granted a six-month permit to travel to India from Pakistan, along with his teenage son, Bashir Mohammad, completely against the flow of refugees still moving in the opposite direction. Leaving his wife and three younger children behind in Lahore, Ahmad Hussain was reunited with his old boss in India, where he resumed his former occupation. Periodically, the factory boss applied to extend the men's permits: 'when large numbers of such Muslims who are not at all of any use to India are being retained in India,' he pleaded, in a revealing letter, 'I see no cause why these only two most useful persons [*sic*] be not retained to train our people. I will stand any surety for these people.' The pay, or the local conditions, must have been to Ahmad Hussain's liking as in 1950 he applied for permanent settlement in India.[17]

Now, though, three years after Partition, borderlines and permit situations had hardened between India and Pakistan and the governments were introducing passports for the first time. Ahmad Hussain's life collided once again with the contingencies of Partition and the state-making processes. In 1951, Ahmad Hussain and Bashir Mohammad had both overstayed their permits, their applications were rejected and father and son were forced to separate from their employer for the final time and were ordered by the police to return to Pakistan.

'I do not consider Pakistan and India as two different countries. If I have to go to the Punjab, I am not going to ask for a passport. And I shall go to Sind also without a passport and I shall go walking. Nobody can stop me.'[18] Gandhi made this declaration to his audience at a daily prayer meeting a fortnight after the plan for Partition had been agreed and, as so often, he captured the prevailing *Zeitgeist*. The creation of Pakistan was now a certainty, yet despite all the violence, the public anticipated soft borders and hoped for a free and easy association with the neighbouring country. In the summer months of 1947 there was the occasional debate in the press about whether passports would be necessary between India and Pakistan but, on the whole, the question was ignored.

The permanent separation of Indians and Pakistanis from each other, and their inability to cross the new border, was the most long-lasting and divisive aspect of Partition although it was barely taken into consideration by the politicians at the time. It is doubtful if even the leaders fully appreciated the full implications of the rubric of the Partition plan as they deferred the question of passports until a later date, leaving it to the two independent dominions to decide their own border defences and immigration controls. In the summer of 1947 few could appreciate the full connotations of the division which would ultimately result in some of the harshest border regulations in the world; indeed one newspaper headline read 'Passport rules believed to be needless at present.'[19]

By this date even less affluent Indians travelled widely around the subcontinent as the railways delivered the possibility of cheap long distance journeys to pilgrimage sites, for trade and to attend and arrange weddings. It seemed unthinkable that destinations mapped in the imagination would become unreachable. 'I did realise that it meant saying goodbye to my home and friends,' recalled one future Pakistani Foreign Minister 'most people didn't think that an iron curtain would come down'.[20] Although the idea of distinct nation states was starting to take root, few thought that India and Pakistan would be hermetically sealed off from each other. A natural corollary to the empirical confusions surrounding Pakistan's territorial extent and Pakistan's intrinsic meaning was that it took a long time for people to come to grips with the idea of India and Pakistan as separate sovereign lands. Members of so-called 'divided families' – often of Kashmiri or North Indian origin – even if they made definitive choices in favour of India or Pakistan, did not antici-pate the weighty consequences of such a decision. 'I went in November,' recalled the renowned Urdu author, Intizar Husain. 'When I left, I had no idea that people who had migrated could never go back to the places they had left behind. That their link with the past had snapped.'[21] In the semi-autobiographical novel *Sunlight on a Broken Column* two Muslim brothers in North India squabble about the future in 1947 and one decides to stay in India while the other opts to migrate to Pakistan:

> 'Can you imagine every time we want to see each other we'll have to cross national frontiers? Maybe even have to get visas,' he added wryly. 'Oh come on Kemal,' Saleem laughed, 'there is no need to be as dramatic as all that. Visas indeed!'[22]

An early permit system devised in 1948 gradually evolved into full-blown citi-zenship legislation. By 1951 Indians and Pakistanis required a passport and visa to cross Radcliffe's infamous line in the west of the country, although the meandering East Bengali border continued to be both more porous and less systematically policed for a longer time and great stretches had not yet been marked out with barbed wire or guarded with border posts. Naturally, the poor and the illiterate could not afford the passport fee and the legal minefield of Pakistani and Indian citizenship caused hardship and complications.

The system of entry and exit permits, which began as a logical attempt to regulate the refugee flow, soon turned into a restrictive administrative regime which became self-sustaining. Now the aim was to keep out terrorists and enemies of the state, as well as stopping people from making claims on national welfare systems or abusing the franchise. Most of all, the govern-ments needed to pin down precisely who was an Indian and who was a Pakistani. There was no room for ambiguities or uncertain grey areas. Excessive red tape tied the hands of those who wished to conduct trade or visit friends and relatives on the other side of the border. At least seven categories of visa existed between India and Pakistan by the mid-1950s. In reality, access became difficult and cast suspicion on those who wanted to cross the border, while strict conditions were attached to the visits and tough regulations limited the goods that could be transported. Carrying gold, for example, was strictly forbidden.

Long after Partition the messy complications of real lives – which did not fit within these paper categories – generated large numbers of court cases, deportations and arrests. The High Courts regularly heard cases in the 1950s and 1960s which hinted at a panoply of human dramas: wives who had migrated with their husbands to Pakistan but now wanted to return to their families in India, complications caused by cross-border marriages and divorces, the defence of people who claimed they were forced to go to India or Pakistan against their own free will, the arguments of those who had entered on false or forged passports, claimed to hold two nationalities or who overstayed their visas.[23]

Indeed, the legacies of these boundary awards have sharpened rather than blunted over time and all the paraphernalia of border control – barbed wire and fencing (more prominent in the west than in the east, but currently expanding along the Indo-Bangladeshi border), land mines, thermal imagers, floodlighting and underground sensors designed to trap 'infiltrators' – have been brought to bear along Radcliffe's pencil lines. Over time the determination with which these borders have been patrolled has ebbed and flowed depending on the climate of relations between the countries but the general trajectory has been towards more heavily guarded borders.

Limbs and lives have been lost as villagers caught in the middle of the border areas try to continue ploughing the land. 'As a major part of the fence remains unlit, chances of anti-national elements sneaking in are there,' commented the Director-General of the Indian Border Security Force interviewed in 2006 about the policing of the Indo-Bangladesh border. 'This year alone we have shot dead 75 people trying to cross the border.'[24] Local people and border guards fall victim to routine border 'scuffles.' Fishermen sailing in the Arabian Sea swept along unknowingly into foreign waters are routinely arrested and imprisoned.

Currently, confidence-building measures agreed by the Indian and Pakistani governments in 2004 give new reasons for optimism and enable separated families to meet, often for the first time in decades; poor fishermen have been freed and repatriated, the limited bus and train services between Amritsar and Lahore resumed and new ones, most significantly the Thar express train which crosses between Sind and Rajasthan and the Pan-Kashmir bus from

Srinigar to Muzaffarabad, have started. Given the language of impermanency surrounding the creation of Partition and the limited way in which the emergent nationalisms related to territory, the monumental permanence of these borders is paradoxical, and has had contemporary consequences barely imaginable to the political protagonists in 1947.

These divisions have, over the years, thrown up some spectacular oddities and ironies: Fazal Mahmood, the legendary fast bowler and cricket captain, was picked to play for India on its maiden tour of Australia in 1947–8, and even attended a conditioning camp in Pune before the team's departure. On his way to Delhi, though, the twenty-year-old player was unable to proceed because of the violence. 'I was informed about the slaughter when I reached the airport,' he recalled much later. 'I could not go to Delhi and Lahore. A kindly passenger gave me his ticket, and I managed to travel to Karachi. The incident changed my life. I decided to stay in Pakistan. I had a lot in India, emotionally and financially, but I had to reconcile myself and settle down in Pakistan.'[25] Heading up the Pakistani national side, he played against India on numerous occasions. Another of the quirks of Partition was that many of the first and second generation of the leading officers in the Indian and Pakistani military facing each other across the Kashmiri line of control in the wars of the twentieth century had been close colleagues and worked alongside each other during the days before Independence. In one such instance, an Indian soldier, General Sinha, was responsible for the custody of an old Pakistani friend, General Niazi, as a prisoner of war after his capture during the 1971 conflict. Prior to Partition the pair had served together as captains in Indonesia during the Second World War.[26]

These borders and demands of statehood persist and are far more than abstractions. Border enclaves on the Indo-Bangladeshi border are perhaps the most extreme and bizarre, yet painfully real, example of Partition's logic. A product of 1947, they continue to exist and shape the lives of South Asians up to the present day. There are 123 border enclaves technically belonging to Bangladesh within India and 74 border enclaves which are legally Indian territories within Bangladesh lying in the eastern border region. These are tiny pieces of land stranded in a wider sea of the 'other' state. They came about as a result of the absorption of the princely state of Cooch Behar, sandwiched between the borderlines of East Pakistan and India in 1949. These scraps of land were legal oddities under the sovereign control of Cooch Behar's ruler, remnants of India's pre-colonial past and reminders of the piecemeal way in which the subcontinent's political map had emerged. With better diplomatic effort they could have been exchanged between the two new states after

Partition. Instead, a 1958 agreement to effect the exchange has not been implemented, and the enclaves have persisted as a technical and legal anachronism, with devastating consequences for the inhabitants. People living in these tiny patches of land have had their lives and identities stretched to the most incredible limits by the demands of nationality and statehood.

Technically 'Indian' but living in Bangladesh, or vice versa, enclave dwellers have found it immensely difficult to travel or trade beyond the limits of their tiny isolated enclaves, and their movement has sometimes been at the risk of danger or death, while criminals and opportunists have taken advantage of lawlessness within these third spaces. Enclave inhabitants have been living tax free so these isolated areas have been abandoned by officials and left without a franchise, policing, roads, healthcare or electricity supplies. The enclaves have, in short, made successive generations of South Asians 'stateless' human beings in a world now defined by nation states.[27]

All these consequences of Partition have reinforced the estrangement of the two nation states. These twists and turns that have followed on from 1947 are far removed from the hopes and dreams of *swaraj* and Pakistan which people rallied to in the late 1940s. Indians and Pakistanis continue to feel the unforeseen repercussions of the 3 June plan. At the same time, they also live alongside memories and amnesia about what took place in 1947.

Remembering and forgetting

Two episodes which took place in 2005 shine a light on the way in which Partition is simultaneously remembered and forgotten in South Asia today.

On 4 June 2005, a remarkable event occurred. A seventy-five-year-old Indian, L.K. Advani, climbed the steps to a glistening white marble monument in Pakistan's chief commercial city and former capital, Karachi. To the sound of bugles blasted by a Pakistani guard of honour, he laid a large wreath of purple and pink flowers at the tomb of Mohammed Ali Jinnah. Honouring a man who has been dead for over half a century can still have dangerous political repercussions as Advani, president and co-founder of the Hindu nationalist Bharatiya Janata Party (BJP), the chief opposition party in present-day India, quickly discovered. In India, Jinnah is, of course, widely reviled as the progenitor of Pakistan and the architect of a mistaken partition of the subcontinent, while Pakistanis cherish his memory as their greatest leader and the founder of their Muslim state. Advani, who later wrote in the visitors' book that Jinnah was a 'great man' who forcefully espoused 'a secular state in which every citizen would be free to practise his own religion', was committing virtual heresy in the eyes of many in his own party who remember Jinnah as a dangerous religious fundamentalist who forced the division of the subcontinent. BJP members called for their party president's immediate resignation.[28]

Advani is not known to be a friend of Pakistan, and is renowned more as a doughty-looking hawk than as a dovish peace campaigner whose personal understanding of Indian nationalism rests upon the bedrock of exclusivist Hindu ideology. His party is usually noted for its demonisation of minority groups, particularly Muslims and, by extension, for a suspicious attitude towards Pakistan. In the past he was nicknamed Demolition Man by the Pakistani press for his role in instigating the brick-by-brick destruction of the sixteenth-century Babri Masjid mosque in the North Indian town of Ayodhya in 1992 so his utterances in Pakistan unleashed widespread speculation about his motives. What had happened? Had Advani made an error of judgement and become sentimental in his old age or was this a calculated strategy to reinvent the party and broaden its electoral base? Did he really believe that Jinnah was secular? In retrospect it seems that he had made a miscalculation while trying to broaden the electoral foundations of the party and cultivate a role for himself as a centrist elder statesman at the hub of national life.

His comments, however, struck at the heart of all the nationalist myths that are held sacred by Indians and Pakistanis, and in both countries the front pages of newspapers were consumed with the story, while reams of editorial revisited the minutiae of Jinnah's character and his political intentions in the 1940s. Roundly condemned across the board by his own party, Advani was forced to resign temporarily as president of the BJP, an embarrassing episode that signalled the beginning of his withdrawal from Indian politics and permanent removal from the post at the end of 2005. Myths of Partition are deeply ingrained and Jinnah is characterised here as a cardboard cut-out hero or anti-hero. Breaking Partition's myths comes with a price.

There was an added twist to the story; Advani, in common with President Musharraf of Pakistan, belongs to a family displaced by the Partition of 1947. Both men and their families were among the twelve million people uprooted. Both have lived the remainder of their lives many miles from their ancestral homes, which are now absorbed into foreign territory. They also belong to that first generation of independent citizens who played a part in consolidating India and Pakistan as distinct nation states and in fashioning these nations from the remnants of the Raj.

Although there are currently reasons to be optimistic about a new *détente* in Indo-Pakistan relations, the unfortunate price of the emergence of these states has been the mutual hostility of the countries. There have been three wars since 1947, the development of nuclear weaponry, and a putative cold war. The movement of people and goods across 2,600 kilometres of international borderline remains highly restricted. Yet, despite persistent animosities, a paradoxical fascination with and attraction to the former homeland lingers. Like Musharraf, who came to India in July 2001 and visited his crumbling ancestral home in the crowded alleys of Old Delhi, Advani desired to see places in his home town of Karachi that he had left behind as a teenager when he departed for India. With his wife and daughter he visited his former house and his old school – the school, coincidentally, that was also attended by Musharraf as a boy – and he expressed genuine emotion in the face of the intervening years: 'I was truly overwhelmed by the warmth and affection of the people . . . I must confess that I am somewhat at a loss to articulate the totality of my feelings and thoughts . . .'[29]

In Pakistan, three months later, another episode equally signalled Partition's deep-seated political significance, which continues to resonate to the present day. On Independence Day 2005, President Musharraf attended a ceremony inaugurating a mammoth 330 million rupee building project in Lahore. The plan, known as Bab-e-Pakistan, has been in the pipeline since 1991. Architectural designs promise a sleek geometric structure, soaring into the sky, which will be reflected in a rectangular ornamental pool below; locals have also been promised a lavish new mosque, library, garden, restaurants and sports facilities. Standing on a platform in front of a large, graphic painting in which a pantheon of national heroes loomed as he inaugurated the start of the construction work, the President of Pakistan invoked the suffering of refugees and their sacrifices at the time of Partition. 'They were fired by passion and had an unswerving hope in Pakistan,' he declared.[30] For the land on which Bab-e-Pakistan will stand is the exact site of the Walton refugee camp, the camp in Lahore through which millions of Pakistanis trudged on their traumatic journey, and the purpose of the project is to memorialise both the camp and the wider story of Partition. The monument (and the library and exhibitions to be hosted within it) will tell a linear story of the triumphal emergence of Pakistan and although the bloodiness of Partition will have a place in this tale, it will be glossed with the language of martyrdom and suffering in the cause of the Pakistani state. The Bab-e-Pakistan project has little to say about the experiences of non-Muslims and avoids delving into the shared responsibility for violence at the time of Partition.

These official versions of history have hardly gone unchallenged; some Pakistani observers immediately called for a more representative memorial. 'If Bab-e-Pakistan has to be built,' suggested a newspaper editorial pointedly, 'let it represent suffering of all refugees from both sides.'[31] Nevertheless, the memories of the squalid refugee camp are to be carefully repackaged in the form of a national monument, and the memories of bewildering social upheaval are to be replaced with a providential, chalked-out destiny.

All memorials and monuments, like history books, have their own rationales, and tell a very particular story. A different criticism sometimes levelled at the governments of South Asia is that they have failed to commemorate the brutality of 1947 in any way at all. In India there is only one official monument to the victims of Partition, the Martyrs' Monument in Chandigarh, the experimental city built after Independence as a symbolic focal point of national regeneration and as a new capital of Indian Punjab. Here, in a square enclosure near to the heart of governance, stone sculptures of a lion, a snake and a prone human figure are intended to symbolise the sufferings of the Punjabis in 1947. However, the lack of other, official, public memorials does not mean that Partition is in any way forgotten.

The political power of the memory of Partition, and the state's ability to appropriate and manipulate these memories, has been graphically shown since 1947. A subtle and diffuse but no less politicised picture of Partition has extremely wide currency. Throughout the length and breadth of South Asia the contents of well-thumbed schoolbooks in children's satchels, regurgitated in undigested chunks for school examinations, tell opposing and sanctified versions of the story of Partition. In India this blends together the tales of the Muslim League's intransigence, its 'communal' or religiously slanted political orientation that made it impervious to cries of unity and resulted in the fracturing of India. In this story, Pakistan's creation is entirely illegitimate and it is the failure of the Leaguers to accept a secular, plural, peace-loving state which is at fault. In this line of thinking, Partition as a violent, human tragedy is spliced together with Partition as a political mistake. For this reason, the Indian child hears very little about the ways in which the violence came about and the polarisation of the League and the Congress in wartime India, or of Congress's own ambivalences about religious nationalism and alliances with militant cadres.

This is at odds with the picture that emerges in Pakistan; here the state proactively engages in rewriting the history of Partition as one of martyrdom, courage and victimhood. Pakistanis, so the story goes, triumphantly created the state, and gave up their lives for it, in the face of a planned attempt to bring

Pakistan to a point of collapse at the moment of the country's inception. In this reading, the Congress was little more than a front for a Hindu and Sikh conspiracy. In the textbooks of both countries, national leaders are extolled as heroes, and at its worst extreme this takes the form of a kind of morality play or fable about the foundational moment of the state. But it is the absences in the schoolbooks that are most striking. As Krishna Kumar, who has turned his critical eye on the production and consumption of these textbooks ironically observes, when it comes to the description of Partition violence, there are more similarities than differences in the way that Indian and Pakistan school histories approach the thorny question of Partition's bloodiness: 'The two narratives come remarkably close in the cursory manner in which they deal with the violence associated with Partition. The horror and suffering that millions of ordinary men and women faced receive no more than a few lines of cold recording in most Indian and Pakistani textbooks.'[32]

The Partition of 1947 cannot simply be regarded as a historical event located in the past. It may appear in history books on sale in every bookshop of India and Pakistan but it is not history if 'history' is considered to consist of past events that are detached from the political decision-making processes of contemporary South Asian life. Advani's *faux pas* underlined how national interpretations of Partition – why it happened and who was responsible – have become ideological shibboleths and have a firm grip on the popular imagination in both countries. There are still strict taboos on what can be said about Partition, and national myths persist, far beyond the limits of the more extreme nationalist parties.

This does not mean that Partition is ignored. Far from it: Partition crops up repeatedly, on South Asian television, in the newspapers, and in a torrent of published memoirs, cinematic and fictional accounts, and these interpretations have a direct bearing on how each neighbour perceives the other. Memories and histories of Partition continue to reinforce and shape each other and are intimately bound to the understandings of nationhood which have come to predominate in both of these countries.

South Asians are simultaneously wary of and hungry for stories of Partition, whether discussing the publication of previously unpublished political diaries or debating the representation of events in the latest Bollywood film or bestselling novel. It is living history that is preserved inside family homes by women and men, many of whom live alongside memories of terrible trauma, which are retold and passed on to descendants. Stories about Pakistan and Partition impress themselves upon the reader during a random browse through any issue of an Indian news magazine: a television show that features debates about Indo-Pakistani relations between guests from both countries, an article about a recent India–Pakistan cricket match, including a story about the experiences of an elderly Indian couple who took the opportunity to return to the Pakistani city of Rawalpindi, 'where they easily located their old family home. To their delight, it still bears their father's nameplate', an article on the suppression of popular Indian satellite channels on Pakistani television.

On the Pakistani side of the border, an equivalent magazine will throw up parallel stories: the construction of a railway station to receive the newly planned cross-border Thar Express train, an article recounting a recent visit to India by a Pakistani artist who enjoyed touring Jaipur and Hyderabad and also took the opportunity to meet up with distant relatives, commenting, 'My cousins in India are now the third generation after partition.'[33] Echoes of Partition resonate in contemporary discourse, and domestic and foreign policy decisions are shaped, and received, by the experience and memories of 1947. Definitions of each country's own nationhood have often been made dialectically, through an engagement with and perception of the other state and for this reason it is difficult to evade the analogies of birth and childhood in descriptions of bilateral relations, and the characterisation of the emergence of the two states as sibling-rivals.

Both national capitals have produced one-dimensional versions of the past. There has been a lot invested in perpetuating false memories and myth. Nevertheless, a broad sweep of Indians and Pakistanis remember 1947 in far more subtle ways. In films, novels and poetry the violence of Partition has seeped deeply into the cultural imagination. Bollywood has approached Partition from many angles; some films, such as Deepa Mehta's *Earth* and Chandra Prakash Dwivedi's *Pinjar*, are beautifully restrained depictions of the times. In the 1980s, the novel *Tamas* was controversially serialised on Indian television to great acclaim. Other films are, however, gung-ho excuses for nationalistic posturing. Sales of translations and new editions of Partition fiction and poetry are booming in both countries, and the work of writers such as Saadat Hasan Manto, Khushwant Singh, Bhisham Sahni and Intizar Husain are as popular as ever, while new writers revisit the perennial yet ever-intriguing themes of lost homelands, regret, the pain of separation and the gross violence. Responses to Partition cannot easily be pigeonholed. They traverse the full range of human emotions from the acrimonious and bitter to the regretful and nostalgic.

Nevertheless, nationalist blinkers have more often than not shaped the way in which the history of Partition's events has been viewed. The master narratives, even if not accepted simplistically or without cynicism, have been remarkably potent. The messy ambiguities of Partition have been under-played, and the anachronistic gloss of nationalism varnishes later accounts. As this book has shown, there is a gulf between these later renderings and the actual experiences of Partition, between the idea and the reality of making two nations in the theatre of decolonisation in 1947.

Epilogue

The Indian Raj was at the centre of the experimental tentative process of forging nation states in the aftermath of empire. Sometimes it has been celebrated – in British thinking at least – as a successful act of British decolonisation, in comparison to the complications that bogged down other European powers in South East Asia and Africa. Alternatively, it has been presented as a series of gruesome horrors far removed from political calculations. These stale views demand reappraisal.

More often than not the history of the Partition of India is read backwards. It is incredibly difficult to see Partition from the perspective of individuals caught up in the post-war whirlwind; people who carried on living daily life through the disintegration of an imperial regime and its replacement by two new nation states. The fog of nationalist myth-making has been thick and coats Partition histories in a dark cloak of inevitability. Partition becomes a stepping stone on a well-trod path and it is too easy to forget how euphoric, confusing, uncertain or strange those days must have been for people who did not know or trust that new states were going to replace the tired and discredited British Raj. Instead, in many history books Partition becomes the end point, or the apex, of a great national struggle and the moment at which one set of historical stories, about achieving liberation from colonial rule ends, and another – about the building up of these new states – starts. As Nehru, the newly appointed Prime Minister of India, and a brilliant practitioner of narrative history, unequivocally stated in 1947, Partition was a 'watershed' which was 'dividing the past from the future'.[1] The result has been that we have taken our cue too readily from the politicians and the creation of the Indian and Pakistani political economies of the 1950s are taken for granted. Partition was, in this reading, a massive but contained historical event. This underestimates the scale of disruption of 1947 and the dangers of the crisis which, arguably, threatened the collapse of the new post-colonial governments. The outcome was never a foregone conclusion.

This book has taken a rather different angle. It has shown how, for several years, South Asia was in a deeply ambiguous, transitional position between empire and nationhood that threatened the very existence of the new states themselves. There was no straightforward exchange of the baton of government. The protracted, unruly end of empire in South Asia was a shock of epic proportions that destabilised life for millions of its inhabitants. In 1946, people felt entirely uncertain about what the future would deliver. It is not implausible that South Asia could have spiralled into an even more devastating civil war, or that Pakistan could have failed to come into existence. It is not improbable that the new states could have been created along entirely different lines or that some of the princely states could have succeeded in their bids for autonomy. There was nothing inevitable or pre-planned about the way that Partition unfolded. Well accustomed as we are nowadays to the contours of these states on the world map, and given the terrific speed with which they acted to establish themselves, it is very challenging to visualise the moment at which they could have been forged in different ways, and what that future might have looked like.

On 15 August 1947 the first part of the British empire was unhooked from the imperial metropolis. This history of Partition has suggested that modern nation states had to be crafted out of a chaotic, diffused situation in which myriad voices made their claims and counter-claims. As the first Asian countries to win their freedom from empire, India and Pakistan pioneered decolonisation. Few aspects of this were preconceived or well mapped out.

The flip-side of the story of liberation from colonial rule was the chaos and violence that engulfed and almost overwhelmed the new states. Nationalism exacted its own blood price. The violence of 1946–8, so regularly and conveniently portrayed by contemporaries and by later historians as the unstoppable thuggery of madmen and hooligans, in an uncanny parody of the colonial language of governance, was, instead, often planned, strategic and linked to middle-class party politics. The black and white imagery of ragged refugees and bloodthirsty peasants should be replaced with a technicolour picture of modern weaponry, strategic planning and political rhetoric, which was used to encourage and legitimise the killers and their actions. Fuelled by appeals to an ideal society and determined to bring about their own interpretations of *swaraj* and Pakistan, some of the murderers no doubt operated with the mistaken idea that they were doing what was best for their nation. Others, living under the shadow of curfew, daily stabbings and bombings, and exposed to misinformation and rumour, turned from a position of strategic self-defence to overt aggression. It is beyond doubt that nationalist politicians and enthusiasts from leading political parties colluded with, and became tangled up in, the massacres.

Individuals and communities felt the full brunt of Partition, far beyond the gravest and most deadly sites of violence in Punjab. Centripetally, its effects radiated out from the nerve centres in the north in a broader arc than is usually presumed. It ripped apart the operation of everyday life in cities across North India and often made ordinary life altogether impossible. The lives of factory workers, teachers, government clerks and shopkeepers were massively, albeit temporarily, disrupted because of the closure of offices and factories, ruptured train lines, the heightened and abnormally anxious circulation of news and rumour. Unfamiliar and desperate batches of refugees speaking strange tongues started to turn up unannounced at local railway stations. Relationships with communities of local people – who were suddenly branded as 'minorities' or 'not one of us' – were cast in a new light, especially when these groups began to cluster together and move to another place for their own safety.

New opportunities to make extra profit or to secure promotion opened up for some. For others, there were major and agonising decisions to make about whether to leave for India or Pakistan. For the refugees, life would never be the same again. In the worst affected places, in an almost carnivalesque manner, relationships between men and women and between families became upended and distorted as every taboo was broken and people clutched at older caste or regional identities while trying to recreate in strange new conditions and alien cities something of their former existence. There were small glimmers of opportunity which enabled, for instance, women to work outside the home, or to seize the political initiative in their new refugee camp or housing colony. But it is difficult to see these attempts at an autonomous, dignified life as anything other than small triumphs in the face of unending adversity.

After Partition, there was a sea change. The new national governments in India and Pakistan worked spectacularly hard at supplanting the endemic confusion with order and at recasting the disorder as the handiwork of thugs and hooligans. Newly emerging nations, economically and politically precarious in 1947, quickly turned from defensive weakness to literal and metaphorical fortification. From the earliest days of Independence, middle-class contemporaries regarded state-building and nation-making as part of their inescapable duty. As this book has argued, new types of nationalism were consolidated in the aftermath of Partition, not only in its prelude. Whether people had previously supported the League or the Congress had become a secondary consideration by 1947. Crucially, Partition had its own intrinsic revolutionary repercussions. It was not just the product of the decades of electrifying change which preceded it.

Pakistan and India are now established facts, distinctive nations, which have followed trajectories that were scarcely dreamed of by their founders and supporters in the 1940s. The Partition plan was, in some ways, a genuine compromise that allowed for a sharing of land and a division of people and materials. It acknowledged the right to self-determination of a large group of Muslims who, albeit in a contradictory and confused manner, had expressed their strong desire to extricate themselves from the Congress's control. For these reasons, the more optimistic onlookers in June 1947 welcomed the settlement as a solution to the problematic tensions that had been plaguing South Asian politics. The blueprint, which was loftily imposed from above in 1947, though, has never escaped the stain of illegitimacy that marred it. It was a plan that went catastrophically wrong: partly because it was sabotaged by militant groups who did not subscribe to it and partly because it did not make detailed allowances for many different grassroots realities that were shaping local politics in the provinces. Even those inside the limited loop of political information in 1947 were shocked by the speed with which Partition was imposed, the lack of clarity and reassurance provided to those living along the borderlines, the paucity of military protection written into the plan, the complete abnegation of duty towards the rights of minorities and failure to elucidate the questions of citizenship. One apparently contradictory aspect of Partition's nature is this tension between speed and sluggishness, decisiveness and prevarication. Far more power had already been devolved by 15 August 1947 than is usually acknowledged. The states that were coming into existence were works in progress. If not entirely responsible for the contending nationalisms that emerged in South Asia (which it certainly contributed to), the British government's most grievous failure was the shoddy way in which the plan was implemented.

In a close approximation of each other, India and Pakistan swiftly moved to consolidate their nations and to define themselves as autonomous states using all the national apparel they could muster – flags, anthems and national histories – and by implementing more concrete measures: the policing of boundaries, the closure of lacunae in the definitions of citizenship and writing constitutions. None of this is too surprising, but the 'other' state necessarily became an object of comparison, a counterpoint, and was, to a greater or lesser extent, vilified in the process. A cornerstone of nation-making was securing control of a separate and powerful army. The Kashmir imbroglio and the subsequent wars since 1947 have, of course, sustained the tensions between India and Pakistan and further entrenched the conflict in new and difficult ways. New grievances and conflicts have arisen because of the growth of militancy, Pakistan's backing for violent atrocities carried out in Kashmir and beyond, Indian human rights abuses in the Kashmir valley, not to forget the complications caused by the creation of Bangladesh after the war of 1971, the acquisition of nuclear weaponry, and the complex interplay of national and regional identities in all three countries.

Not all of South Asia's current problems can be laid at the feet of Partition. Events have moved on from 1947 and difficulties created by the Radcliffe line – such as the maintenance of illogical and tricky boundaries – instead of being salved with the balm of diplomacy have become running sores. Yet, the way in which Kashmir is usually cited as the cause of these problems overlooks the way in which Partition itself was the site for, and the origin of, so many of the ongoing conflicts in South Asia, not least because it was the source of the suspicions and national myths that are deeply rooted in the definition of one state against the other.

Today a peace process is under way in earnest and there are reasons for optimism as the confidence-building measures agreed between the two governments are gradually implemented. New bus, rail and air services link up the two nations. The prospects for commerce are excellent and the surge in bilateral trade, which crossed the 500 million dollar mark in 2004–5, has outstripped earlier levels of economic interaction. Chambers of Commerce send eager delegations across the border. Film, entertainment and tourism all have wide attraction for Indians and Pakistanis who have a shared taste in humour, music and film. Pilgrims want to visit temples and sacred sites, artists would welcome the chance to perform to the transnational audience, businessmen know full well the market for their goods and services across the border which is confirmed by the thriving black market in everything from textiles to food products and electronics. There are recent signs that the ban on showing Indian films in Pakistani cinemas, which has boosted a thriving pirate industry, may be lifted and Pakistani cinemas have been able to screen selected Bollywood movies for the first time in forty years.

Nevertheless, Indians and Pakistanis are still, despite the ongoing and encouraging liberalisation of the visa regime in 2006, kept apart. For sixty years Indians and Pakistanis have been largely segregated in a manner unthinkable to the protagonists who agreed to the plan at the fateful meeting on 3 June 1947. The way in which Pakistan and India have evolved as nation states and the literal, pedantic, policing of nationality in the interim seems in retrospect a product of the anxieties and insecurities of Partition. The failure at the time to define Indian and Pakistani citizenship fully, the contradictions of imagined nationalisms and the territorial realities of state-making left a difficult and acrimonious legacy. Today, queues outside visa offices remain long and depressing as families camp out from early in the morning trying to acquire the necessary paperwork to cross the border, while the visa regime explicitly favours the wealthy and cosmopolitan. Visas, when issued, still restrict visitors to specific cities, only allow trips of a short duration and involve complicated and dispiriting registration with the local police on arrival. It has become ever harder to recover a sense of what it was like to be a pre-Indian or a pre-Pakistani.

Partition deserves renewed consideration and closer attention for abundant reasons. It was one of the twentieth century's darkest moments. The millions of people killed and forced to leave their homes merit greater recognition and a place closer to the heart of history writing for their own sake. The Partition of 1947 is also a loud reminder, should we care to listen, of the dangers of colonial interventions and the profound difficulties that dog regime change. It stands testament to the follies of empire, which ruptures community evolution, distorts historical trajectories and forces violent state formation from societies that would otherwise have taken different – and unknowable – paths. Partition is a lasting lesson of both the dangers of imperial hubris and the reactions of extreme nationalism. For better or worse, two nations continue to live alongside each other in South Asia and continue to live with these legacies.

Notes

Introduction: The Plan

1. USSA 845.00/6–647 Box 6070. Gordon Minnigerode to US Secretary of State, 6 June 1947.
2. Khwaja Ahmad Abbas, 'Who Killed India', in Mushirul Hasan, ed., *India Partitioned: The Other Face of Freedom* (Delhi: Lotus Collection, 1995), vol. 2, p. 232.
3. IOR L/PJ/5/140, Akbar Hydari to Mountbatten, 5 June 1947.
4. Alan Campbell-Johnson, *Mission with Mountbatten* (London: Robert Hale, 1951), p. 106.
5. N. Mansergh, ed., *TOP*, vol. 11, pp. 86–101.
6. Ibid.
7. Ibid., p. 96.
8. Ibid., pp. 97–8.
9. As the historian Gyanendra Pandey has stressed, Independence and Partition marked out the problematic beginning of a process, 'the normalization of particular communities and particular histories . . .' See Gyanendra Pandey, *Routine Violence: Nations, Fragments, Histories* (Stanford, Calif.: Stanford University Press, 2006), p. 52.
10. *Times of India*, 4 June 1947.
11. *SWJN*, 1st ser., vol. 15, p. 506; Pakistan Assembly debate, 11 August 1947 reproduced in M. Rafique Afzal, ed., *Speeches and Statements of Quaid-i-Millat Liaquat Ali Khan 1941–1951* (Lahore: University of Punjab, 1967), p. 118.
12. The numbers of people who died during Partition are ultimately unknowable. Figures discussed by contemporaries and historians range from 200,000 to one million. On the difficulties with these figures see G. Pandey, *Remembering Partition: Violence, Nationalism and History in India* (Cambridge, Cambridge University Press, 2001), pp. 88–91. Paul Brass also discusses the problem of counting the dead in 'The Partition of India and Retributive Genocide in the Punjab, 1946–7,' *Journal of Genocide Research*, 5.1 (2003), pp. 75–6.
13. M. Hasan, *India Partitioned: The Other Face of Freedom* (Delhi: Lotus Collection, 1995), vol. 2, p. 156; *The Journey to Pakistan: A Documentation on Refugees of 1947* (Islamabad: National Documentation Centre, Govt of Pakistan, 1993), p. 258. These incidents are discussed in Chapters 8 and 9.
14. *TOP*, vol. 11, p. 159. Viceroy's Personal Report, 5 June 1947. For a perceptive critique of Partition historiography after fifty years of Independence, see David Gilmartin, 'Partition, Pakistan, and South Asian History: In Search of a Narrative', *Journal of Asian Studies*, 57.4 (1998), 1068–1095.

15. These examples are taken from Steven Wilkinson's data set reproduced in S. Wilkinson, ed., *Religious Politics and Communal Violence* (Delhi and Oxford: Oxford University Press, 2005), pp. 405–44. This lists towns with reported 'communal' riots in India (and for the pre-1947 period) Pakistan and Bangladesh; based on two data sets compiled by Wilkinson and Ashutosh Varshney using colonial and archival records, published government records, Indian and British papers and other secondary sources. Wilkinson acknowledges the many problems in deciding what constitutes a 'communal riot'.

16. J. Greenberg, 'Generations of Memory: Remembering Partition in India/Pakistan and Israel/Palestine', *Comparative Studies of South Asia, Africa and the Middle East*, 25.1 (2005), p. 90. Joya Chatterji similarly highlights the misleading use of surgical metaphors to describe the making of the international borderline between the two countries and the 'clinical detachment' with which the operation was presented by the British. Joya Chatterji, 'The Fashioning of a Frontier: The Radcliffe Line and Bengal's Border Landscape, 1947–52', *Modern Asian Studies*, 33.1. (Feb. 1999), p. 185.

17. Urvashi Butalia, *The Other Side of Silence: Voices from the Partition of India* (London: Hurst, 2000), p. 15. The phrase is from Roland Barthes.

Chapter 1: In the Shadow of War

1. M. Darling, *At Freedom's Door* (Oxford: Oxford University Press, 1949), pp. xiii, 35–6, 51, 68, 80, 194.

2. Ibid., p. 109.

3. Tan Tai Yong, *The Garrison State: The Military, Government and Society in Colonial Punjab, 1849–1947* (New Delhi and London: Sage, 2005), pp. 284–5.

4. *Times of India*, 8 Jan. 1946; *Statesman*, 2 March 1946.

5. *SWGBP*, vol. 10, p. 392. Speech at Agra, 13 Nov. 1945.

6. USSA 845.105/8–1547 – 845.105/12.3149 Box 6082, 13 Nov. 1946.

7. Winston W. Ehrmann, 'Post-War Government and Politics of India', *Journal of Politics*, 9.4 (Nov. 1947), p. 660.

8. Daniel Thorner, 'Problems of Economic Development in India', *Annals of the American Academy of Political and Social Science*, 268 (March 1950), pp. 96–7.

9. Ibid., p. 98.

10. *Searchlight*, 9 March 1946. Cited in Vinita Damodaran, *Broken Promises: Popular Protest, Indian Nationalism and the Congress Party in Bihar, 1935–1946* (Delhi and Oxford: Oxford University Press, 1992), pp. 290–1.

11. Rahi Masoom Reza, *The Feuding Families of Village Gangauli: Adha Gaon*, trans. from Hindi by Gillian Wright (Delhi: Penguin, 1994), p. 140.

12. *Times of India*, 31 Jan. 1946; *Wavell: The Viceroy's Journal* ed. P. Moon (London: Oxford University Press, 1973), p. 224.

13. *Times of India*, 25 March 1946.

14. *The Statesman*, 12 March 1946.

15. Indivar Kamtekar, 'A Different War Dance: State and Class in India, 1939–45', *Past and Present*, 176 (Aug. 2002), pp. 187–221. On the Indian role in the Second World War see also, Judith Brown, 'India', in I.C.D. Dear and M.R.D. Foot, eds, *The Oxford Companion to the Second World War* (Oxford: Oxford University Press, 1995), pp. 557–65 and Ashley Jackson, *The British Empire and the Second World War* (London: Hambledon, 2005).

16. By 1938–9 the All India membership figures for the Indian National Congress were 4,511,858. Source: B.R. Tomlinson, *The Indian National Congress and the Raj, 1929–1942: The Penultimate Phase* (London: Macmillan, 1976), p. 86.

17. Andrew Whitehead, *Oral Archive: India, a People Partitioned* (London: School of Oriental and African Studies, 1997, 2000), A.S. Bakshi interviewed in Chandigarh, 16 March 1997.
18. The colonial applications and implications of the decennial census are discussed in N. Barrier, ed., *The Census in British India* (Delhi: Manohar, 1981). *CWMG*, vol. 85, p. 448, 1946.
19. The British granted the principle of representative government to Indians in 1861, 1892, 1909 and more substantially by the parliamentary Acts of 1919 and 1935, although the franchise was always highly selective and powers were carefully curtailed.
20. The literature on the growth of Muslim and Hindu nationalism and the use of religious symbolism by nationalist parties prior to 1947 is extensive. For a variety of perspectives see, P. Brass, *Language, Religion and Politics in North India* (Cambridge: Cambridge University Press, 1974); S. Freitag, *Collective Action and Community: Public Arenas and the Emergence of Communalism in North India* (New York: Oxford University Press, 1989); William Gould, *Hindu Nationalism and the Language of Politics in Late Colonial India* (Cambridge: Cambridge University Press, 2004); Christophe Jaffrelot, *The Hindu Nationalist Movement and Indian Politics* (London: Hurst, 1996); Ayesha Jalal, *Self and Sovereignty: Individual and Community in South Asian Islam since 1850* (London: Routledge, 2000); Gyanendra Pandey, *The Construction of Communalism in Colonial North India* (Oxford: Oxford University Press, 1992); Peter Van der Veer, *Religious Nationalism: Hindus and Muslims in India* (Berkeley: University of California Press, 1994); Farzana Shaikh, *Community and Consensus in Islam: Muslim Representation in Colonial India, 1860–1947* (Cambridge: Cambridge University Press, 1989); Francis Robinson, *Islam and Muslim History in South Asia* (New Delhi and Oxford: Oxford University Press, 2000); Mushirul Hasan and Asim Roy, eds, *Living Together Separately: Cultural India in History and Politics* (New Delhi and Oxford: Oxford University Press, 2005). On Indian community relations prior to the arrival of European colonialism, see David Gilmartin and Bruce B. Lawrence, eds, *Beyond Turk and Hindu: Rethinking Religious Identities in Islamicate South Asia* (Gainesville: University Press of Florida, 2000). For an excellent analysis of some of the major theoretical debates, see Gail Minault, 'Some Reflections on Islamic Revivalism vs. Assimilation among Muslims in India', *Contributions to Indian Sociology*, 18 (1984), pp. 301–2, and Francis Robinson, 'Islam and Muslim Society in South Asia: A Reply to Das and Minault', *Contributions to Indian Sociology*, 20 (1986), pp. 97–104.
21. On the terms 'communal', 'ethnic' and 'ethno-religious', and their relative merits, see Amartya Sen, *Identity and Violence: The Illusion of Destiny* (New York: W.W. Norton, 2006) and Ayesha Jalal, 'Secularists, Subalterns and the Stigma of "Communalism": Partition Historiography Revisited', *Modern Asian Studies*, 30. 3 (1996), pp. 681–9.
22. C.H. Philips and M.D. Wainwright, eds, *The Partition of India: Policies and Perspectives, 1935–1947* (London: Allen and Unwin, 1970), pp. 409–10.

Chapter 2: Changing Regime

1. A.K. Azad, *India Wins Freedom* (First published 1959, edition cited, Delhi: Orient Longman, 1989), pp. 92, 122.
2. *Times of India*, 27 March 1946.
3. Circular to all Provincial Congress Committees, 11 Jan. 1947, reprinted in *Congress Bulletin* (AICC, Delhi, 1947), pp. 10–15.
4. *CWMG*, vol. 85, p. 35. Letter to V. Patel, 21 July 1946.
5. *SWJN*, 1st ser., vol. 15, p. 2; Malcolm Darling, *At Freedom's Door* (London, 1949), p. 17.

6. *Wavell: The Viceroy's Journal*, ed. P. Moon (London: Oxford University Press, 1973), p. 202.
7. Memoir of B.C. Dutt, one of the leaders of the Royal Indian Navy mutiny, quoted in S. Kuwajima, *Muslims, Nationalism and the Partition: 1946 Provincial Elections in India* (Delhi: Manohar, 1998) pp. 114–15.
8. Sumit Sarkar, *Modern India, 1885–1947* (Delhi: Macmillan, 1983) pp. 405–8.
9. A.K. Gupta, *The Agrarian Drama: The Leftists and the Rural Poor in India, 1934–1951* (Delhi: Manohar, 1996), p. 287.
10. USSA 845.105/8–1547 – 845.105/12.3149 Box 6082.
11. Gail Omvedt, *Reinventing Revolution: New Social Movements and the Socialist Tradition in India* (New York: M.E. Sharpe, 1993), p. 23. Sumit Sarkar, *Modern India*, pp. 442–6.
12. Lawrence James, *Raj: The Making and Unmaking of British India* (London: Little, Brown, 1997), p. 597.
13. *TOP*, vol. 6, p. 393. Twynam to Wavell, 25 Oct. 1945.
14. *Times of India*, 8 March, 1946.
15. Desmond Young, *Try Anything Twice* (London: Hamish Hamilton, 1963), p. 330.
16. *TOP*, vol. 6, p. 554. Wavell to Pethick-Lawrence, 27 Nov. 1945
17. *TOP*, vol. 6, p. 576. Clow to Wavell, 1 Dec. 1945; IOR, L/PJ/5/168 Colville to Wavell, 3 Feb. 1947.
18. *SWGBP*, vol. 10, pp. 378–9. Speech at a public meeting in village Syed Raja, Varanasi district, 27 Oct. 1945.
19. Sumit Sarkar, *Modern India, 1885–1947*, pp. 418–23.
20. *TOP*, vol. 6, pp. 512, 516. Intelligence Bureau, Home Dept 20 Nov. 1945. It was also reported that leaders at most of the 160 political meetings held in the Central Provinces during the first half of October demanded the release of INA men.
21. *TOP*, vol. 6, pp. 554, 555.
22. Address by King George VI at Opening of Parliament, 15 August 1945, *The Times*, 16 August 1945.
23. The total electorate for the provincial elections was 41,075,839. As a proportion of the adult population over twenty years old, this may have been approximately 28 per cent of men and 16 per cent of women. See Kuwajima, *Muslims, Nationalism and the Partition*, p. 47.
24. See for instance J.P. Narayan's far-sighted note on the communal question, AICC, G–23 (1946–8). On the CPI's relationship with Nehru, see Benjamin Zachariah, *Nehru* (London: Routledge, 2003), pp. 123–5.
25. Extract from an Urdu poem *c.* 1946 trans. Kedarnath Komal and Rukmani Nair in Mushirul Hasan, ed., *India Partitioned: The Other Face of Freedom* (Delhi: Lotus Collection, 1995), vol. 1, p. 43.
26. An extract from the election bill of the Palamu district Kisan Sabha, translated from the Hindi in Kuwajima, *Muslims, Nationalism and the Partition*, p. 242.
27. Statement of A.K. Azad, 4 April 1946 quoted ibid. p. 144.
28. Speech of Jinnah quoted ibid., p. 134. On the expedient use of Islamic motifs during this election, see also Ayesha Jalal, *Self and Sovereignty: Individual and Community in South Asian Islam since 1850* (Delhi: Oxford University Press, 2001), pp. 386–471.
29. *Times of India*, 8 Jan. 1946.
30. *SWGBP* vol. 10, p. 378; Speech at a public meeting in Varanasi district, 27 Oct. 1945; *Times of India*, 27 Feb. 1946.
31. Andrew Whitehead, *Oral Archive: India, a People Partitioned* (London: School of Oriental and African Studies, 1997, 2000), Zawwar Zaidi interviewed in Islamabad, 7 April 1997.
32. *SWGBP*, vol. 11, p. 414. Speech in Kakori, 22 Feb. 1946.

33. Ian Talbot, *Khizr Tiwana: The Punjab Unionist Party and the Partition of India* (Karachi and Oxford: Oxford University Press, 2002), p. 195.
34. William Gould, *Hindu Nationalism and the Language of Politics in Late Colonial India* (Cambridge: Cambridge University Press, 2004).
35. Cited in Khalid Bin Sayeed, *Pakistan: The Formative Phase* (London: Oxford University Press, 1968), pp. 203–4.
36. Quoted in Usha Sanyal, *Devotional Islam and Politics in British India: Ahmad Riza Khan Barelwi and his Movement, 1870–1920* (Delhi: Oxford University Press, 1996), p. 310.
37. Cited in Khalid Bin Sayeed, *Pakistan*, p. 199. On 'Nationalist Muslims' and the subtle divisions among Muslim thinkers in the lead up to 1947 see Barbara Daly Metcalf, *Islamic Contestations: Essays on Muslims in India and Pakistan* (New Delhi and Oxford: Oxford University Press, 2004); Aziz Ahmad, *Muslim self-statement in India and Pakistan 1857–1968* (Wiesbaden, 1970).
38. For a convincing critique of the term 'Nationalist Muslim' see Gyanendra Pandey, *Remembering Partition: Violence, Nationalism and History in India* (Cambridge: Cambridge University Press, 2001), pp. 154–5; Pandey, 'The Prose of Otherness', in David Arnold and David Hardiman, eds, *Subaltern Studies VIII* (Delhi: Oxford University Press, 1994), pp. 118–221; and A. Jalal, 'Exploding Communalism: The Politics of Muslim Identity in South Asia', in S. Bose and A. Jalal, eds, *Nationalism, Democracy and Development: State and Politics in India* (Delhi: Oxford University Press, 1997).
39. AICC, P-17 (1947–8).
40. M. Hasan, ed., *India Partitioned: The Other Face of Freedom* (Delhi: Lotus Collection, 1995), vol. 2, p. 45.
41. AICC, G–23 (1946–8), J. P. Narayan's note on the communal question, 1946.
42. Kuwajima, *Muslims, Nationalism and the Partition*, p. 160.
43. AICC, G 22 (1945–6) Delhi Congress Committee to Secretary AICC, 16 Feb. 1946.
44. *Times of India*, 12 March 1946.
45. The Muslim League won all 30 reserved seats in the Central Legislative Assembly and 86.6 per cent of votes cast. It also won 442 of 509 reserved seats in the provinces. The Congress won 57 of the 102 seats in the Central Legislative Assembly and 91.3 per cent of the non-Muslim votes cast.
46. On the provincial strategies of the different parties see Ayesha Jalal, *The Sole Spokesman: Jinnah, the Muslim League and the Demand for Pakistan* (Cambridge: Cambridge University Press, 1985), pp. 126–73; Jalal, *Self and Sovereignty*; Ian Talbot, *Provincial Politics and the Pakistan Movement: The Growth of the Muslim League in North-West and North-East India 1937–47* (Karachi and Oxford: Oxford University Press, 1988); and Kuwajima, *Muslims, Nationalism and the Partition*.
47. *TOP*, vol. 6, p. 771.

Chapter 3: The Unravelling Raj

1. On Aligarh in the 1940s, see works by Paul Brass, especially *Language, Religion and Politics in North India* (Cambridge: Cambridge University Press, 1974). Also, E.A. Mann, *Boundaries and Identities: Muslims Work and Status in Aligarh* (New Delhi: Sage Publications, 1992) and M. Hasan 'Negotiating with Its Past and Its Present: The Changing Profile of the Aligarh Muslim University' in M. Hasan, ed., *Inventing Boundaries: Gender, Politics and the Partition of India* (New Delhi and Oxford: Oxford University Press, 2000). *SWJN*, 2nd ser., vol. 1, pp. 49–50. Letter to Rafi Ahmad Kidwai, 28 Sept. 1946.

2. *Dawn*, 28 Jan. 1946.
3. *Times of India*, 11 April 1946. See also S.S. Pirzada, ed. *Foundations of Pakistan: All-Indian Muslim League Documents: vol. 2 1924–1947* (First published, Karachi, 1970); edition cited, New Delhi: Metropolitan Book Co., 1982), pp. 521–2.
4. Pirzada, ed. *Foundations of Pakistan*, p. 524.
5. Khalid Bin Sayeed, *Pakistan: The Formative Phase* (London: Oxford University Press, 1968) pp. 181–2.
6. *JP* 2nd ser., vol. 12, p. 643. M.A. Ishaque to Jinnah, 8 March 1946.
7. Ayesha Jalal, *The Sole Spokesman: Jinnah, the Muslim League and the Demand for Pakistan* (Cambridge: Cambridge University Press, 1985). Ayesha Jalal's revisionist interpretation of Jinnah's motives caused shock waves when it was published, yet it was also successful, and persuasive, because Jinnah's actions had hitherto been interpreted in a one-dimensional way. The ambiguity surrounding the Lahore Resolution and the uncertain attitudes to the meanings of Pakistan had been noted by contemporary observers, but Jalal gave these new credibility and scholarly authority, so much so that her interpretation of Jinnah has become the new orthodoxy. The Jinnah who hovers malevolently like a bad spirit in Attenborough's epic Oscar-winning film, *Gandhi*, has been replaced by an astute lawyer, who managed to sit upon the powderkeg of diverse Muslim interests, and subtly bartered with the British in order to win the best possible deal for Muslims. In the event, his preferred dream of a federated India with parity for Muslims was shattered and he accepted the option of a Pakistani state with greatly curtailed borders and inherent limitations, resolving to make the best of a bad situation.
8. Ata-ur-Rehman, ed., *A Pictorial History of the Pakistan Movement* (Lahore: Dost Associates), p. 103.
9. Shaista Suhrawardy Ikramullah, *From Purdah to Parliament* (Karachi: Oxford University Press, 1963), p. 135.
10. AICC, G–42 (1945–6).
11. Rajeshwar Dayal, *A Life of Our Times* (Delhi: Orient Longman, 1998), p. 78.
12. Ibid., Rajeshwar Dayal was appointed Home Secretary to the United Provinces government in 1946.
13. C.H. Philips and M. Wainwright, eds., *The Partition of India: Policies and Perspectives, 1935–1947* (London: Allen and Unwin, 1970)p. 410–1.
14. *Times of India*, 3 April 1946.
15. Malcolm Darling, *At Freedom's Door* (Oxford: Oxford University Press, 1949), p. 11.
16. Ibid., pp. 13–14.
17. Ibid., pp. 14, 24.
18. Inverview with Sarfaraz Nazine in Mukulika Banerjee, *The Pathan Unarmed: Opposition and Memory in the North West Frontier* (Oxford and Delhi: James Currey, 2000), p. 170.
19. P. Moon, ed., *Wavell: The Viceroy's Journal* (London: Oxford University Press, 1973), p. 494.
20. IOR L/PJ/5/168, S.V. Ramamurty to Mountbatten, 30 May 1947.
21. D. Potter, *India's Political Administrators: 1919–1983* (Oxford: Oxford University Press, 1986), p. 135.
22. A.K. Azad, *India Wins Freedom* (first published 1959; edition cited) (Delhi: Orient Longman, 1989), pp. 134–5.
23. AIHM, C–190 (1946–7), Undated note on Ram Sena. UP Hindu Mahasabha Papers, P–108 (part 2) (1946–7).
24. IOR L/PJ/5/275, FNR, first half Jan. 1946.
25. *TOP*, vol. 8, p. 519.

26. Andrew Whitehead, *Oral Archive: India, a People Partitioned* (London: School of Oriental and African Studies, 1997, 2000), Kewal Malkani interviewed in Delhi, 16 Jan. 1997. The RSS, founded in 1925 by K.B. Hedgewar, has a persistent presence in India and still trains up the young foot-soldiers of Hindutva or Hindu nationalism today. Hindutva conflates a thoroughly modern idea of 'race' with 'Indianness'. It means relegating all those who fall outside the Hindu civilisational pale – including Christians, *dalits* and Muslims – to the status of minorities or second-class citizens.

27. Tapan Raychaudhuri, 'Shadows of the Swastika: Historical Perspectives on the Politics of Hindu Communalism', *Modern Asian Studies*, 34.2 (May 2000), pp. 259–79.

28. Trans. from Urdu by Hira Lal Seth, *The Khaksar Movement* (Lahore: Hero Publications, 1946), p. 61.

29. Markus Daechsel, *The Politics of Self-Expression: The Urdu Middle-Class Milieu in Mid-twentieth century India and Pakistan* (London: Routledge, 2006); M.S. Golwalkar, *We, or Our Nationhood Defined* (Nagpur, 1939).

30. Bhisham Sahni, *Tamas* (Delhi: Penguin, 2001), pp. 57–8.

31. *JP*, 2nd ser., vol. 12, p. 624. Durrani to Jinnah, 1 March 1946.

32. S.C. Sharma, *Pandit Ravi Shankar Shukla: Life and Times* (Delhi: Bharatiya Bhasha Peeth, 1991), p. 207. Speech of Shukla at a press conference, 27 April 1946.

33. *SWJN*, 1st ser., vol. 15, 5 Aug. 1946; 2nd ser., vol. 1. 25 Sept. 1946. Speech at a meeting of Congress volunteer organisations, Delhi 25 Sept. 1946.

34. Banerjee, *The Pathan Unarmed*, p. 186.

35. *Civil and Military Gazette*, 9 May 1947.

36. AICC, G–53 (1946). Nehru to K. Chatterji, 30 Aug. 1946.

37. *Times of India*, 15 Jan. 1946; 5 Feb. 1946.

38. Ruchi Ram Sahni, *To the British Cabinet Mission* (Lahore: Dewan Ram, 1946), pp. 13, 91.

39. *Times of India*, 19 March 1946; *TOP*, vol. 7, p. 23. Note by Major Wyatt, 28 March 1946.

40. *Times of India*, 15 April 1946.

41. J.P. Chander, *Cabinet Mission in India* (Lahore: Indian Printing Works, 1946), p. 107.

42. Ibid., p. 108.

43. *TOP*, vol. 7, pp. 592–4.

44. *TOP*, vol. 7, p. 766. Meeting of Cabinet Delegation, Wavell, Wylie and Twynam, 1 June 1946.

45. *Times of India*, 17 May 1946.

46. On G.D. Birla's role during Partition see Medha M. Kudaisya, *The Life and Times of G.D. Birla* (Oxford and Delhi: Oxford University Press, 2003).

47. Moon, ed., *Wavell: The Viceroy's Journal*, p. 239.

48. *TOP*, vol. 7, p. 858; *Times of India*, 18 May 1946.

49. Nasim Ansari, *Choosing to Stay: Memoirs of an Indian Muslim* (first published in 1987; edition cited trans. from Urdu by Ralph Russell, Karachi: City Press, 1999), pp. 17–18.

50. *TOP*, vol. 8, p. 161. Wylie to Wavell, 31 July 1946.

51. *TOP*, vol. 7, p. 655. Wavell to Henderson, 21 May 1946.

52. *CWMG*, vol. 85, p. 54.

Chapter 4: The Collapse of Trust

1. Suranjan Das, *Communal Riots in Bengal 1905–1947* (Oxford: Oxford University Press, 1994), p. 171.

2. See Bidyut Chakrabarty, *The Partition of Bengal and Assam, 1932–1947: Contour of Freedom* (London: RoutledgeCurzon, 2004), p. 98.

3. *Dawn*, 16 Aug. 1946; *Eastern Times*, 16 Aug. 1946.

4. Das, *Communal Riots in Bengal*, p. 168.
5. From a League pamphlet entitled *Let Pakistan Speak for Herself* (1946) cited in Chakrabarty, *The Partition of Bengal and Assam*, p. 99.
6. Andrew Whitehead, Oral Archive: *India: A People Partitioned* (London: School of Oriental and African Studies, 1997, 2000); Jugal Chandra Ghosh, interviewed in Calcutta, 24 May 1997.
7. Ibid.; Syed Nazimuddin Hashim interviewed in Dhaka, 22 April 1997. On ethno-religious conflict in Bengal see John H. Broomfield, *Elite Conflict in a Plural Society: Twentieth Century Bengal* (Berkeley, 1968); Joya Chatterji, *Bengal Divided: Hindu Communalism and Partition, 1932–1947* (Cambridge: Cambridge University Press, 1994); Das, *Communal Riots in Bengal;* Taj I. Hashmi, *Pakistan as a Peasant Utopia: The Communalization of Class Politics in East Bengal, 1920–1947* (Boulder, Colorado: Westview, 1992).
8. Andrew Whitehead, 'The Butchers of Calcutta', *Indian Express*, 1 July 1997.
9. Whitehead, *India: A People Partitioned*; Syed Nazimuddin Hashim interviewed in Dhaka, 22 April 1997.
10. M. Daechsel, *The Politics of Self-Expression: The Urdu Middle-Class Milieu in Mid-twentieth-century India and Pakistan* (London: Routledge, 2006), p. 75.
11. *Times of India*, 25 May 1946.
12. Saumya Gupta, 'The "Daily" Reality of Partition: Politics in Newsprint, in 1940s Kanpur', in S. Sengupta and G. Lovink, eds, *The Public Domain: Sarai Reader 01* (New Delhi: Centre for the Study of Developing Societies, 2001), p. 83.
13. Ibid.
14. AICC G–10 (1947) Bengal Provincial Congress Committee Papers, 15 Oct. 1946.
15. Suranjan Das, *Communal Riots in Bengal*, p. 193.
16. Ashoka Gupta, 'Those Days in Noakhali', *Indian Seminar*, 510 (2002).
17. Whitehead, *India: A People Partitioned*; Sailen Chatterjee interviewed in Delhi, 25 Jan. 1997; *CWMG*, vol. 86, p. 138, 20 Nov. 1946. See also *India Today*, 18 Aug. 1997.
18. *SWJN*, 2nd ser., vol. 1, pp. 47–112. Speeches at Bakhtiarpur and Fatwa, 4 Nov. 1946; letter to Vallabhbhai Patel, 5 Nov. 1946.
19. Cited in Vinita Damodaran, *Broken Promises: Popular Protest, Indian Nationalism and the Congress Party in Bihar, 1935–1946* (Delhi and Oxford: Oxford University Press, 1992), p. 356. Damodaran describes post-war Bihar and the growth of agricultural and ethnic conflict in detail, pp. 284–369.
20. IOR L/PJ/5/275, Wylie to Wavell, 21 Nov. 1946. My description is drawn from accounts of the violence in AICC, G–10 (1947), Congress Reports on Garhmukhteshwar; IOR L/PJ/8/575, Reports on the disturbances in Bihar and UP, and IOR L/PJ/8/650, UP Ministerial and Political Affairs, 1946–7. For an analysis of the different interpretations placed on the violence by the Congress, League and British, see Gyanendra Pandey, *Remembering Partition: Violence, Nationalism and History in India* (Cambridge: Cambridge University Press, 2001), pp. 92–120.
21. A.P. Jain, *Rafi Ahmad Kidwai: A Memoir of his Life and Times* (London: Asia Publishing House, 1965), p. 75.
22. AICC, G–10 (1946). Report of B.B. Jetley, Superintendent of Police, Meerut, 19 Dec. 1946.
23. For example the Government of Bombay immediately after Independence described 'the three great vices of modern times' as 'prostitution, gambling and drinking', enforced prohibition in six districts of Bombay and made it illegal to advertise liquor in newspapers, while the film censor banned drinking scenes from films.
24. S.S. Ikramullah, From *Purdah to Parliament* (Karachi: Oxford University Press, 1963), p. 143.

25. Sarfaraz Mirza, *Muslim Women's Role in the Pakistan Movement* (Lahore: Research Society of Pakistan, University of the Punjab, 1969), p. 83.
26. C.H. Philips and M. Wainwright, eds, *The Partition of India: Policies and Perspectives, 1935–1947* (London: Allen and Unwin, 1970), p. 377.
27. *TOP*, vol. 8, p. 849. Jenkins to Wavell, 31 Oct. 1946.
28. IOR L/PJ/5/167.
29. Chatterji, *Bengal Divided*, pp. 240–59.
30. Ibid., pp. 242, 244.
31. Daechsel, *The Politics of Self-Expression*, pp. 141–6.
32. Ibid., pp. 18–59.
33. IOR Mss Eur. D724/13, Hume Papers, 10 Nov. 1946.
34. AICC, CL–10 (1946–7); AICC, G–10 (1947).
35. AICC G–10 (1947). Note on Noakhali.
36. IOR L/PJ/5/167, Clow to Wavell, 4 Nov. 1946.
37. IOR L/PJ/5/139, FNR, second half Oct. 1946.
38. Gupta, 'The "Daily" Reality of Partition', p. 86.
39. Medha Kudaisya, *The Life and Times of G.D. Birla* (Delhi and Oxford: Oxford University Press, 2003), p. 234; Letter to Rajagopalachari, 21 Nov. 1946.
40. Penderel Moon, *Divide and Quit: An eyewitness account of the Partition of India* (Delhi: Oxford University Press, 1998), p. 74.
41. IOR L/PJ/5/275, FNR, first half Jan. 1946.
42. IOR Mss Eur. D724/13, Hume Papers, Jan.–Dec. 1946.
43. *TOP*, vol. 8, p. 750. Patel to Stafford Cripps, 19 Oct. 1946; IOR L/PJ/5/276 Wylie to Wavell, 22 Jan. 1947; *JP*, 1st ser., vol. 3, p. 224. Mountbatten to Jinnah, 9 July 1947.
44. *CWMG*, vol. 85 p. 282. 15 Sept. 1946; Cantwell Smith, *Modern Islam in India*, p. 292.

Chapter 5: From Breakdown to Breakdown

1. Pran Nevile, *Lahore: A Sentimental Journey* (Delhi: Penguin, 2006), p. xx.
2. IOR L/PJ/5/276, FNR, second half April 1947; IOR, Mss Eur. C290, Unpublished memoirs of C. Pearce (UP Police), *c.* 1977.
3. Ian Copland, *State, Community and Neighbourhood in Princely North India, c.1900–1950* (London: Palgrave Macmillan, 2005), p. 115.
4. Wm Roger Louis, 'The Partitions of India and Palestine', in *Ends of British Imperialism: The Scramble for Empire, Suez and Decolonization* (New York, 2006), p. 407.
5. Penderel Moon, *Divide and Quit: An eyewitness account of the Partition of India* (Delhi: Oxford University Press, 1998), pp. 62–3.
6. Andrew Whitehead, *Oral Archive: India: A People Partitioned* (London: School of Oriental and African Studies, 1997, 2000); Amjad Husain, interviewed in Lahore, 11 Oct. 1995.
7. Raghuvendra Tanwar, *Reporting the Partition of Punjab, 1947: Press, Public and Other Opinions* (Delhi: Manohar, 2006), pp. 143, 152.
8. IOR FNR L/PJ/5/168 and USSA 845.00/7–3047, Box 6070.
9. IOR L/PJ/5/168, Fortnightly report 3 March 1947. *Civil and Military Gazette*, 13 May 1947.
10. Bhisham Sahni, *Tamas* (Delhi: Penguin edn, 2001), p. 162.
11. Ibid., p. 103.
12. This has resonance with Paul Brass's description of an 'institutionalised riot system' in contemporary India. See Paul Brass, *The Production of Hindu-Muslim Violence in Contemporary India* (Seattle: University of Washington Press, 2003); and Paul Brass,

Theft of an Idol: Text and Context in the Representation of Collective Violence (Princeton: Princeton University Press, 1997).

13. Asim Roy, 'The High Politics of India's Partition', *Modern Asian Studies*, 24.2 (May 1990), pp. 385–408, p. 404.
14. Seth Ramkrishna Dalmia, *Some Notes and Reminiscences* (Bombay: Times of India Press, 1948), pp. 29–30.
15. Congress resolution on Partition of Punjab, 8 March 1947.
16. UP Hindu Mahasabha Papers, P–108 (Part 1) (1947); Gist of conversation between Sampurnanand and Mahasabha leaders, 22 July 1947 agreed by Sampurnanand. Prithwiraj was the last Rajput (and therefore 'Hindu') ruler of Delhi. He ruled in the twelfth century, was killed in battle with Afghans and was succeeded by Mohammed Ghori. For a close interpretation of Sampurnanand's political ideology see William Gould, *Hindu Nationalism and the Language of Politics in Late Colonial India* (Cambridge, Cambridge University Press, 2004), pp. 166–80.
17. Alan Campbell Johnson, *Mission with Mountbatten* (London: Robert Hale, 1951), pp. 64–73.
18. Ibid., p. 47.
19. *JP*, 1st ser., vol. 2, p. 416. Jinnah to Patrick Lacey, 22 June 1947.
20. L. Carter, ed., *Mountbatten's Report on the Last Viceroyalty 22 March to 15 August 1947* (Delhi: Manohar, 2003), p. 188.
21. *Times of India*, 4 June 1947.
22. *JP*, 1st ser., vol. 2, p. 51, 4 June 1947.
23. *Times of India*, 5 June, 1947.
24. Moon, *Divide and Quit*, p. 68.
25. S.S. Ikramullah, *From Purdah to Parliament* (Karachi: Oxford University Press, 1963), p. 154.
26. *JP*, 1st ser., vol. 3, pp. 842–3. Minutes of the meeting of the All India Muslim League, 9 June 1947.
27. *JP*, 1st ser., vol. 2, pp. 141–2, 10 June 1947.
28. S.M. Burke, ed., *Jinnah: Speeches and Statements, 1947–8* (Karachi: Oxford University Press, 2000), p. 25. Constituent Assembly Address, 11 Aug. 1947.
29. IOR L/PJ/5/276, FR, second half June 1947.
30. IOR L/PJ/5/276, FR, second half May 1947.
31. IOR L/PJ/5/168, Fortnightly report, 3 June 1947.
32. A. Jalal, *Self and Sovereignty: Individual and Community in South Asian Islam Since 1850* (Delhi: Oxford University Press, 2001), pp. 539, 543.
33. *Times of India*, 9 June 1947.
34. Shahid Hamid, *Disastrous Twilight: A Personal Record of the Partition of India* (London: Cooper and Secker and Warburg, 1986), p. 178.
35. Ibid. p. 180.
36. *Civil and Military Gazette*, 17 July 1947.
37. *JP*, 1st series, vol. 2, p. 609, letter to Jinnah, 30 June 1947.
38. AICC Resolution on 3 June plan, passed 14 June 1947. *TOP*, vol. 11, p. 398.
39. USSA 845.006-647 Box 6070, Gordon Minnigerode to US Secretary of State, 6 June 1947. Reactions in Karachi and Sind to the British Plan for the Partition of India.
40. Sumathi Ramaswamy, 'Maps and Mother Goddesses in Modern India,' *Imago Mundi*, vol. 53 (2001), pp. 97–114. On the intersections between gender and the shaping of nationalism see also Mrinalini Sinha, *Specters of Mother India: The Global Restructuring of an Empire* (Durham, NC: Duke University Press, 2006).
41. IOR L/PJ/5/168, Fortnightly report 18 July 1947.
42. USSA, 845.00/5–147 – 845.00/7–3047 Box 6070, State Department Records.
43. *Hindustan Times*, 11 June 1947.

44. T. Tan and G. Kudaisya, *The Aftermath of Partition in South Asia* (London and New York: Routledge, 2000), p. 163.
45. Rajendra Prasad, 3 June 1947, cited in Raghuvendra Tanwar, *Reporting the Partition of Punjab, 1947* (New Delhi: Manohar, 2006), p. 167.
46. J. Chatterji, *Bengal Divided: Hindu Communalism and Partition, 1932–1947* (Cambridge: Cambridge University Press, 1994), p. 260; *Times of India*, 9 June 1947.
47. *CWMG*, vol. 88, p. 374. Speech at prayer meeting, 19 July 1947; UPSA General Administration, Box 659, 169/1. Resolution passed 10 Aug. 1947.
48. Malcolm Darling, *At Freedom's Door* (Oxford: Oxford University Press, 1949), p. 307.
49. L. Carter, ed., *Mountbatten's Report on the last Viceroyalty: 22 March–15 August 1947* (Delhi: Manohar, 2003), p. 157; IOR L/PJ/5/168, Fortnightly report, 18 July 1947.
50. Ian Copland, *The Princes of India in the Endgame of Empire 1917–1947* (Cambridge: Cambridge University Press, 1997), pp. 229–60.
51. Quoted ibid., p. 257.
52. See W.A. Wilcox, *Pakistan: The Consolidation of a Nation* (New York, 1963) on the assimilation of the Pakistani princely states.
53. For analysis of these princely schemes during the Raj's disintegration see Copland, *State, Community and Neighbourhood* especially chapters 4 and 5.
54. Moon, *Divide and Quit*, p. 104.
55. *Times of India*, 5 June 1947.
56. *TOP*, vol. 12, p. 125, Governor of Central Provinces and Berar to Mountbatten, 12 July 1947.
57. USSA 845.00/5–147 – 845.00/7–3047 Box 6070, Encl. to dispatch dated 19 June by American Consul-General, Bombay.
58. *JP*, 1st ser., vol. 2, p. 541, 27 June 1947.
59. *Civil and Military Gazette*, 6 May 1947.
60. Moon, *Divide and Quit*, pp. 93–4.
61. *Civil and Military Gazette* 21 June 1947; USSA 845.00/6–647 Box 670 Gordon Minnigerode to US Secretary of State, 6 June 1947. Reactions in Karachi and Sind to the British Plan for the Partition of India.
62. NMML, Pant Papers, File IV, doc. 96. Enclosure on the Indo-Pakistan Muslim League, 1948.
63. USSA 845.00/5–147 – 845.00/7–3047 Box 6070, Attlee in conversation with US Ambassador and Sir Paul Patrick in conversation with State Department representatives, 29 May 1947.
64. *Civil and Military Gazette*, 5 July 1947.

Chapter 6: Untangling Two Nations

1. Penderel Moon, *Divide and Quit: An eyewitness account of the Partition of India* (Delhi: Oxford University Press, 1998), pp. 90–1.
2. *CWMG*, vol. 88, p. 135, Speech at a prayer meeting, 11 June 1947.
3. Moon, *Divide and Quit*, pp. 90–1.
4. IOR L/PJ/5/140 Hydari to Mountbatten, 1 Aug. 1947.
5. *TOP*, vol. 11, p. 26. Jenkins to Mountbatten, 31 May 1947.
6. Ibid., p. 136. Jenkins to Mountbatten 5 June 1947.
7. Moon, *Divide and Quit*, p. 114.
8. *TOP*, vol. XI, pp. 561–3, Nehru to Mountbatten, 22 June 1947; *JP*, 1st ser., vol. 2, p. 829, Mountbatten to Jenkins, 24 June 1947.
9. Ibid., p. 51, 10 June 1947.
10. *JP*, 1st ser., vol. 1, p. 903. A.A. Quddoosi to Jinnah, 22 May 1947.

11. *CWMG*, vol. 88, p. 113, Speech 11 June 1947.
12. Sir Muhammad Zafrullah Khan's recollections republished in Ahmad Salim, ed., *Lahore, 1947* (Delhi: tara-india research press, 2006), pp. 232–4.
13. IOR R/3/1/157, Radcliffe to Bengal Boundary Commission, 17 July 1947; *Dawn*, 19 July 1947; Joya Chatterji, 'The Making of a Borderline', in I. Talbot and G. Singh, eds, *Region and Partition: Bengal, Punjab and the Partition of the Subcontinent* (Oxford and Delhi: Oxford University Press, 1999), p. 172.
14. IOR R/3/1/157.
15. IOR R/3/1/157, Appeal forwarded to Mountbatten, 23 June 1947; *Dawn*, 17 July 1947.
16. IOR R/3/1/157, Maharaja of Patiala to Mountbatten, 7 Aug. 1947.
17. IOR R/3/1/157, on some aspects of untouchable/scheduled caste politics at Partition see R.S. Rawat, 'Partition Politics and Achhut Identity: A Study of the Scheduled Castes Federation, and Dalit Politics in UP, 1946–8', in S. Kaul, ed., *The Partitions of Memory: The Afterlife of the Division of India* (Delhi: Permanent Black, 2001), pp. 111–39.
18. AICC, G 11 (1946–8), undated letter from Lahore, c. mid-1947.
19. *Dawn*, 17 July 1947.
20. *TOP*, vol. 12, p. 148.
21. Diary of Fikr Taunsvi, 11 Aug. 1947 reproduced in Salim, ed., *Lahore, 1947*, p. 19.
22. The authorities in Lahore prohibited noises made by all these items in May 1947.
23. Diary of Fikr Taunsvi, 11 Aug. 1947 reproduced in Salim ed. *Lahore, 1947*, pp. 14–15.
24. Andrew Whitehead, *Oral Archive: India: A People Partitioned* (London: School of Oriental and African Studies, 1997, 2000); Shanti Seghal interviewed by Anuradha Awasthi in Delhi, 1 Feb. 1947.
25. IOR Mss Eur. C290; unpublished manuscript of William Chaning Pearce.
26. USSA 845.00/8–147 – 845.00/12–3147 Box 6071, 13 Aug. 1947.
27. Moon, *Divide and Quit*, p. 115.
28. L. Carter, ed. *Mountbatten's Report on the last Viceroyalty, 22 March to 15 August 1947* (New Delhi: Manohar, 2003), p. 79.
29. Epstein Papers (Private Collection), Col. G.S.N Hughes to Mr Bowen, 24 June 1947.
30. Epstein Papers (Private Collection) Anthony Epstein to family, 14 Oct. 1947.
31. Whitehead, *India: A People Partitioned*; Sahabzada Yaqub Khan, interviewed in Delhi, 15 March 1997.
32. Indian Emergency Committee Meeting Minutes, 6–7 Sept. 1947, reprinted in H.M. Patel, *Rites of Passage: A Civil Servant Remembers* (New Delhi: Vedam, 2005), pp. 280, 284; *Civil and Military Gazette*, 29 May 1947.
33. Letter from a British police officer quoted in Francis Tuker, *While Memory Serves* (London: Cassell, 1950), pp. 486–7.
34. IOR, Mss Eur. C290, Unpublished memoirs of C. Pearce (UP Police, 1945–7), c. 1977.
35. USSA 845.00/8–147 – 845.00/12–3147, Box 6071, Phillips Talbot to Institute of Current World Affairs on the Indian political situation, 22 July 1947. Talbot would later become a diplomat and specialist on South Asian affairs.
36. *JP*, 1st ser., vol. 3, pp. 668–9. Recommendations of the Muslim members of the Health Committee.
37. *TOP*, vol. 11, pp. 682–5. USSA 845.00/5–147 – 845.00/7–3047 Box 6070. Charles Thomson, Consul in Calcutta, 30 June 1947.
38. *JP*, 1st ser., vol. 4, p. 126. 'Agha' to Fatima Jinnah, 1 Aug. 1947. Attia Hosain's novel, *Sunlight on a Broken Column* (London: Chatto and Windus, 1961) also vividly depicts the indecision among Muslim families confronting the prospect of moving to Pakistan.
39. *JP*, vol. 2, p. 521. S. M. Hasan to Jinnah, 26 June 1947.
40. Manzoor Alam Quraishi, *Indian Administration, Pre and Post Independence: Memoirs of an ICS* (Delhi: BR Publishing, 1985), p. 155.
41. Anwar Ahmed Hanafi interviewed by Patrick French, *Liberty or Death: India's journey to Independence and division* (London: HarperCollins, 1997), p. 315.

42. *Dawn*, 11 Aug. 1947, cited in Tan Tai Yong and G. Kudaisya, *The Aftermath of Partition in South Asia* (London and New York: Routledge, 2000), p. 48.
43. Intizar Husain interviewed in Alok Bhalla, *Partition Dialogues: Memories of a Lost Home* (New Delhi: Oxford University Press, 2006), p. 105.
44. Carter, ed., *Mountbatten's report on the last Viceroyalty*, p. 216.
45. *TOP*, vol. 11, p. 404.
46. *TOP*, vol. 7, p. 169. Note on Meeting of Cabinet Delegation, 8 April 1946.
47. *Hindustan Times*, 20 June 1947.
48. W.C. Smith, *Modern Islam in India* (London: Victor Gollancz, 1946), p. 266; Intizar Husain interviewed in Bhalla, *Partition Dialogues*, p. 94.
49. *TOP*, vol. 11, pp. 193–4; USSA 845.00/8–147 – 845.00/12–3147, Box 6071, Phillips Talbot to Institute of Current World Affairs on the Indian political situation, 22 July 1947.
50. Ravinder Kaur, 'Planning Urban Chaos: State and Refugees in Post-partition Delhi', in E. Hust and M. Mann, eds, *Urbanization and Governance in India* (New Delhi: Manohar, 2005), p. 236.
51. M. Bourke-White, *Halfway to Freedom: A report on the new India* (New York: Simon and Schuster, 1949), pp. 22–3.
52. *JP*, 1st ser., vol. 3, p. 343. Nawab of Bhopal to Jinnah, 12 July 1947.
53. Quoted in M. Hasan, 'Memories of a Fragmented Nation', in S. Settar and I. Gupta, eds, *Pangs of Partition* (New Delhi: Manohar, 2002), vol. 2, p. 182.
54. *Civil and Military Gazette*, 15 Aug. 1947; USSA 845.00/8–147 – 845.00/12–3147 Box 6071, Note by American Consul, Calcutta 13 Aug. 1947.
55. *TOP*, vol. 12, p. 190.
56. IOR L/PJ/5/140, Hydari to Mountbatten, 1 Aug. 1947.
57. Satish Gujral in Hasan, ed., 'Memories of a Fragmented Nation', pp. 47–8.
58. Quoted ibid., p. 182.
59. Bhisham Sahni, *Tamas* (New Delhi: Penguin edn, 2001), pp. 127–8
60. *Report of the Punjab Boundary Commission* (Govt of India, 1947), p. 10.
61. *The Journey to Pakistan; A documentation on refugees of 1947* (Islamabad: Govt of Pakistan, 1993), p. 150.
62. Moon, *Divide and Quit: An eye-witness account of the Partition of India* (Delhi and Oxford: Oxford University Press, 1998) p. 186.
63. M. Hasan, *Legacy of a Divided Nation: India's Muslims Since Independence* (London and Delhi: Oxford University Press, 1997), p. 128.
64. Butalia, *The Other Side of Silence: Voices from the Partition of India* (London: Hurst, 2000), p. 236.
65. Alan Campbell-Johnson, *Mission with Mountbatten* (London: Robert Hale, 1951), p. 167.
66. Broadcast speech of Jinnah on 2 Sept. 1947, in *The Journey to Pakistan: A Documentation on Refugees of 1947* (Islamabad: Govt of Pakistan, 1993), p. 241.
67. Shail Mayaram, 'Speech, Silence and the Making of Partition Violence in Mewat', in Shahid Amin and Dipesh Chakrabarty, eds, *Subaltern Studies IX: Writings on South Asian History and Society* (Delhi: Oxford University Press, 1996), p. 149.

Chapter 7: Blood on the Tracks

1. L. Carter, ed., *Mountbatten's Report on the Last Viceroyalty: 22 March–15 August 1947* (New Delhi: Manohar, 2003), p. 266.
2. Ibid., p. 191.

3. For a convincing account of the severe limitations of this force see Robin Jeffrey, 'The Punjab Boundary Force and the Problem of Order, August 1947', *Modern Asian Studies*, 8.4 (1974), pp. 491–520. The Boundary Force had an operational existence of 32 days, covered only the twelve most 'disturbed' districts of Punjab and included, at its peak, up to 25,000 men, which meant that 'At its greatest strength, the Boundary Force was in a position to allot four men to every three villages or fewer than two men to a square mile; to the population [of these districts], it stood in a ratio of 1:630', p. 500.

4. Moon, *Divide and Quit: An eye witness account of the Partition of India* (Delhi: Oxford University Press, 1998), p. 95.

5. Official state-sponsored accounts have shown a resilient amnesia and 'massacres' comprise a subsidiary appendix tacked on to the greater story of the freedom struggle. There are immense difficulties in disentangling the slivers of memory, anecdotes and fictional accounts preserved by survivors and witnesses. Mapping what took place and placing it in an explanatory framework is no easy task. The jigsaw puzzle of regional and district-level snapshots is still being painstakingly pieced together by historians who are starting to disaggregate the sweeping generalisations and stock imagery of 1947, and realising through sifting through oral history interviews, government archives, personal letters and newspapers that the violence had very particular characteristics; riots and pogroms varied in their intensity, in their precise relationship to the handiwork of local politicians, and in the havoc that they unleashed. For works which specifically address violence in Punjab at the time of Partition see Urvashi Butalia, *The Other Side of Silence: Voices from the Partition of India* (London: Hurst, 2000); Ian Talbot, *Freedom's Cry. The Popular Dimension in the Pakistan Movement and the Partition of the Subcontinent* (Karachi: Oxford University Press, 1999); Paul Brass, 'The Partition of India and Retributive Genocide in the Punjab, 1946–7', *Journal of Genocide Research*, 5.1 (2003); Pippa Virdee, 'Partition and Locality: Studies of the Impact of Partition and its Aftermath in the Punjab region 1947–61' (Unpublished Ph.D. thesis, Coventry University, 2004); Ian Talbot, *Divided Cities: Partition and its Aftermath in Lahore and Amritsar* (New York: Oxford University Press, 2007); Ayesha Jalal, 'Nation, Reason and Religion: The Punjab's Role in the Partition of India', *Economic and Political Weekly*, 8 Aug. 1998; Anders Bjørn Hansen, *Partition and Genocide: Manifestation of Violence in Punjab, 1937–1947* (Delhi, 2002); Swarna Aiyar, "August Anarchy": The Partition Massacres in Punjab, 1947', in D.A. Low and H. Brasted eds, *Freedom, Trauma, Continuities: Northern India and Independence* (Delhi: Sage, 1998); Ian Copland, 'The Master and the Maharajas: The Sikh Princes and the East Punjab Massacres of 1947', *Modern Asian Studies*, 36. 3 (2002); Indivar Kamtekar, 'The Military Ingredient of Communal Violence in Punjab, 1947', *Proceedings of the Indian History Congress*, 56 (1995), pp. 568–72.

6. Moon, *Divide and Quit*, pp. 134–5.

7. Ishtiaq Ahmed, 'Forced Migration and Ethnic Cleansing in Lahore in 1947: Some First Person Accounts', in I. Talbot and Shinder Thandi, eds, *People on the Move: Punjabi Colonial and Post Colonial Migration* (Karachi and Oxford: Oxford University Press, 2004), pp. 132–4.

8. Urvashi Butalia, *The Other Side of Silence*, p. 237.

9. Whitehead, *Oral Archive: India: A People Partitioned* (London: School of Oriental African Studies, 1997, 2000); Harcharan Singh Nirman interviewed in Chandigarh, 17 March 1997.

10. Ibid., Ram Dev interviewed in Chandigarh, 17 March 1947.

11. Bhisham Sahni, *Tamas* (Delhi: Penguin, 2001), p. 229.

12. Whitehead, *India: A People Partitioned*; Krishna Baldev Vaid interviewed in Delhi, 12 Jan. 1997.

13. Jon Stallworthy, *Louis MacNeice* (London: Faber and Faber, 1995), pp. 357–8.

14. Whitehead, *India: A People Partitioned*; Mrs Ashoka Gupta interviewed in Calcutta, 24 April 1997.
15. Extract from interview with Taran in Menon and Bhasin, *Borders and Boundaries*, pp. 46–7.
16. Whitehead, *India: A People Partitioned*; Kuldip Nayar interviewed in Delhi 14 Aug. 1996; Menon and Bhasin, *Borders and Boundaries*, p. 32.
17. Menon and Bhasin, *Borders and Boundaries*, p. 76.
18. Official figures ibid., p. 70. Urvashi Butalia cites 75,000 abductions in *The Other Side of Silence*, p. 3. In 1948, Mridula Sarabhai, who organised the Indian recovery operation, believed that the official figure of women abducted in Pakistan – 12,500 – could have been ten times that in reality.
19. Ian Copland, 'The Further Shores of Partition: Ethnic Cleansing in Rajasthan, 1947', *Past and Present*, 160 (1998), pp. 203–39. The violence in Alwar and Bharatpur is also analysed in S. Mayaram, 'Speech, Silence and the Making of Partition Violence in Mewat'; Shahid Amin and Dipesh Chakrabarty, eds, *Subaltern Studies IX: Writings on South Asian History and Society* (Delhi: Oxford University Press, 1996), pp. 128–61.
20. Copland, 'The Further Shores of Partition', pp. 203–39. There are similarities here with events in the princely states of East Punjab, which Ian Copland has also described in 'The Master and the Maharajas: The Sikh Princes and the East Punjab Massacres of 1947', *Modern Asian Studies*, 36. 3 (2002).
21. IOR Mss Eur. C290, Unpublished memoirs of C. Pearce (UP Police, 1945–7) *c.* 1977.
22. Whitehead, *India: A People Partitioned*, B.L. Dutt interviewed at home in Chandigarh, 15 March 1997.
23. Moon, *Divide and Quit*, p. 164.
24. IOR Mss Eur. F161. Notes of E.S. Thomson, Railway Protection Force, *c.* Sept. 1947 [undated] see also IOR Mss Eur. 147, Demi official reports by D. Cruickshank, East India Railways, 13 Sept. and 22 Sept. 1947.
25. Ibid.
26. Ian Copland, *State Community and Neighbourhood in Princely North India, c. 1900–1950* (London: Palgrave Macmillan, 2005), pp. 156–7.
27. USSA 845.105/8–1547 – 845.105/12.3149 Box 6082, 8 Sept. 1947.
28. *SPC*, vol. 6, p. 319. Patel to Nehru, 4 May, 1948.
29. IOR L/PJ/5/167, Fortnightly reports, Oct. 1946.
30. *The Rape of Rawalpindi* (Lahore: Punjab Riot Sufferers' Relief Committee, *c.* 1947), unpaginated.
31. G.D. Khosla, *Stern Reckoning: A survey of events leading up to and following the Partition of India* (Delhi and Oxford: Oxford University Press, 1989), p. 133.
32. AICC, CL-9 (File 1) (1946–7).
33. BBC news online: 'Indian director Mahesh Bhatt is hoping to make the first ever Indian film shot entirely in Pakistan – a project he described as a "South Asian Schindler's List".' 16 May 2003.
34. M. Hasan, ed., *India Partitioned: the Other Face of Freedom* (Delhi: Lotus Collection, 1995), vol. 2, p. 96.
35. AICC, G–18, Part 2 (1947–8), M. Brelvi to Sadiq Ali, 24 Oct. 1947.
36. Whitehead, *India: A People Partitioned*, Dalit Joginder, interviewed 18 March 1997.
37. Ian Talbot's introduction to Ahmad Salim, ed., *Lahore, 1947* (Delhi: tara-india research press, 2006), p. 6.
38. Whitehead, *India: A People Partitioned*, Shanti Seghal interviewed in Delhi, 1 Feb. 1947.
39. Moon, *Divide and Quit*, p. 120.
40. AICC, G–10 (1947), Report of Meerut District Magistrate, 13 Feb. 1947.
41. IOR L/PJ/5/168, Colville to Wavell, 16 March 1947.
42. *SPC*, vol. 6, p. 266. R. Prasad to V. Patel, 14 May 1948.

Chapter 8: Leprous Daybreak

1. P.N. Chopra, ed., *Inside Story of Sardar Patel: The Diary of Maniben Patel: 1936–50* (New Delhi: Vision Books, 2001), pp. 164–9.
2. Richard Symonds, *In the Margins of Independence: A Relief Worker in India and Pakistan, 1942–1949* (Karachi: Oxford University Press, 2001), p. 34.
3. Partition Emergency Committee Minutes, 16 Sept. 1947, reprinted in appendix to H.M. Patel, *Rites of Passage: A Civil Servant Remembers* ed. Sucheta Mahajan (New Delhi: Rupa and Co., 2005), p. 360.
4. Partition Emergency Committee Minutes, 16 Sept. 1947, reprinted in appendix to Patel, *A Civil Servant Remembers*, p. 360.
5. Alan Campbell-Johnson, *Mission with Mountbatten* (London: Robert Hale, 1951), p. 180; Judith Brown, *Nehru: A political life* (London and New Haven: Yale University Press, 2003), p. 176.
6. Symonds, *In the Margins of Independence*, pp. 33–4. Many stories of Nehru's agitated state were in circulation at this time, including one that he had kicked a group of *sadhus*, or Hindu holy men, who had blockaded the entrance to his house and refused to move: see USSA 845.00/8–147 – 845.00/12–3147 Box 6071, 5 Aug. 1947.
7. Ayub Khan, *Friends Not Masters: A Political Autobiography* (New York and Oxford: Oxford University Press, 1967), p. 17.
8. M.M. Kudaisya, *The Life and Times of G.D. Birla* (Delhi and Oxford: Oxford University Press, 2003), p. 243. Birla to Katju, 29 Sept. 1947.
9. Penderel Moon, *Divide and Quit: An eye-witness account of the Partition of India* (Delhi: Oxford University Press, 1998), p. 154.
10. Extract written by the Urdu journalist Shorish Kashmiri reproduced in M. Hasan, *India Partitioned: The Other Face of Freedom* (Delhi: Lotus Collection, 1995), vol. 2, p. 156.
11. S.M. Burke, ed., *Jinnah: Speeches and Statements, 1947–8* (Karachi: Oxford University Press, 2000), p. 14. Press conference, 14 July 1947.
12. Suhasini Das, 'A Partition Diary', trans. Kumkum Chakravarti, *Seminar*, 510 (Feb. 2002).
13. F. Tuker, *While Memory Serves* (London: Cassell, 1950), p. 530.
14. M. Hasan, ed., *India Partitioned*, vol. 2, p. 194.
15. Epstein Papers (Private Collection), Letter to Parents, 15 May 1947.
16. IOR Mss Eur. 147 Demi-official reports by D. Cruickshank, East India Railways, 13 Sept. and 22 Sept. 1947.
17. Mahatma Gandhi, *Delhi Diary: Prayer speeches from 10 Sept. 1947 to 30 Jan. 1948* (Ahmedabad: Navajivan Publishing House, 1948), 28 Oct. 1947.
18. Symonds, *In the Margins of Independence*, p. 33.
19. *SWJN*, 2nd ser., vol. 4, p. 441. Letter to Provincial Premiers, 15 Oct. 1947.
20. Campbell-Johnson, *Mission with Mountbatten*, pp. 178–9.
21. *The Journey to Pakistan: A documentation on refugees of 1947* (Islamabad: Govt of Pakistan, 1993), p. 256. Jinnah's speech, 14 Sept. 1947 on the establishment of the Quaid e Azam Relief Fund.
22. *Millions on the Move: The Aftermath of Partition* (Govt of India, Delhi, 1948), photograph and caption facing p. 4.
23. R. Menon and K. Bhasin, *Borders and Boundaries: Women in India's Partition* (Delhi: Kali for Women, 1998), p. 232.
24. Symonds, *In the Margins of Independence*, p. 54; Tuker, *While Memory Serves*, p. 476.
25. USSA, 845.00/8–147 – 845.00/12–3147 Box 6071, Howard Donovan to Secretary of State, Washington, 30 Sept. 1947. Encl. extracts from a personal letter written by a retired British officer (unidentified), Simla 17 Sept. 1947.

26. *Millions on the Move*, p. 55.
27. *Pakistan Times*, 26 Aug. 1947.
28. Andrew Whitehead, *Oral Archive: India: A People Partitioned* (School of Oriental and African Studies, 1997, 2000); Sahabzada Yaqub Khan, interviewed in Delhi, 15 March 1947; Burke, ed., *Jinnah: Speeches and Statements*, p. 35.
29. Mangla Prasad, United Provinces Provincial Congress Secretary, Lucknow, to all district and town Congress committees, 30 July 1947. Quoted in Tan Tai Yong and G. Kudaisya, *The Aftermath of Partition in South Asia* (London and New York: Routledge, 2000), p. 37.
30. *Times of India*, 13 Aug. 1947; 18 Aug. 1947.
31. Syed Mahmud to S.K. Sinha, *c.* 1948 (undated) in V.N. Datta and B.E. Cleghorn, eds, *A Nationalist Muslim and Indian Politics: Selected Letters of Syed Mahmud* (Delhi: Macmillan, 1974), pp. 263–4.
32. UPSA, Home Department Police (A), Box 22, 63/1948.
33. *Hindustan Times*, 22 July 1947. Cited in Tan and Kudaisya, *The Aftermath of Partition in South Asia*, p. 42. For a very detailed account of Independence Day ceremonies and celebrations, on which my account draws, see ibid., pp. 29–77.
34. Tan and Kudaisya, *The Aftermath of Partition*, pp. 29–77.
35. Moon, *Divide and Quit*, p. 115.
36. A.N. Bali, *Now it can be told* (Jullundur: Akash Vani Prakashan, 1949), p. 39.
37. Andrew Whitehead, *Oral Archive: India: A People Partitioned*; Amjad Husain, interviewed in Lahore, 11 Oct. 1995.
38. Ibid., Saroj Pachauri interviewed in Delhi, 28 Jan. 1997.
39. Moon, *Divide and Quit*, p. 125.
40. *Times of India*, 12 Aug. 1947.
41. Constituent Assembly of Pakistan debates, 11 Aug. 1947 in M Rafique Afzal, ed., *Speeches and Statements of Quaid-i-Millat Liaquat Ali Khan, 1941–51* (Lahore: University of Punjab, 1967), p. 117.
42. Alok Bhalla, *Partition Dialogues: Memories of a Lost Home* (New Delhi: Oxford University Press, 2006), p. 162.
43. IOR FNR, L/PJ/5/276, Wylie to Mountbatten, 10 Aug. 1947.
44. Aycsha Jalal, Gyanendra Pandey and Mushirul Hasan have analysed these conflations and confusions which were worsened by setting up 'nationalism' as a binary to 'communalism'. See, for instance, Ayesha Jalal, 'Exploding Communalism: The Politics of Muslim Identity in South Asia', in S. Bose and A. Jalal, eds, *Nationalism, Democracy and Development: State and Politics in India* (Delhi: Oxford University Press, 1997); G. Pandey, 'Can a Muslim be an Indian?' *Comparative Studies in Society and History*, 41.4 (1999), and M. Hasan, *Legacy of a Divided Nation: India's Muslims Since Independence* (London and Delhi: Oxford University Press, 1997).
45. Burke, ed., *Jinnah: Speeches and Statements*, p. 28. Speech to Constituent Assembly, 11 Aug. 1947.
46. Abdul Quaiyum Khan to Syed Mahmud, 8/10 Feb. 1948 in Datta and Cleghorn, eds, *A Nationalist Muslim*, p. 267.
47. Whitehead, *India: A People Partitioned*, Danial Latifi interviewed in Delhi, 23 Dec. 1996.
48. Figures are taken from tables and appendices in *After Partition* (Delhi: Publications Division, Govt of India, 1948) and *The Journey to Pakistan* (Govt. of Pakistan).
49. Khushwant Singh, *Train to Pakistan* (first published in 1956; edition cited Ravi Dayal and Permanent Black, New Delhi, 1988), p. 57.
50. *JP*, 1st ser. vol. 2, pp. 824–5, 'Jinnah Anxious to have non Muslims live in Pakistan'.
51. *SWJN*, 2nd ser., vol. 4, p. 442. Letter to Premiers of Provinces, 15 Oct. 1947.
52. Butalia, *The Other Side of Silence*, p. 80.

53. Ibid., p. 92.
54. Emergency Committee minutes, 7 Sept. 1947, reprinted in H. M. Patel, *A Civil Servant Remembers*, p. 292.
55. *Millions on the Move*, p. 6.
56. Whitehead, *India: A People Partitioned* Harcharan Singh Nirman interviewed in Chandigarh, 17 March 1997.
57. Symonds, *In the Margins of Independence*, p. 55.
58. Sarah Ansari, *Life after Partition: Migration, Community and Strife in Sindh, 1947–1962* (Karachi and Oxford: Oxford University Press, 2005), p. 54.
59. Moon, *Divide and Quit*, pp. 180–1.
60. *The Journey to Pakistan*, p. 34.
61. M. Bourke-White, *Halfway to Freedom. A Report on the New India in the Words and Photographs of Margaret Bourke-White* (New York, 1949), p. 20.
62. Ibid., pp. 17–18.
63. Whitehead, *India: A People Partitioned*, Kuldip Nayar, interviewed in Delhi, 29 Oct. 1996.
64. Khushwant Singh, *Train to Pakistan*, p. 57.
65. Whitehead, *India: A People Partitioned* Nasreen Azhar, interviewed in Islamabad, 25 Sept. 1995.
66. Moon, *Divide and Quit*, pp. 110–11.
67. Shaista Suhrawardy Ikramullah, *From Purdah to Parliament* (Karachi: Oxford University Press, 1963), p. 158; Mian Amiruddin's 'Memories of Partition', in Ahmad Salim, ed., *Lahore, 1947* (Delhi, 2006), pp. 257, 251.
68. *Millions on the Move*, p. 67.
69. Whitehead, *India: A People Partitioned*, Khorshed Mehta, interviewed in Delhi, 18 Jan. 1997.
70. The Indian government estimated at the end of 1947 that there were 1.25 million refugees in 160 camps in India and the Pakistani government estimated that there were 1,116,500 refugees in 16 camps in West Punjab (Sources: *After Partition* and *The Journey to Pakistan*).
71. Report by K.M. Malik Khuda Baksh, 4 Oct. 1947, reproduced in *The Journey to Pakistan*, p. 209.
72. Anis Kidwai, 'In the Shadow of Freedom', trans. from Urdu and reproduced in Hasan, ed., *India Partitioned*, vol. 2, pp. 167–80.

Chapter 9: Bitter Legacies

1. Note by Delhi's Superintendent of Police, 4 Jan. 1948 enclosed in *SPC*, vol. 6, pp. 260–1.
2. *SPC*, vol. 6, p. 162.
3. Catherine Rey-Schirr, 'The ICRC's Activities on the Indian Subcontinent following Partition (1947–1949)', *International Review of the Red Cross*, 323 (1998), pp. 267–91, p. 268.
4. *SPC*, vol. 6, p. 244. Nehru to V. Patel, 12 Jan. 1948.
5. Ibid., pp. 119–20. Bardoloi to Patel, 5 May 1948.
6. Sarah Ansari, *Life after Partition: Migration, Community and Strife in Sindh, 1947–1962* (Karachi and Oxford: Oxford University Press, 2005), pp. 46–121.
7. *The Journey to Pakistan: A Documentation on Refugees of 1947* (Islamabad: Govt of Pakistan, 1993), pp. 310–11.
8. Quoted in Urvashi Butalia, 'An Archive with a Difference: Partition Letters', in Suvir Kaul, ed., *The Partitions of Memory: The Afterlife of the Division of India* (Delhi: Permanent Black, 2001), p. 219. Urvashi Butalia's brilliant account of these letters

suggests that, 'notwithstanding their sense of reproach, and sometimes alienation', through all the letters 'ran a thread of commitment to the new nation, and to the newly-forming state'.

9. A classic example of this thinking is *Rehabilitation of Displaced Persons in Bombay State: A Decennial Retrospect* (Govt of Bombay, 1958), p. 28: 'The rehabilitation of millions of displaced persons from Pakistan, who have migrated to our country, no doubt, has presented special problems but viewed broadly, it has to be regarded as an essential aspect of development of the economy of the country as a whole.' On the intellectual consensus around 'development' as a state goal, the prioritisation of scientific expertise and state welfare, and its interpretation by nationalist elites in the late colonial state, see in particular, Benjamin Zachariah, *Developing India: An Intellectual and Social History c. 1930–50* (New Delhi and Oxford: Oxford University Press, 2005).

10. *Rehabilitation of Displaced Persons* (Publications Division, Ministry of Information and Broadcasting, Govt of India, 1948), p. 17.

11. The Indian and Pakistani governments also used Victorian terms such as 'the deserving poor' and 'sloth' (no doubt inherited from the lexicon of the Raj) in their discussion of the displaced. Hard-working refugees who would stand on their own two feet were to be rewarded and encouraged while 'measures to eliminate forced idleness' were essential. While touring the kitchens of refugee camps in Lahore, Jinnah instructed the staff to, 'Make the refugees work. Do not let them nurse the idea that they are guests for all time.'
   Dependency on the state was an expensive sin to be discouraged, and this official mindset was entirely compatible with socialistic, centralised planning projects.

12. AICC, G–18 (Part 1), Frontier and Punjab Riot Sufferer Committee to Pant, 4 Oct. 1947; UPSA, Relief and Rehabilitation, 197(18)/47, Pakistan Sufferers Cooperative Housing Society.

13. Ravinder Kaur, 'Planning Urban Chaos: State and Refugees in Post-partition Delhi', in E. Hust and M. Mann, eds, *Urbanization and Governance in India* (New Delhi: Manohar, 2005), p. 235. This attitude was most pronounced in the different way that Bengali and Punjabi refugees were treated by the Indian government. Punjabis had the lion's share of these schemes and benefited most from government help while the Bengalis were often left to fend for themselves. Less money was spent, per head, on Bengali than Punjabi refugees. The Punjabi crisis was more visible in the national capital than the Bengali one as the region was closer and Partition's damage was more concentrated, bloody and horrifying. But as the historian Joya Chatterji has illustrated, Congress politicians also drew on old colonial stereotypes and blatantly discriminated between the hardy Punjabis and the 'weak', 'dependent' Bengalis. Joya Chatterji, 'Right or Charity? Relief and Rehabilitation in West Bengal', in Kaul, ed., *The Partitions of Memory*.

14. NMML AIHM C–177. The Hindu Mahasabha claimed that 15 were killed and 60 injured in the firing.

15. L. C. Jain, *The City of Hope: the Faridabad Story* (Delhi: Concept Publishing Co., 1998), p. 75.

16. UPSA Relief and Rehabilitation, Box 68 153/51, Disbanding of women's home at Darbhangha Castle, Allahabad.

17. UPSA Relief and Rehabilitation C, File MC/50 14 July 1951.

18. UPSA Relief and Rehabilitation Dept, 273/48 Box 18, 12 March 1950.

19. Ata-ur-Rehman, ed., *A Pictorial History of Pakistan Movement* (Lahore and Karachi: Dost Associates, c. 1998).

20. *The Journey to Pakistan*, p. 296.

21. Ibid., Letter to the editor of the *Pakistan Times* on conditions at Walton camp, 23 Aug. 1947 from Mohammad Qureshi, p. 231.

22. *The Journey to Pakistan*, 19 Sept. 1947 p. 258.
23. W. Anderson and S. Damle, *The Brotherhood in Saffron: the Rashtriya Swayamsevak Sangh and Hindu Revivalism* (Boulder: Westview, 1987), p. 50.
24. Mawdudi's statement, 7 Oct. 1947, reproduced in *The Journey to Pakistan*, pp. 267–8. On Jam 'at-i Islami and refugee rehabilitation in Pakistan, see Seyyed Vali Reza Nasr, *The Vanguard of the Islamic Revolution: The Jama'at-i Islami of Pakistan* (London: I.B. Tauris, 1994), pp. 88–9.
25. Mudie to Jinnah, 5 Sept. 1947, cited in Khalid B. Sayeed, *Pakistan: the Formative Phase, 1857–1948* (London: Oxford University Press, 1968), p. 262.
26. I. Talbot, *Freedom's Cry: The Popular Dimension in the Pakistan Movement and Partition Experience in North-West India* (Karachi and Oxford: Oxford University Press, 1996), p. 174.
27. *SWJN*, 2nd ser., vol. 4, p. 441.
28. Emergency Committee minutes, 18 Sept. 1947, reproduced in H. Patel, *Rites of Passage: A Civil Servant Remembers* (New Delhi: Vedam, 2005), p. 367.
29. V.N. Datta and B.E. Cleghorn, eds, *A Nationalist Muslim and Indian Politics. Selected Letters of Syed Mahmud* (Delhi: Macmillan, 1974), Nehru to Syed Mahmud, 26 Feb. 1948, p. 268.
30. *SPC*, vol. 8, pp. 46–7.
31. *SPC*, vol. 8, pp. 49–50, 1 Dec. 1949.
32. Ayub Khan, *Friends Not Masters: A Political Autobiography* (New York and Oxford: Oxford University Press, 1967), p. 48.
33. *After Partition* (Delhi: Publications Division, Govt of India, 1948), p. 35.
34. Ashis Nandy, 'Final Encounter: The Politics of the Assassination of Gandhi', in *At the Edge of Psychology: Essays in Politics and Culture* (Delhi: Oxford University Press, 1980), pp. 70–98.
35. *SWJN*, 2nd ser., vol. 5, pp. 1–15.
36. The contrast with Liaquat Ali Khan's assassination could not have been more striking: he too died of gunshots to the chest, in October 1951. The motive of the assassin, a civil servant from NWFP, remained obscure, and the death of the premier did little to assuage social tensions.
37. M. Rafique Afzal, ed., *Speeches and Statements of Quaid-i-Millat Liaquat Ali Khan, 1941–51* (Lahore: University of Punjab, 1967), p. 121, Radio broadcast, 7 Oct. 1947.
38. 'Gandhi Foresees Race for Armaments', *Civil and Military Gazette*, 9 July 1947.
39. Quoted in Ayesha Jalal, *The State of Martial Rule: The Origins of Pakistan's Political Economy of Defence* (Cambridge: Cambridge University Press, 1996), p. 42. Jalal analyses the partition of the armed forces and implications for the Pakistani state in detail. See especially pp. 25–48.
40. Liaquat Ali Khan's Speech to the Pakistan Muslim League Council, 20 Feb. 1949 in Afzal, ed., *Speeches and Statements*, p. 211.
41. F. Tuker, *While Memory Serves* (London: Cassell, 1950), p. 497.
42. *SPC*, vol. 6, p. 210. Patel to Baldev Singh, 12 Jan. 1948.

Chapter 10: Divided Families

1. G.D. Khosla quoted in R. Kaur, 'Planning Urban Chaos: State and Refugees in Post-partition Delhi', in E. Hust and M. Mann, eds, *Urbanization and Governance in India* (New Delhi: Manohar, 2005), p. 231.
2. M. Bourke-White, *Halfway to Freedom: A report on the new India in the words and photographs of Margaret Bourke-White* (New York: Simon & Schuster, 1949), p. 32;

R. Menon and K. Bhasin, *Borders and Boundaries: Women in India's Partition* (Delhi: Kali for Women, 1998), p. 178.

3. Menon and Bhasin, *Borders and Boundaries*, p. 196.
4. M.A. Quraishi, *Indian Administration Pre and Post Independence: Memoirs of an ICS* (Delhi: BR Publishing, 1985), p. 154.
5. From Urvashi Butalia, *The Other Side of Silence: Voices from the Partition of India* (London: Hurst, 2000), p. 204, cited in S. Kamra, *Bearing Witness*, pp. 165–200. In an interesting discussion on the psychology of Partition, and in contrast to my argument here, Kamra argues that recovery, or at least the ability to live alongside the past, was possible and did occur with the passage of time, so that these events are 'fixed' in the past for many survivors. She also argues that the strong social cohesion of communities who were collectively displaced helped to mitigate the impact of trauma.
6. *SWJN*, 2nd ser., vol. 7, p. 258. Broadcast from Delhi, 18 Sept. 1948.
7. *SWJN*, 2nd ser., vol. 14, part 2, p. 111. Nehru to Attlee, 20 March 1950.
8. Richard Symonds, *The Making of Pakistan* (London: Faber and Faber, 1951), pp. 112–13.
9. Ibid.
10. *SWJN*, 2nd ser., vol. 14, pt. 2, p. 23. Nehru to Rajagopalachari, 11 April 1950.
11. Resignation letter of J.N. Mandal to Government of Pakistan, 8 Oct. 1950, Tathagata Roy, *My People Uprooted: A Saga of the Hindus of Eastern Bengal* (Kolkata: Ratna Prakashan, 2001), pp. 353–76; M. Rafique Afzal, ed., *Speeches and statements of Quaid-i-Millat Liaquat Ali Khan, 1941–51* (Lahore: University of Punjab, 1967), p. 311.
12. See the acrimonious letters exchanged between Nehru and Liaquat Ali Khan in 1950 reproduced in Afzal, ed. *Speeches and Statements*, p. 585. Liaquat Ali Khan writes: 'the whole country was ravaged by fire and sword. Vast numbers were butchered and countless women were abducted', and blames India for the violence; to which Nehru replies: 'any impartial person familiar with the tragic happenings in the Punjab will recognise the complete baselessness of the suggestion that India organised the wholesale massacre of the Muslim population in any part of its territories' and describes the violence against Muslims carried out, 'by way of retaliation'. Other officially produced publications that accuse the 'other side' of initiating and sustaining Partition's violence include: *Note on the Sikh Plan: An Account of the Secret Preparations of the Sikhs* (Lahore: Govt Print, West Punjab, 1948); *The Sikhs in Action: Showing the Sikh Plan in Actual Operation* (Lahore: Govt Print, 1948).
13. *Concerning Evacuee Property: problem and solution* (Ministry of Information and Broadcasting, Govt. of India, Delhi, 1950) p. 4.
14. *After Partition* (Delhi: Publications Division, Govt of India, 1948), p. 40.
15. *National Herald*, 10 May 1950.
16. UPSA, Home Police C, Box 2, File 128(PT)/49. Extension of stay for Pakistan artisans. Amar Nath Bindra to Govt of UP, 24 May 1949.
17. Ibid., Amar Nath Bindra to Govt of UP, 24 July 1949.
18. *CWMG*, vol. 88, p. 164, Speech at a prayer meeting, 15 June 1947.
19. *Civil and Military Gazette*, 29 June 1947.
20. Andrew Whitehead, *Oral Archive: India: A People Partitioned* (London: School of Oriental and African Studies, 1997, 2000), Sahabzada Yaqub Khan, interviewed in Delhi 15 March 1997.
21. Alok Bhalla, *Partition Dialogues: Memories of a Lost Home* (New Delhi: Oxford University Press, 2006), p. 91.
22. Attia Hosain, *Sunlight on a Broken Column* (London: Chatto and Windus, 1961), p. 287.
23. See cases in Mazhar Husain, ed., *The Law relating to Foreigners in India and the Citizenship Laws of India and Pakistan* (Delhi and Lucknow: Eastern Book Co., 4th edn, 1967).

24. *The Statesman,* Interview with the Director-General of the Border Security Force, 28 Oct. 2006.
25. *Guardian,* 2 June 2005, Obituary of Fazal Mahmood.
26. *The Hindu,* 29 Aug. 2004.
27. Willem van Schendel, 'Stateless in South Asia: The Making of the India–Bangladesh Enclaves', *Journal of Asian Studies,* 61.1 (Feb. 2002), pp. 115–47. See also W. van Schendel, *The Bengal Borderland: Beyond State and Nation in South Asia* (London: Anthem, 2005).
28. Speech of L.K. Advani quoted in Bharatiya Janata Party (BJP) press release, Karachi, 4 June 2005.
29. L.K. Advani's speech at the South Asian Free Media Association, Islamabad, 2 June 2005. See also 'Musharraf's Family Ties to Delhi', BBC News, 13 July 2001.
30. *The Nation,* 16 Aug. 2005. See also www.bab-e-pakistan.gov.pk.
31. *Daily Times,* 17 Nov. 2005.
32. Krishna Kumar, 'Peace with the Past', *Seminar,* 522 (2003). See also Krishna Kumar, *Prejudice and Pride: School Histories of the Freedom Struggle in India and Pakistan* (New Delhi and London: Penguin, 2002).
33. *Outlook,* 27 Feb. 2006; *Dawn* magazine, 19 March 2006.

Epilogue

1. *SWJN,* 2nd ser., vol. 3, p. 99.

Select Bibliography

Primary material

Afzal, M. Rafique (ed.) *Speeches and Statements of Quaid-i-Millat Liaquat Ali Khan [1941–1951]* (Lahore: University of the Panjab, 1967)

Azad, A.K., *India Wins Freedom* (Delhi: Orient Longman, 1989), 1st edn, 1959

Bourke-White, M., *Halfway to Freedom: A report on the new India* (New York: Simon and Schuster, 1949)

Burke, S.M. (ed.), *Jinnah: Speeches and Statements, 1947–8* (Karachi: Oxford University Press, 2000)

Cantwell Smith, W., *Modern Islam in India: a social analysis,* (London: Victor Gollancz, 1946)

Carter, L. (ed.), *Mountbatten's Report on the Last Viceroyalty 22 March to 15 August 1947* (New Delhi: Manohar, 2003)

Choudhary, V. (ed.), *Dr Rajendra Prasad Correspondence and Select Documents* (Delhi: Allied Books, 1984–92)

Darling, M., *At Freedom's Door. The story of a ride across northern India in the winter of 1946–7.* (London: Oxford University Press, 1949)

Das, D. (ed.), *Sardar Patel's Correspondence, 1945–50* (Ahmedabad: Navajivan, 1971)

Datta, V.N. and Cleghorn, B.E. (eds), *A Nationalist Muslim and Indian Politics: Selected Letters of Syed Mahmud* (Delhi: Macmillan, 1974)

Dayal, R., *A Life of Our Times* (Delhi: Orient Longman, 1998)

Ebright, D.F., *Free India: The First Five Years: An Account of the 1947 Riots, Refugees, Relief and Rehabilitation* (Nashville: Parthenon Press, 1954)

Gandhi, M., *The Collected Works of Mahatma Gandhi,* (New Delhi: Publications Division, Ministry of Information and Broadcasting, Govt of India, 1958–)

Gopal, S. (ed.), *Selected Works of Jawaharlal Nehru* (1st ser.) (Delhi: Orient Longman, 1972–82); 2nd ser. (New Delhi: Jawaharlal Memorial Fund, 1984–)

Harvani, Ansar, *Before Freedom and After: Personal Recollections* (Delhi: Gian Publishing House, 1989)

Ikramullah, S.S., *From Purdah to Parliament* (Karachi: Oxford University Press, 1963)

Jain, A.P., *Rafi Ahmad Kidwai: A Memoir of his Life and Times* (London: Asia Publishing House, 1965)

Johnson, Alan Campbell, *Mission with Mountbatten* (London: Robert Hale, 1951)

Khaliquzzaman, Choudhry, *Pathway to Pakistan* (Karachi: *The Journey to Pakistan: A Documentation on Refugees of 1947* (Islamabad: Govt of Pakistan, National Documentation Centre, 1993; Longman, 1961)

Khan, Mohammad Ayub, *Friends, Not Masters: A Political Autobiography* (New York and Oxford: Oxford University Press, 1967)

Khosla, G.D., *Stern Reckoning* (Delhi: Oxford University Press, 1989), 1st edn, 1949

Mansergh, N. (ed.), *Transfer of Power, 1942–1947: Constitutional Relations between Britain and India* (London: HM Stationery Office, 1970–83)

Moon, P., *Divide and Quit: An eyewitness account of the Partition of India* (Delhi: Oxford University Press, 1998)

Nanda, B.R. (ed.), *Selected Works of Govind Ballabh Pant* (Delhi: Oxford University Press, 1993–)

Patel, H., *Rites of Passage: A Civil Servant Remembers* (New Delhi: Vedam, 2005)

Patel, Maniben, *Inside Story of Sardar Patel: The Diary of Maniben Patel: 1936–50*, chief ed., P.N. Chopra; ed. Prabha Chopra (New Delhi, 2001)

Pirzada, Syed Sharifuddin (ed.), *Foundations of Pakistan: All-Indian Muslim League Documents: 1906–1947. vol 2, 1924–1947* (New Delhi: Metropolitan Book Co., 1982)

Quraishi, M.A., *Indian Administration Pre and Post Independence: Memoirs of an ICS* (Delhi: BR Publishing, 1985)

Rao, B., *The Story of Rehabilitation* (Delhi: Government of India, 1962)

Rasul, A., *From Purdah to Parliament* (Delhi: Ajanta, 2001)

Symonds, Richard, *The Making of Pakistan* (London: Faber and Faber 1951)

Tuker, F., *While Memory Serves* (London: Cassell, 1950)

Wavell: The Viceroy's Journal, ed. Penderel Moon (London: Oxford University Press, 1973)

Wynne, M. (ed.), *On Honourable Terms: The Memoirs of Some Indian Police Officers, 1915–1948* (London: BACSA, 1985)

Young, D., *Try Anything Twice* (London: Hamish Hamilton, 1963)

Zaidi, Z.H. (ed.), *Quaid-i-Azam Mohammad Ali Jinnah Papers* (Islamabad: National Archives of Pakistan, 1993–2001)

Secondary Material

Ahmad, Aziz, *Muslim Self-statement in India and Pakistan 1857–1968* (Wiesbaden, 1970)

Ahmed, I., Dasgupta, A. and Sinha-Kerkhoff, K. (eds), *State, Society and Displaced People in South Asia* (Dhaka: Dhaka University Press, 2004)

Aiyar, S., '"August Anarchy": The Partition Massacres in Punjab, 1947', in D.A. Low, and H. Brasted (eds), *Freedom, Trauma, Continuities: Northern India and Independence* (Delhi: Sage, 1998)

Andersen, W. and Damle, S., *The Brotherhood in Saffron: The RSS and Hindu Revivalism* (Boulder: Westview, 1987)

Ansari, S., 'The Movement of Indian Muslims to West Pakistan after 1947: Partition-related Migration and its Consequences for the Pakistani Province of Sind', in J. Brown and R. Foot (eds), *Migration: The Asian Experience* (New York: St Martin's, 1994)

Ansari, S., 'Partition, Migration and Refugees: Responses to the Arrival of the Mohajirs in Sind 1947–8' *South Asia,* 18 (1995)

Ansari, S., *Life after Partition: Migration, Community and Strife in Sindh, 1947–1962* (Karachi and Oxford: Oxford University Press, 2005)

Aziz, K.K., *The Making of Pakistan: A Study in Nationalism* (London: Chatto and Windus, 1967)

Aziz, K.K., *Party Politics in Pakistan, 1947–1958* (Islamabad: National Commission on Historical and Cultural Research, 1976)

Bagchi, Jasodhara and Dasgupta, Subhoranjan, *The Trauma and the Triumph: Gender and Partition in Eastern India* (Kolkata: Stree, 2003)

Banerjee, Mukulika, *The Pathan Unarmed: Opposition & Memory in the North West Frontier* (New Delhi and Oxford: James Currey, 2000)

Basu, Aparna, *Mridula Sarabhai, Rebel with a Cause* (Delhi: Oxford University Press, 2005)

Bhalla, A., *Partition Dialogues: Memories of a Lost Home* (New Delhi: Oxford University Press, 2006)

Brass, P., *Factional Politics in an Indian State* (Berkeley: University of California Press, 1965)

Brass, P., *Language, Religion and Politics in North India* (Cambridge: Cambridge University Press, 1974)

Brass, P., *Theft of an Idol: Text and Context in the Representation of Collective Violence* (Princeton: Princeton University Press, 1997)

Brass, P., *The Production of Hindu–Muslim Violence in Contemporary India* (Seattle: University of Washington Press, 2003)

Brass, P., 'The Partition of India and Retributive Genocide in the Punjab, 1946–7', *Journal of Genocide Research*, 5.1 (2003)

Brennan, L., 'From One Raj to Another: Congress Politics in Rohilkhand, 1930–50', in D.A. Low (ed.), *Congress and the Raj: Facets of the Indian Struggle 1917–47* (London, 1977)

Brennan, L., 'The Illusion of Security: The Background to Muslim Separatism in the United Provinces', *Modern Asian Studies*, 18. 2 (1984)

Brennan, L., 'The State and Communal Violence in Uttar Pradesh: 1947–1992', in J. Macguire et al. (eds), *Political Violence from Ayodhya to Behrampada* (Delhi, 1996)

Brown, J.M., *Nehru: A Political Life* (New Haven: Yale University Press, 2003)

Butalia, U., *The Other Side of Silence: Voices from the Partition of India* (London: Hurst, 2000)

Chakrabarti, P., *The Marginal Men: The Refugees and the Left Political Syndrome in West Bengal* (Calcutta, 1990)

Chakrabarty, B., *The Partition of Bengal and Assam, 1932–1947: Contour of Freedom* (London: RoutledgeCurzon, 2004)

Chakravartty, Gargi, *Coming Out of Partition: Refugee Women of Bengal* (New Delhi: BlueJay Books, 2005)

Chatterjee, P., *Nationalist Thought and the Colonial World: A Derivative Discourse?* (London: Zed Books, 1986)

Chatterjee, P., *The Nation and its Fragments: Colonial and Postcolonial Histories* (Princeton: Princeton University Press, 1993)

Chatterji, J., *Bengal Divided: Hindu Communalism and Partition, 1932–1947* (Cambridge: Cambridge University Press, 1994)

Chatterji, J., 'The Fashioning of a Frontier: The Radcliffe Line and Bengal's Border Landscape, 1947–52', *Modern Asian Studies*, 33. 1 (Feb. 1999)

Chatterji, J., 'Right or Charity? Relief and Rehabilitation in West Bengal,' in S. Kaul. (ed.), *The Partitions of Memory* (Delhi: Permanent Black, 2001)

Chester, L., 'The 1947 Partition: Drawing the Indo-Pakistani Boundary', *American Diplomacy*, 7.1 (Feb. 2002)

Copland, I., '"Communalism" in Princely India: The Case of Hyderabad, 1930–40', in M. Hasan, (ed.), *India's Partition: Process, Strategy and Mobilization* (Delhi: Oxford University Press, 1993)

Copland, I., *The Princes of India in the Endgame of Empire, 1917–1947* (Cambridge: Cambridge University Press, 1997)

Copland, I., 'The Further Shores of Partition: Ethnic Cleansing in Rajasthan, 1947' *Past and Present*, 160 (1998)

Copland, I., 'Crucible of Hindutva? V.D. Savarkar, the Hindu Mahasabha and the Indian Princely States', *South Asia*, 25.3 (2002)

Copland, I., 'The Master and the Maharajas: The Sikh Princes and the East Punjab Massacres of 1947', *Modern Asian Studies*, 36. 3 (2002)

Copland, I., *State, Community and Neighbourhood in Princely North India, c.1900–1950* (London: Palgrave Macmillan, 2005)

Daechsel, Markus, 'Military Islamisation in Pakistan and the Spectre of Colonial Perceptions', *Contemporary South Asia* 6.2 (1997), pp. 141–60

Daechsel, Markus, *The Politics of Self-Expression: The Urdu Middle-class Milieu in Mid-twentieth-century India and Pakistan* (London: Routledge and Royal Asiatic Society, 2006)

Das, S., *Communal Riots in Bengal 1905–1947* (Oxford: Oxford University Press, 1994)

Das, V. (ed.), *Mirrors of Violence: Communities, Riots and Survivors in South Asia* (Delhi: Oxford University Press, 1992)

Das, V., *Critical Events: An Anthropological Perspective on Contemporary India* (Delhi: Oxford University Press, 1995)

Faruqi, Ziya-ul-Hasan, *The Deoband School and the Demand for Pakistan* (Bombay: Asia Publishing House, 1963)

Fraser, Bashabi (ed.), *Bengal Partition Stories: An Unclosed Chapter* (London: Anthem Press, 2006)

Freitag, S., *Collective Action and Community: Public Arenas and the Emergence of Communalism in North India* (New York: Oxford University Press, 1989)

Gilmartin, D., *Empire and Islam: Punjab and the Making of Pakistan* (London: I. B. Tauris, 1988)

Gilmartin, D., 'Partition, Pakistan and South Asian History: In Search of a Narrative', *Journal of Asian Studies*, 57.4 (1998)

Gould, W., 'Congress Radicals and Hindu Militancy: Sampurnanand and Purushottam Das Tandon in the Politics of the United Provinces, 1930–47', *Modern Asian Studies*, 36.3 (2002)

Gould, W., *Hindu Nationalism and the Language of Politics in Late Colonial India* (Cambridge: Cambridge University Press, 2004)

Graham, B., *Hindu Nationalism and Indian Politics: The Origins and Development of the Bharatiya Jana Sangh* (Cambridge: Cambridge University Press, 1993)

Greenberg, J., 'Generations of Memory: Remembering Partition in India/ Pakistan and Israel/Palestine', *Comparative Studies of South Asia, Africa and the Middle East*, vol. 25.1 (2005)

Gupta, S., 'The "Daily" Reality of Partition: Politics in Newsprint, in 1940s Kanpur', in *The Public Domain: Sarai reader 01* (New Delhi: Centre for the Study of Developing Societies (CSDS), 2001)

Hasan, M. (ed.), *India's Partition: Process, Strategy and Mobilization* (Delhi: Oxford University Press, 1993)

Hasan, M. (ed.), *India Partitioned: The Other Face of Freedom*, 2 vols, (Delhi: Lotus Collection, 1995)

Hasan, M., *Legacy of a Divided Nation: India's Muslims since Independence* (London and Delhi: Oxford University Press, 1997)

Hasan, M. (ed.), *Inventing Boundaries: Gender, Politics and the Partition of India* (Delhi: Oxford University Press, 2000)

Hashmi, Taj I., *Pakistan as a Peasant Utopia: The Communalization of Class Politics in East Bengal, 1920–1947* (Boulder, Colorado: Westview, 1992)

Jaffrelot, C., *The Hindu Nationalist Movement and Indian Politics* (London: Hurst, paperback edn, 1996)

Jalal, A., *The Sole Spokesman: Jinnah, the Muslim League and the Demand for Pakistan* (Cambridge: Cambridge University Press, 1985)

Jalal, A., *The State of Martial Rule: The Origins of Pakistan's Political Economy of Defence* (Lahore:Vanguard, 1991)

Jalal, A., 'Secularists, Subalterns and the Stigma of "Communalism": Partition Historiography Revisited', *Modern Asian Studies*, 30. 3 (1996)

Jalal, A., 'Exploding Communalism: The Politics of Muslim Identity in South Asia', in S. Bose and A. Jalal (eds), *Nationalism, Democracy and Development: State and Politics in India* (Delhi: Oxford University Press, 1997)

Jalal, A., *Self and Sovereignty: Individual and Community in South Asian Islam since 1850* (London: Routledge, 2000)

Kamra, S., *Bearing Witness: Partition, Independence, End of the Raj* (Calgary, University of Calgary Press, 2002)

Kamtekar, I., 'A Different War Dance: State and Class in India, 1939–45', *Past and Present* 176 (Aug. 2002)

Kamtekar, I., 'The Military Ingredient of Communal Violence in Punjab, 1947', in *Proceedings of the Indian History Congress*, 56 (1995)

Kaul, S. (ed.), *The Partitions of Memory: The Afterlife of the Division of India* (Delhi: Permanent Black, 2001)

Kaur, R., 'Planning Urban Chaos: State and Refugees in Post-partition Delhi', in E. Hust and M. Mann (eds), *Urbanization and Governance in India* (New Delhi: Manohar, 2005)

Kaur, R. (ed.), *Religion, Violence and Political Mobilisation in South Asia* (Delhi: Sage, 2005)

Kesavan, Mukul, 'Invoking a Majority: The Congress and the Muslims of the United Provinces' (unpublished) Occasional Papers on History and Society, 2nd ser., Nehru Memorial Museum and Library

Kudaisya, Medha M., *The Life and Times of G.D. Birla* (Delhi and Oxford: Oxford University Press, 2003)

Kumar, Krishna, *Prejudice and Pride: School Histories of the Freedom Struggle in India and Pakistan* (New Delhi and London: Penguin, 2002)

Kuwajima, Sho, *Muslims, Nationalism and the Partition: 1946 Provincial Elections in India* (New Delhi: Manohar, 1998)

Louis, Wm Roger, 'The Partitions of India and Palestine', in *Ends of British Imperialism: The Scramble for Empire, Suez and Decolonization* (New York: I.B. Tauris, 2006)

Low, D.A. (ed.), *Congress and the Raj: Facets of the Indian Struggle, 1917–47* (Columbia: South Asia Books, 1977)

Low, D.A. and Brasted, H. (eds), *Freedom, Trauma, Continuities: Northern India and Independence* (Delhi, 1998)

Mayaram, S., 'Speech, Silence and the Making of Partition Violence in Mewat', in S. Amin and D. Chakrabarty (eds), *Subaltern Studies IX* (Delhi: Oxford University Press, 1997)

Mayaram, S., *Resisting Regimes. Myth, Memory and the Shaping of a Muslim Identity* (Delhi: Oxford University Press, 1997)

Mazower, M., 'Violence and the State in the Twentieth Century', *American Historical Review*, 107.4 (2002)

Memon, M.U. (ed.), *An Epic Unwritten. The Penguin Book of Partition Stories* (Delhi: Penguin, 1998)

Menon, R. and Bhasin, K., *Borders and Boundaries: Women in India's Partition* (Delhi: Kali for Women, 1998)

Menon, R. (ed.), *No Woman's Land: Women from Pakistan, India and Bangladesh Write on the Partition of India* (New Delhi: Women Unlimited, 2004)

Metcalf, Barbara Daly, *Islamic contestations: Essays on Muslims in India and Pakistan* (New Delhi and Oxford: Oxford University Press, 2004)

Minault, G., 'Some Reflections on Islamic Revivalism vs. Assimilation among Muslims in India', *Contributions to Indian Sociology*, 18 (1984)

Mirza, Sarfaraz Hussain, *Muslim Women's Role in the Pakistan Movement* (Lahore: Research Society of Pakistan, University of the Punjab, 1969)

Naidu, M., *Mahatma Gandhi and Hindu–Muslim Unity: During Transfer of Power and Partition of India (1944–48)* (New Delhi: Manak, 2005)

Nandy, Ashis, 'Final Encounter: The Politics of the Assassination of Gandhi', in *At the Edge of Psychology: Essays in Politics and Culture* (Delhi: Oxford University Press, 1980), pp. 70–98

Page, D., *Prelude to Partition: The Indian Muslims and the Imperial System of Control 1920–1932* (Delhi and New York: Oxford University Press, 1982)

Pandey, G., *The Ascendancy of the Congress in Uttar Pradesh: A Study in Imperfect Mobilization* (Oxford: Oxford University Press, 1978)

Pandey, G., *The Construction of Communalism in Colonial North India* (Oxford: Oxford University Press, 1992)

Pandey, G., 'The Prose of Otherness', in D. Arnold and D. Hardiman (eds), *Subaltern Studies VIII* (Delhi, 1994)

Pandey, G., *Remembering Partition: Violence, Nationalism and History in India* (Cambridge: Cambridge University Press, 2001)

Pandey, G., *Routine Violence: Nations, Fragments, Histories* (Stanford, Calif.: Stanford University Press, 2006)

Philips, C.H. and Wainwright, M.D. (eds), *The Partition of India: Policies and Perspectives, 1935–1947* (London: Allen and Unwin, 1970)

Potter, D., *India's Political Administrators, 1919–1983* (Oxford: Oxford University Press, 1986)

Qadiri, K.H., *Hasrat Mohani* (Delhi: Idarah-I Adabiyat-I Delli, 1985)

Rahman, M.D. and Van Schendel, W., 'I Am Not a Refugee: Rethinking Partition Migration', *Modern Asian Studies*, 37.3 (2003), pp. 551–84.

Ramaswamy, Sumathi, 'Maps and Mother Goddesses in Modern India' *Imago Mundi*, 53 (2001), pp. 97–114.

Robinson, F., *The Politics of the United Provinces Muslims, 1860–1923* (London: Cambridge University Press, 1973)

Robinson, F., 'Islam and Muslim Society in South Asia: A Reply to Das and Minault', *Contributions to Indian Sociology*, 20 (1986)

Robinson, F., *Islam and Muslim History in South Asia* (New Delhi and Oxford: Oxford University Press, 2000)

Roy, B., *Some Trouble with Cows: Making Sense of Social Conflict* (Berkeley: University of California Press, 1994)

Salim, A., *Lahore, 1947* (Delhi: tara-india research press, 2006)

Samaddar, Ranabir (ed.), *Reflections on Partition in the East* (Dehli: Sangam Books, 1997)

Sarkar, S., *Modern India, 1885–1947* (Delhi: Macmillan, 1983)

Sayeed, Khalid B. *Pakistan: The Formative Phase, 1857–1948* (London: Oxford University Press, 1968)

Scechtman, J.B., 'Evacuee Property in India and Pakistan', *Pacific Affairs*, 24.4 (Dec. 1951)

Seminar 'Partition' number (August 1994)

Sen, Amartya, *Identity and Violence: The Illusion of Destiny* (New York : W. W. Norton, 2006.)

Settar, S. and Gupta, I.B. (eds), *Pangs of Partition*, 2 vols (Delhi: Manohar, 2002)

Smith, Wilfred Cantwell, *Pakistan as an Islamic State* (Lahore: Ashraf, 1951)

South Asia, 18 (1995), special issue on 'North India: Partition and Independence'

Talbot, I., *Punjab and the Raj, 1849–1947* (Delhi: Manohar, 1988)

Talbot, I., *Freedom's Cry: The Popular Dimension in the Pakistan Movement and Partition Experience in North-West India* (Karachi: Oxford University Press, 1999)

Talbot, I., *Khizr Tiwana: The Punjab Unionist Party and the Partition of India* (Karachi and Oxford: Oxford University Press, 1996)

Talbot, I., *Divided Cities: Partition and its Aftermath in Lahore and Amritsar* (New York: Oxford University Press, 2007)

Talbot, I. and Thandi, S. (eds), *People on the Move: Punjabi Colonial, and Post-colonial Migration* (Oxford: Oxford University Press, 2004)

Tan, T.Y. and Kudaisya, G., *The Aftermath of Partition in South Asia* (London and New York: Routledge, 2000)

Tan, T.Y., *The Garrison State: The Military, Government and Society in Colonial Punjab, 1849–1947* (New Delhi and London: Sage, 2005)

Tanwar, R., *Reporting the Partition of Punjab 1947: Press Public and Other Opinions* (Delhi: Manohar, 2006)

Van der Veer, P., *Religious Nationalism: Hindus and Muslims in India* (Berkeley: University of California Press, 1994)

Van Schendel, W., 'Stateless in South Asia: The Making of the India–Bangladesh Enclaves', *Journal of Asian Studies*, 61.1 (Feb. 2002)

Van Schendel, W., *The Bengal Borderland: Beyond State and Nation in South Asia* (London: Anthem, 2005)

Verkaaik, O., 'A People of Migrants: Ethnicity, State and Religion in Karachi', *Comparative Asian Studies*, 15 (1994)

Virdee, Pippa, 'Partition and the Absence of Communal Violence in Malerkotla', in Ian Talbot (ed.), *The Deadly Embrace: Religion, Politics and Violence in India and Pakistan, 1947–2002* (Karachi: Oxford University Press, 2007)

Whitehead, A., *Oral Archive: India: A People Partitioned* (London School of Oriental and African Studies, 1997, 2000)

Zachariah, B., *Nehru* (London: Routledge, 2003)

Zachariah, B., *Developing India: An Intellectual and Social History* (New Delhi and Oxford: Oxford University Press, 2005)

Zamindar, Vazira, 'Rite of Passage: The Partition of History and the Dawn of Pakistan', in *Interventions: International Journal of Postcolonial Studies*, vol. 1, no. 2 (1999)

Index